'Florence Violet McKenzie should be a household name! This comprehensive retelling of her incredible and inspiring life is helping to make that so. Dufty's new biography captures her unwavering dedication in the face of adversity and the sheer force and scope of her determination. Florence Violet McKenzie is one of my Australian touchstones, and I hope through this book she will be yours too!'

Genevieve Bell
Distinguished Professor and Florence Violet McKenzie Chair
College of Engineering and Computer Science,
Australian National University

About the author

David Dufty has a PhD in psychology, and has worked as a social researcher at the University of Memphis, Newspoll, and the Australian Bureau of Statistics. His book *The Secret Code Breakers of Central Bureau* won the 2017 Nib Military History Prize. He also wrote *How to Build an Android: The true story of Philip K. Dick's robotic resurrection* (published in the UK as *Losing the Head of Philip K. Dick*, and originally published in Australia as *Lost in Transit: The strange story of the Philip K. Dick android*).

DAVID DUFTY

RADIO
GIRL

The story of the
extraordinary Mrs Mac,
pioneering engineer and
wartime legend

ALLEN&UNWIN
SYDNEY•MELBOURNE•AUCKLAND•LONDON

First published in 2020

Copyright © David Dufty 2020

Allen & Unwin
83 Alexander Street
Crows Nest NSW 2065
Australia
Phone:(61 2) 8425 0100
Email:info@allenandunwin.com
Web:www.allenandunwin.com

A catalogue record for this
book is available from the
National Library of Australia

ISBN 978 1 76087 665 4

Internal design by Post Pre-press Group
Set in 12/16 pt Palatino by Post Pre-press Group, Australia
Printed and bound in Australia by Griffin Press, part of Ovato

10 9 8 7 6 5 4 3

The paper in this book is FSC® certified.
FSC® promotes environmentally responsible,
socially beneficial and economically viable
management of the world's forests.

To Jenny and Joan

CONTENTS

PREFACE

•— —•—•••—••••—•• —•—••

Before we begin, I have to tell you how this book came to be written.

In 2014, a retired spy suggested the idea to me, as we had a cup of tea in her living room. I was there to interview her about Australia's code-breaking activities during World War II, a topic in which she was well versed. Incidentally, her life also would have made a cracking story, but unlike the one told here, it won't be published.

As the afternoon shadows lengthened, she changed the topic from wars and codes and long-lost friends. She said abruptly, 'You know, you should do something on Mrs Mac.' I confessed that I had no idea who she was talking about.

She gave an enthusiastic potted summary of the deeds of Violet McKenzie, apparently nicknamed 'Mrs Mac' by the thousands of young men and women who encountered her during the war. She'd had something to do with the WRANS—the Women's Royal Australian Naval Service— and had trained lots of women in Morse code. At least, that seemed to be the gist.

I was deep in the throes of writing my book *The Secret Code-Breakers of Central Bureau*, and wasn't looking for a new project, but when I returned to Canberra I looked into the story of Mrs Mac, and discovered that she was tangentially related to my topic. It turned out that she trained the first women code-breakers in Australia (in signals, I should add, not in code-breaking as such), and that she personally persuaded the navy to set up the WRANS in the first place. That was intriguing. Who on earth talks a navy into establishing a new defence service?

The more I dug, the more nuggets popped to the surface. She was Australia's first woman electrical engineer. She wrote a bestselling cookbook. She was an ABC presenter in its first year of existence. The list goes on and on, but I'll resist the temptation to tell you more, because these and other surprises await you in the pages that follow. As I explored the little nooks and alleyways of her life, new leads would turn up, suggesting yet more twisting backstreets of which I hadn't been aware.

My exploration of this fascinating woman's life was helped at the start by the work of Catherine Freyne, a journalist who had investigated Mrs Mac several years earlier and had produced a documentary about her for *Hindsight*, a history show on ABC Radio National. Freyne's work provided the pointers to the many directions one could go in exploring the life of this extraordinary woman.

Violet McKenzie made an appearance in my code-breaking book, in a chapter titled 'Mrs Mac and her Girls in Green'. It is possibly the most talked-about chapter in the whole thing.

When I gave presentations, I was somewhat nonplussed to find that many in the audience were more interested in Mrs Mac than in the code-breakers themselves, whose lives and works I'd spent the previous five years piecing together. And when the Department of Veterans' Affairs printed an extract of my book in their monthly magazine, they chose to publish the chapter about Mrs Mac. The message was unmistakable: there was something about Violet McKenzie that got people excited. She needed a book of her own.

It turned out that, while I—and most Australians—had not heard of Violet McKenzie, her memory had been kept alive to a fervent, almost fanatical degree by two separate subcultures: the women of the Ex-WRANS Association, and the men and women of the amateur radio community.

In 1987, the Ex-WRANS Association submitted an application for Violet McKenzie to be considered in a list of 200 great Australians for the bicentennial celebrations the following year. They were unsuccessful, but their work had a happy by-product, at least for me: in the process of writing the application, they had compiled an extensive portfolio of documents about her life. That portfolio was safely stored away in a cardboard box at the naval repository on Spectacle Island in Sydney Harbour, which is where I perused it 30 years later. After being escorted to Spectacle Island on a navy ferry, and while sorting through that lovingly compiled collection housed at the back of a dusty navy building, I was struck by an overwhelming sense that I was holding something important and beautiful that had been forgotten.

There was a time, now long gone, when Violet McKenzie was quite well known to the public. Luckily for me as a biographer, she was the subject of sporadic media attention over more than six decades, commencing with a 1920 feature in Sydney's *The Sun* newspaper titled 'Mademoiselle Edison'.[1]

When, in 2018, *The Sydney Morning Herald* printed my appeal to hear from people who had known Violet McKenzie (I threw caution to the wind and let them publish my phone number), I received calls over the next few weeks from people all over Australia, wanting to tell me their own stories about Mrs Mac. I visited many of them for in-person interviews. They spoke with admiration and awe, the most frequent descriptors of her being 'amazing', 'wonderful' and 'marvellous'. The closest anyone came to criticism was a veteran of the WRANS who described her as 'cunning', but only after having first sung her praises to the same extent as the others.

This had to be hyperbole. Nobody is perfect. Perhaps it was a collective effort to compensate for her lack of modern-day acclaim. Or perhaps it was in recognition of her rags-to-riches-to-rags story; maybe, if she'd died wealthy, the eulogising might have been more muted. But she didn't. She made a fortune as an entrepreneur in the 1920s and 1930s, and then spent it all establishing and running her signalling school. This school was vital to the war effort, but nobody in government or defence had the wit or insight to run it themselves.

The reason for the praise is now clear. Some individuals simply are extraordinary, and Violet McKenzie was such a person.

As I delved into her life, I sometimes had an embarrassing sense of prying, of spying on someone who was quite private and whose life was carefully compartmentalised. And yet, even so, some things remained out of reach. Not all leads could be followed.

Nonetheless, here is her story—as complete as it can be—for you to enjoy and marvel at, just as I have done.

THE MORSE CODE

A	•—		T	—
B	—•••		U	••—
C	—•—•		V	•••—
D	—••		W	•——
E	•		X	—••—
F	••—•		Y	—•——
G	——•		Z	——••
H	••••			
I	••			
J	•———		1	•————
K	—•—		2	••———
L	•—••		3	•••——
M	——		4	••••—
N	—•		5	•••••
O	———		6	—••••
P	•——•		7	——•••
Q	——•—		8	———••
R	•—•		9	————•
S	•••		0	—————

1

AUSTINMER

•— ••— ••• — •• —• —— •—•

*I was born on the same day as Confucius, so it seemed
only natural that I became a teacher.*

Florence Violet McKenzie[1]

The Wallace family arrived in the village of Austinmer,
on the south coast of New South Wales, around the year
1892. They were George, Marie Annie (known as Annie) and
their children, Walter Reginald (aged three) and Florence
Violet (aged two, and known throughout her life as Violet).
They explained to the locals that they had recently emigrated
from Britain, Annie hailing from Shropshire in England, and
George from Scotland.[2]

In due course, they became upstanding members of the
community. Since the opening of a nearby coalmine a few
years earlier, the village had been going through a brief

mining boom. George worked as a clerk for the mine, and later as a salesman for the Vacuum Oil Company (the first company to sell retail petrol in Australia). He was one of the founding members of the local surf-lifesaving club, and was elected to the town council.

Discovering that the village had no church, Annie made arrangements with a pastor from a nearby parish to come to Austinmer on a regular basis on Sunday afternoons, and to hold church services in her living room. Once the services had become established as a regular event, she launched a fund to raise money for the construction of an Anglican church. As Austinmer's population was small, her plan met with scepticism, and the scheme was nicknamed by some 'the church that would never be built'.

A local Catholic, Mr Patsy Kennedy, told Annie, 'I hear that you are trying to get an Anglican church in Austinmer, but you never will, with so few people here.'

Annie replied, 'Oh yes we will, Mr Kennedy. Please do not discourage me.'

As there was no Catholic church nearby, he told her that he would donate to her fund once construction had actually commenced. When in due course the building work began, he kept his word. The church—named All Saints in keeping with the ecumenical spirit of the congregation—was opened in 1904.[3]

•—•

Although they were known to all as Mr and Mrs Wallace, unbeknown to the townsfolk of Austinmer George and Annie were not actually married, a scandalous situation for a churchgoing family of the time. In fact, it is not clear how old they were, where they met or who was the real father of the children.

A few months after All Saints Anglican Church opened, George and Annie snuck off to Sydney, where they quietly got married at the Wesley Chapel. They returned to Austinmer that afternoon as the husband and wife they had been pretending to be all along.[4]

The children had both been born in Melbourne, Walter Reginald on 28 July 1889 and Florence Violet on 28 September 1890. Walter's birth record asserts that he was the illegitimate son of Annie Giles (aged 25) and James Greville (aged 45). 'Annie Giles' was no doubt the same Marie Annie Wallace under her maiden name of 'Giles'. But when she gave birth to Florence Violet fourteen months later, her name was recorded as 'Annie Granville' and she was still aged 25.[5] When she married George Wallace four years after that, she told the minister at the Wesley Chapel that she was 26 years of age. George was recorded as being 36 years of age.

In fact, on the available evidence (which is sketchy), Annie was born in Shropshire in 1874, making her fifteen when she had her first child in Melbourne, on the other side of the world from her birthplace. How and why she came to Melbourne are unknown.[6]

As for her first husband, James Granville (or perhaps 'James Greville', the handwritten name of the father on Walter's birth register), he is even more of a mystery, and may never have existed at all. There are no records confirming his existence— whether for immigration, birth, marriage, death, censuses, run-ins with the law or any other matter—other than the name appearing on the birth registers for Annie's two children. Maybe 'James Granville' was George all along, covering his tracks for his impregnation of an underage, unmarried girl. Or maybe George had nothing to do with Annie's teenage pregnancies but was simply a man who became smitten with a young single mum from a poor inner-city neighbourhood.

There's reason to suspect that he may have been on the wrong side of the law, because a 'George Wallace' was remanded and bailed in Melbourne in 1892, charged with bribing a police officer to turn a blind eye to something. Maybe it's a coincidence. Or maybe he was caught with his young lover, skipped bail with her and left the colony.

Whatever the truth, their secrets are now lost. But whether they were on the run from the law, from social scandal or from economic hardship, the Wallaces moved to the quiet mining village of Austinmer hoping to make a fresh start. And that's exactly what they did.

•—•

Austinmer Station had opened only a few years before as part of the new Sydney-to-Wollongong railway line, providing the township with easy access to both cities. Young Violet Wallace was entranced by the trains as well as the signals near the station. These remained some of her earliest childhood memories, presaging her lifelong interest in engineering and signalling systems.[7]

Walter and Violet attended Thirroul Public School, a single, long classroom in a brick building, on a grassy hill by the beach. It was also new, having been completed only a year before they arrived, the previous schoolhouse having been destroyed by termites. The school's only teacher was Mr Fuller, who lived in the schoolmaster's residence next door.[8]

The adults in the community respected Mr Fuller, in part because of his kindly and progressive views on education. For example, each morning he made the children recite the Bible's 'Golden Rule': 'Do unto others as you would have others do unto you.'[9]

Mr Fuller was so compassionate that he refused to administer 'the cane' to girls who misbehaved, instead merely making them stand in the fireplace with their back to the class. And so it was that, under Mr Fuller's innovative regime, Violet would pay for her infractions by standing in the cold, charred remains of the winter's fire, facing the sooty brick-work, wondering what eyes were staring at her back from the classroom behind her. Walter, being a boy, was provided no such luxury and would receive the sting of Mr Fuller's cane whenever he was judged to deserve it.

•—•

Hard times came upon the country. The property boom of the 1880s ended in a bust in 1890; the slow-motion collapse of the financial sector began, with a string of building societies and then banks hitting the wall. By the mid-1890s, the downturn had become a full-blown depression, and companies were going out of business all over the place.

The Austinmer mine, which was the largest local employer, wound back its operations, resulting in lay-offs. The unions fought back, embroiling the mine in a series of strikes and industrial disputes, but nothing could stave off the reckoning: in 1895, the mine closed altogether. Miners and their families moved away, the population shrank, and enrolments at the school plummeted.

Mr Fuller left Austinmer in 1897 and was replaced by Mr William G. Masters, who found himself in charge of a school with a student population of 'almost zero'. When the Department of Education closed the school in 1899, Mr Masters' brief tenure as schoolmaster came to an end.[10]

Unhappy with the lack of educational opportunities for their children, a group of local families banded together to remedy the situation. They lobbied the Department of Education and doorknocked Austinmer households to impress on their neighbours the importance of sending their children to school. Their efforts paid off when the Department of Education reopened the school the following year and appointed Mrs Sarah Carroll as schoolmistress.

In the interim, the closure had not halted Violet's education so much as diverted it, giving her plenty of opportunities to learn at home. She loved playing with her father's tools and would often carry a hammer and a pocketful of nails around with her. She also learned, presumably from George, how to rig simple electric circuits and became obsessed with them. Her mother would open cupboards to discover a light inside switching on as she did so, and had to be on the lookout for electric 'burglar alarms' on the floor.[11]

Violet remembered much later in life:

> I used to play about with bells and buzzers and things around the house. My mother would sometimes say, 'Oh, come and help me find something, it's so dark in this cupboard'—she didn't have very good eyesight . . . So I'd get a battery and I'd hook a switch, and when she opened that cupboard door a light would come on . . . I started sort of playing with those things.[12]

When the school reopened, the new teacher discovered that Violet had an aptitude for mathematics. Mrs Carroll helped her apply for a scholarship to Sydney Girls High School, which she won in 1904.[13]

Sydney Girls High School was—and still is—a prestigious public school whose mission was to provide high-quality education to girls, including those who could not afford expensive private education. It held annual entrance examinations and granted scholarships to the applicants with the highest scores. As one of its former students recounted on the occasion of the school's 50th anniversary: 'When the Sydney

Girls High School was founded 50 years ago, it marked a new epoch in the education of Australian women. It meant that a liberal education was available to girls of all classes, and was no longer a special privilege for the daughters of people wealthy enough to pay for governesses and tutors.'[14]

Many of its alumnae had already made an impact on Australian society. These included Isa Coghlan, who had been one of the first two Australian women to become doctors, in 1893; Ada Evans, who was the first woman in Australia to qualify as a lawyer, completing her legal studies despite knowing that, as a woman, she would be prohibited from practising; and Ethel Turner, who wrote the classic Australian children's book *Seven Little Australians*.[15]

The school was across the road from Sydney's Hyde Park, on the site where the David Jones store stands today. Violet would eat lunch with her friends in the shade of a large fig tree with a view of the rear of a theatre in Castlereagh Street. She would watch the theatre's actresses put their wigs out to dry in the sun on a washing line overlooking the schoolyard.[16]

Violet had chronic health problems that caused her to miss so much school that she had to repeat a year. Nonetheless, she successfully completed her senior year in 1909, and decided to become a mathematics teacher.[17]

The Sydney Teachers' College had opened three years earlier, with the aim of improving the quality of the state's teaching force. Like the other Australian states, New South Wales had long suffered from a chronic shortage of well-trained teachers. Most teachers were trained under variations of an apprenticeship system, either learning to teach while attending one-teacher bush schools, or undertaking supervised teaching at a specialised so-called model (or 'normal') school before being assigned elsewhere.

Violet's cohort was seen as the future, a new breed of teachers that would transform the state's schools for the better. At college, Violet learned educational theory and attended university classes in mathematics.

Meanwhile, her brother, Walter, had completed a different kind of training course. In the same year that Violet was accepted into Sydney Girls High School, Walter had departed for England, where George had arranged an apprenticeship for him in electrical engineering. Walter returned to Australia six years later as an electrical engineer, just as Violet began her Teaching diploma.[18]

2

A TALE OF TWO ENGINEERS

•— — •— •—•• • ——— ••—• — •—— ———
• —• — —• •• —• • • • —• • •••

You can learn anything from books.

Florence Violet McKenzie[1]

After qualifying as a mathematics teacher in 1913, Violet was assigned a teaching position in the town of Armidale in the lush grazing country of the state's northern tablelands. The train journey from Sydney to Armidale, with numerous stops at small towns along the central coast and up the Hunter Valley, took fourteen hours, departing from Central Station twice a day.

Perhaps she hoped that attending the local Anglican church (her family's denomination) would alleviate the effects of rural isolation. Whether through loneliness or boredom, by mid-year she had had enough.

At church one Sunday morning, she had a revelation: her life was on the wrong track. She was wasting her time as a schoolteacher in Armidale, and should instead go back to university. In an interview in 1922, she recalled, 'a strong feeling came over me that I ought to study science'.[2]

But why, on that occasion, did she say that 'science' was her goal? In many other interviews throughout her life, she made it clear that she wanted to be an electrical engineer all along. For example, in an interview for *The Sun* in 1920, she said, 'When I was asked, "What do you want to do?" I said, "Engineering, please."'[3]

A 1971 *Woman's Weekly* feature about Violet stated: 'She wanted to do Engineering but couldn't because she would have had to be apprenticed to a firm and no one would take her on.'[4]

And in 1979 she was visited in a nursing home by two 'old girls' from Sydney Girls High School, Louise Lansley and Islay Wybenga, who interviewed her to record her oral history. They asked her about studying science at The University of Sydney. Violet replied, 'Yes, that was because of the electrical engineering. I couldn't afford to do it full time. Anyhow, they wouldn't have women then, they wouldn't have anyone unless they were apprenticed to, or working at it.'[5]

Perhaps, as a rising young professional in 1922, she was either too polite or too embarrassed to say that she had not gained admission into the Engineering program. At any rate, the university did not accept her into either Science or Engineering for the 1914 intake, but instead offered her a place in the Arts faculty. She accepted it because she knew that, with a judicious choice of subjects and good grades, she might be able to switch faculties down the track.

Violet returned home and commenced part-time university study in 1914. Her two first-year subjects, mathematics and physics, were unusual choices for an undergraduate Arts student, but they happened to be the two foundational subjects required by the university's Engineering course. She passed both of them—or at least we can presume she did, given her academic record and her later accounts of this time in her life—but there is actually no paper trail, because the university's records have long since been destroyed.

Given that the Engineering course was her ultimate goal, she presumably applied for a transfer to Engineering. Again she was unsuccessful, but she secured a transfer to the Science faculty, which was at least closer to her ultimate goal than Arts. The following year she completed chemistry and geology, two subjects that would also count towards an Engineering degree if she were able to transfer into it.

•—•

There was an alternative pathway to becoming an engineer, through a diploma from the nearby technical college. The material in the college and university courses overlapped, as did the teaching staff, so that students in the degree program often attended classes across the road at the college. The engineering subjects at the college, like the science subjects Violet had done, could also count as credit towards an Engineering degree, if a student decided to upgrade from a diploma to the more prestigious qualification.

Violet decided to enrol in the Engineering diploma as a backup plan for the following year. If she was knocked back a third time to enrol for an Engineering degree, she could withdraw and just do the diploma instead.

Violet visited the college and met with the Head of Engineering to discuss her plans. Although he was sympathetic, there were rules about who could study at the college.

He told her, 'You can't come here and do engineering unless you're working at it.'

The catch was the same as with the university: to enrol in the diploma course, she first needed to secure an apprenticeship with a local employer and, as they both knew, no employer would take on a woman as an apprentice. Despite Violet being a woman, the Head of Engineering had no problem with her enrolling in the course, as long as she met the requirements. If, however, nobody would give her an apprenticeship, that was not his problem.

But Violet proposed a workaround that she hoped he would accept, even though it had cut no ice at the university: she intended to acquire a local engineering firm and then apprentice herself to her own firm. She asked him, 'Well now, suppose I had an electrical engineering business and I'm working at it, would that be all right?'

He cautiously replied, 'Yes,' but then added, 'If you produce proof.' He made it clear to her that, when it came to 'proof', hiring herself as an apprentice was in itself insufficient. He insisted that she produce a contract for electrical work, to prove that her business was genuine.

With this verbal assurance, she put her scheme into effect. The first step was to acquire Walter's engineering business, which had fallen on hard times due to some rather poor decisions her brother had made.

•—•

After returning from England with an electrical engineering qualification, Walter had found employment for a while with the Sydney City Council before moving into the blossoming new world of cinema.

Cinema was a booming new technology, and its reliance on electrical machinery meant that electrical engineers were in demand. The first cinema in Australia, running an Edison Kinetoscope imported from the United States, had opened in 1894 in Pitt Street, showing a very short silent film. By the time Walter had returned to Australia in 1910, there were over 100 cinemas in Sydney and another 30 either in planning or under construction.

Around that time, Walter met the Reverend Charles Jones, a charismatic figure who took Walter under his wing and promised that he would help the impressionable young man achieve greatness. But, despite the title 'Reverend', Jones was not a preacher; he was a con man and well known to the constabulary further south.

Jones had a long history of frauds and scams in the state of Victoria involving a string of fake businesses. He had even registered his own church, the Reformed Church of England, through which he had registered himself as a clergyman, gaining the right to officiate at marriages and funerals. He opened a business called The Marriage Shop, with a sign in the window that proclaimed:

Rev Charles T. Jones.
Marriages Solemnised.
Marry early and often!

The Victorian attorney-general launched an investigation into Reverend Jones, only to cause a public outcry when the police could not find any crimes with which to charge him. But he was eventually convicted and sentenced to two months in prison for running a scam involving a non-existent aviation school.[6]

After his release, Reverend Jones judiciously relocated to Sydney, where his exploits were relatively unknown. He could not believe his luck when he came across the young and gullible engineer, Walter Wallace, to whom Jones proposed a foolproof money-making plan.

They acquired a cinema projector, known at the time as a flickergraph, and opened a 'flickergraph training school' in Liverpool Street. For a modest fee, students could enrol in a one-week course with Walter as their instructor to learn how to operate the machine. Reverend Jones collected the enrolment fees and paid Walter a meagre 20 per cent of the takings, pocketing the remainder as management costs.

Some students lodged complaints with the police about the course, claiming that they had not learned anything. When plain-clothes police visited to investigate, Reverend Jones greeted them warmly and gave them a tour of the facilities. He led them upstairs, where several students were practising on the flickergraph; there was a second machine nearby, but Jones explained that it was broken.

One of the officers noticed a piano and asked why it was there. Reverend Jones replied, 'Oh, that's to teach piano tuning. We can teach you anything at all if you pay. We also have a hairdressers' school in the basement, with four or five chairs.'

The astonished police officer asked where Reverend Jones recruited people for the hairdressing students to practise on. Jones answered, 'Oh, they come from deadbeats in the park.' He added, 'It's free, and we get more than we want.'

The officers informed Reverend Jones and Walter that they were both being charged with conspiracy to defraud, arrested them and escorted them to the station. In a rare moment of altruism, Jones protested that they should not be arresting Walter because 'he was only an instructor'.

Walter nervously asked one officer, 'How do you think I'll get on?' The officer replied that he didn't know. Walter continued, 'I was always frightened that something like this would happen. But I did the best I could with the two old machines.'

At their trial in November that year, Walter had legal representation while Reverend Jones represented himself, dazzling and beguiling the jury with heartfelt proclamations of innocence. To counter the prosecutors, he produced—as if by magic—a parade of supposed 'former students' who praised his flickergraph school. If the 'former students' on the stand bore any resemblance to the park vagrants he some-times employed, such resemblance was purely coincidental. Besides, they hardly looked like vagrants with those lovely neat haircuts.

Walter and Reverend Jones were both acquitted, but the ordeal took a toll on Walter. The arrest and trial had featured prominently in the news; in addition to the lost time and the stress, his professional reputation was tarnished.[7]

He moved back in with his parents, George and Annie. This incident might have been the catalyst for his excessive drinking, which over subsequent years morphed into alco-holism, doing more to sabotage his career than the trial.

So when Violet, at the age of 23, moved back to her parents' house to attend university, Walter was living there, too. In an effort to reset his career, he set up an engineering business and applied for contracting work, but—probably because of his sullied reputation around town—he could not get trac-tion. Each morning, Violet and Walter caught the train from Austinmer to Sydney's Central Station. From there, Violet walked to the university campus for science classes, while Walter continued his futile search for engineering contracts.

In June 1915, Walter relinquished ownership of 'W.R. Wallace & Co' to his sister, and even gave her his small collec-tion of tools.[8] Violet never explained in detail the transfer of Walter's business to her, other than to say rather cryptically

21

that a 'specific circumstance arose'. But whatever Walter's reasons for selling the business, for Violet it was a ticket into the engineering world.

She acquired an office at Rawson Chambers, which was a three-storey labyrinth of workshops and small businesses located in Sydney's Haymarket. When she begged the manager for some furniture to get her started, he gave her a desk and some chairs.

The next step was to win a contract. The business, such as it was, had no existing clients, so she started from scratch, applying for tenders advertised in the daily newspapers.

Her first break came from a job that no one else wanted. The brief was to install electrical wiring for a house in Undercliffe (now part of Earlwood), on the south-western outskirts of the city beyond Marrickville. Violet caught the tram as far as she could and then walked the rest of the way, carrying Walter's toolbox. She later recalled that first job: 'It was a fearfully hot day, and the house was about two miles [3.2 kilometres] from the tram. I got the job because I was the only contractor to arrive there. I employed a lad to help me and—well, there were no complaints when it was done.'[9]

With a contract in hand, she returned to the technical college and lodged it with her application to enrol in the Electrical Engineering diploma course. When she was accepted, she became the first woman in Australia to enrol in an Engineering course. She used the earnings from her first contract to buy more tools.[10]

After enrolling at the college, she withdrew from the university. She told people that she could not afford it, but a more likely reason was her failure yet again to get a transfer to the Engineering degree. However, there were advantages to the new pathway she had adopted. Although she would get an Engineering diploma instead of a degree, she would gain more practical experience along the way and be able to support herself as well.[11]

•—•

One of Violet's classes was a 'practical night'. The tutor showed the class some soldering equipment, briefly described the task, and then asked Violet to demonstrate to everyone how to solder. It was a set-up, of course. She was a young woman in a man's domain—*his* domain, in fact—and he wanted to embarrass her. One of the other students anxiously offered to assist her, but she reassured him, 'I'll be all right, thanks. I think I can manage this.'[12]

Violet had learned how to solder years before at her father's workbench in Austinmer. For her, it was literally child's play. Deftly wielding the soldering iron as the men watched in awe, she sealed her place in the Engineering course.

The male students were fascinated and confused by her presence. She remembered later: 'Naturally, the men were curious about me at first. They used to peep at me over the partition and through the doors, but I just waved back at them and pretty soon they were treating me as one of themselves.'[13]

Later on, Violet never held back her sardonic jabs about sexist tutors and college administrators, but she never spoke ill of her male fellow students. She enjoyed their eagerness to help and was amused by their awkwardness around her.

The war had slashed student numbers at the college. Many young men had enlisted in the army and had departed in huge, packed convoys to the other side of the world, where they fought and died in France, Belgium and Gallipoli. Violet was one of only three students to complete the subject 'Electrical Engineering I' in 1916, the course component of her first year of the seven-year diploma.[14]

The obstacles that Violet faced with her newly acquired

contracting business were the same obstacles met by every new business owner, namely that nobody had heard of her and she had no track record. Besides that, she wasn't even a certified engineer, only an apprentice engineer, and to top it all off she was a woman, the only one in the industry. For all these reasons, the early days were tough going. The only slight advantage she had was that her competition was thinned by the departure of many young men for the war.

She took any jobs she could, starting with those from her dad, and from her dad's friends and acquaintances around Austinmer. Elsewhere she judiciously applied for the worst contracts going: ones that were too small, too remote or otherwise too inconvenient or annoying for other contractors to take on. Within a few years, she had a solid reputation, steady work and a staff of several men.

The Great War—as people were calling it—finally ended with the armistice on 11 November 1918. Some, including writer H.G. Wells and US President Woodrow Wilson, called it 'The War to End all Wars', expressing the rather naive view that the unprecedented scale of destruction and misery would quell the desire in human hearts to ever again wage war against each other. The people of 1918 would have been disheartened to learn that their Great, Final, Last-Ever, Never-To-Be-Repeated War to End All Wars was later renamed with the more prosaic title of World War I, thanks to the sequel that commenced after an interim of just two decades.

Young men came home with the eyes of old men. They returned to their old jobs, or to jobs that they might have taken earlier had a war not come along. Violet's engineering classes, sparsely populated during the war, swelled with male students returning to careers and coursework that had been interrupted by a spell of unspeakable violence.

By then, Violet was four years into the diploma, and

her business was steaming along. She was taking on large projects, such as wiring up factories, houses, apartments and office blocks, including the top floor of Rawson Chambers, where her office was based. She frequently had two contracts going at the same time, running separate teams at each site and going between them in her loose-fitting overalls.

The Sun ran a feature article on her in 1920, in which she talked about being a woman in a male-dominated industry:

> Of course all my hands are men, and I never have any bother. Now and again, engaging labour, I have overheard the query, 'Say, what's it like working for a woman?' and the reply, 'She'll do. Come in.'
>
> Only once did I strike the jealous masculine opposition that I had feared. A city council inspector told me I ought to be home in my proper place, washing dishes; but he didn't find any fault with my work.
>
> Another time I asked a gentle workman to put in a little overtime on a job, and he was so disgusted at the injury and insult of my sex and the request that he threw a coil of wire at me. But that's all in the game, and breaks any monotony that might threaten.[15]

3

THE WIRELESS SHOP

– •••• • •–– •• •–• • •–•• • ••• •••

••• •••• ––– •––•

Nearly every boy who owns a crystal set knows Miss Wallace.

The Bulletin, 1924[1]

An opportunity to expand into a new line of business arrived in 1921 in the form of a failed engineering-supply shop. Two engineers, Raymond McIntosh and Charles Briot, had opened an equipment and parts outlet in the Royal Arcade on George Street, but soon they had a falling-out. Briot exited the partnership, leaving McIntosh to run it alone.

Unfortunately, McIntosh had no idea how to run a business. In fact, he admitted to the bankruptcy registrar that 'The books weren't properly kept; that is the trouble'. He also admitted that he had no idea whether various contracts ran at a profit or loss, saying, 'It would be hard to pick any individual contract and say what the loss was, but I don't think any of them paid at all.' He did not keep a proper ledger of accounts, and sometimes literally stuffed payments into his pockets and then lost track of the cash.

Creditors—led by an army captain's widow—pursued McIntosh through the courts, forcing his bankruptcy in November 1921, by which time he had already disposed of his assets, a situation that earned him a reprimand in the Supreme Court. One of the main benefactors of his fire sale of assets was Miss F.V. Wallace, who purchased most of his inventory at rock-bottom prices, as well as the lease on his shop.[2]

Alas, the Royal Arcade no longer exists, having been demolished and replaced by the Sydney Hilton Hotel; however, in 1921 it was a prominent retail hub on George Street. The shop in the arcade that Violet had acquired from Raymond McIntosh was Shop 18, located one floor above ground level. She had secured a prime real-estate location for a bargain price.

Violet relinquished her office space in the teeming hive of Rawson Chambers to operate from her more upmarket acquisition on the first floor of the arcade, while trying her hand at retail at the same time. The inventory she had inherited was mostly industrial machinery, such as generators and motors, with an assortment of other electrical goods. The shopfront provided her with an opportunity to experiment with various products, and she soon developed a keen understanding of what was selling, and what was not.

Among other things, McIntosh had been trying to sell motor-car circuits, which was not exactly a good fit for an upstairs shop in a city arcade. The same was true for the generators and other heavy equipment that he had in stock.

An engineer looking for such a thing would probably visit a shop where they would not have to carry the generator downstairs and out through city streets. As she suspected would be the case, Violet was not selling large numbers of generators. On the other hand, she was doing a brisk trade in home appliances and small electrical parts.

One of her first retail customers was a merchant sailor who was using his shore leave to do some shopping. He asked if she had iron pyrite crystals in stock. Not only did she not have any, but she also didn't know what he was talking about. He was annoyed, and her questions—trying to clarify his request—only annoyed him more. The frustrated sailor turned around and left.

Asking around her network of colleagues, Violet soon learned what an iron pyrite crystal was used for. It was a component for a homemade wireless set (the word 'wireless' was gradually replaced by 'radio').

A crystal set is a kind of radio set that anyone can make, and requires no cord, plug, battery or any other power source. The radio waves themselves, captured by an aerial, provide the power by causing the pyrite crystals to vibrate. A metal wire resting against the crystal transmits the vibrations to the listener's headphones, where they are turned into sound.

Crystal sets were simple to construct, required no electricity to run and were undetectable, yet wireless sets were the subject of strict government regulation. During World War I, simply owning a radio set—even a crystal set—was illegal, as all broadcasting and receiving of wireless signals had been banned in 1916 as a wartime security measure. Only in September 1920, almost two years after the signing of the armistice in Europe, did the government reverse the wartime prohibition on radios. Yet, even when the ban was lifted, it was hardly a free-for-all. From 1920 onwards, an individual who wanted to build a radio had to first apply for a receiver's licence. The licence fee was originally set at £2—an exorbitant amount—but was slashed two years later to 10 shillings.[3]

Two schoolboys provided Violet with another lesson in wireless, one that would shape the course of her life. They brought a Morse key into the shop, put it on the counter and tapped out rapid bursts of clicks.

Violet had never seen such a gadget before and asked what they were doing.

The boys said, 'That's Morse code! Don't you know it?'

'No,' she admitted, but added, 'I'd like to, though.'

So the boys explained how Morse code worked and gave her a lesson.[4]

●—●

When the first undersea cables were laid for long-distance communication in the second half of the nineteenth century, conversations by voice were not feasible. Instead, messages were sent by Morse code, a system whereby letters and numbers are converted into strings of dots and dashes. The most famous of these is the Morse code for the distress signal SOS. In Morse code, the letter S is three dots (dot-dot-dot or, as Morse experts say, *dit-dit-dit*), while the letter O is three dashes (Morse people will tell you that is *dah-dah-dah*). SOS is therefore:

●●●———●●●

When radio came into being, Morse code was essential. In the early days, no method existed for sending voice or music by radio; that came much later. All that could be transmitted was a hum on a single frequency, a sort of long beep. The only way of turning that into a message was to rapidly switch the transmission on and off, punctuating the hum with dots and dashes. A short beep was a *dit*, while a long beep was a *dah*. A radio was useless if you didn't know Morse code.

The boys in Violet's shop showed her how to use their Morse key. They explained that to send a message, you tap your Morse code message out on the key. When you press your finger down on the key, this closed a circuit and caused the radio signal to send. If you tapped the key then released it quickly, that would send a short burst, a dot (*dit*). But if you tapped it and held it down for about three times longer, you would send a longer burst of signal, and that was a dash (*dah*).

Radio technology matured in the later decades of the twentieth century. But Morse code retained its place for a long time in both wire and wireless transmission, because it was the only precise way of transmitting text.

It was the dawn of a new era of communication, and it set Violet's imagination on fire. She applied for a 'wireless experimenter's licence' to build and own radio equipment, becoming the first woman in Australia to hold one. As for the shop, she got rid of all the engineering stock—it wasn't selling anyway—and replaced it with a range of small components related to radio. She changed the trading name to 'The Wireless Shop—Miss F.V. Wallace'.

There were no other shops in Australia specialising in radio and electrical parts. They would in time proliferate, with names such as Radio Shack, Radio House, Dick Smith and Jaycar; but before all of those there was The Wireless Shop, the first of its kind, showing the way.

•—•

The timing of Violet's pivot towards radio could not have been better. Once the new regulations were in place, demand for electrical components boomed overnight. When that wave hit, Violet was ready for it; her shop was well stocked with crystals and all the other parts needed to construct a wireless set. Within a few months, The Wireless Shop was the go-to location in New South Wales for wireless enthusiasts, retaining that market-leader status even while other outlets tried to mimic its success.

For Violet, this wasn't just business. She had been bitten by the wireless bug and was as crazy about it as any of her customers.

A subculture of amateur wireless enthusiasts sprang into being. Members of this community exchanged ideas, tips and parts, and organised gatherings with the fervour of religious converts. While their friends and relatives made do with the old of communication—such as handwritten letters— they tinkered with crystal sets, turning the dial in the hope of picking up a transmission from other experimenters or, if they were lucky, a snatch of a broadcast from America.

Family members and friends looked on them as oddballs and fantasists, but the wireless amateurs understood each other. Through wireless, they had glimpsed the future. They knew what was coming, and they knew it would be wonderful. With their binary packets of information (Morse code) and their network of data channels (radio frequency bands), they created ham radio, an ad hoc precursor to the internet of today.

In Sydney, the epicentre of the amateur wireless community was The Wireless Shop.

●—●

Licences were also introduced for so-called 'experimental stations'. The first such licence was issued to Charles Maclurcan, a man whom Violet would become friends with over the following years. He installed an array of transmitter masts in the backyard of his house in Strathfield, where he lived with his wife and children; he broadcast pre-recorded and live music on his station, 2CM, for 90 minutes every Sunday afternoon.

Maclurcan was no newcomer to wireless. Ten years earlier, he had been part of a small group of experimenters who had formed an amateur association they called the Wireless Institute of Australia. They had built their own transmitters and aerials, sending each other messages in Morse code and trying to catch snippets of broadcasts from elsewhere in the world.

Maclurcan's parents owned Sydney's Wentworth Hotel. This building provided an ideal location for a wireless station, so in 1910 he installed two transmitting masts on the roof. In doing so, he was several steps ahead of the government, which did not get around to the construction of a network of ship-to-shore wireless stations until the following year.[5]

With civilian wireless activity curtailed during World War I, Maclurcan had been ordered to dismantle his equipment and take down the masts. Unable to experiment with wireless, he concentrated on his many other interests, including figure-skating. He was a national champion figure-skater, and he built Australia's first skating rink; he was later a figure-skating judge at the Olympic Games.

Maclurcan was also one of the first people in Australia to own a motor vehicle, importing a Renault Landaulette before the driver's licence had been introduced. He was caught on one occasion speeding around Circular Quay in his imported car doing 24 miles per hour (about 38 kilometres an hour). The horrified magistrate exclaimed, 'That's the speed of an express train!' before issuing him with a fine of £4. However, that was only an *estimated* speed, because the police had calculated it with a stopwatch by timing his laps as he sped from one end of Circular Quay to the other.[6]

Certainly, money made all of this possible. Charles Maclurcan could invest in wireless stations, skating rinks, ski trips and automobiles only because of his parents' immense wealth. On the other hand, to be fair, he didn't waste any of the opportunities that he was lucky enough to get, achieving much for both himself and the community. These achievements would in time be eclipsed by those of a girl from a poor family in Austinmer, a girl who started with nothing at all—but credit should still be given where it's due.[7]

Maclurcan and Violet shared a background in engineering, a fascination with wireless and an entrepreneurial mindset. As he was Sydney's leading wireless experimenter and she was Sydney's leading wireless retailer, it was only natural that they would become acquainted.

One morning, a spectacular display was installed in Violet's shop: a detailed scale replica of Maclurcan's Strathfield radio station. It must have taken many painstaking hours to construct. It is not known who made the beautiful little diorama, but—given his involvement in sport, business and broadcasting—it is unlikely to have been Maclurcan himself. The display was one of a number of clues that Violet's admiration for Charles Maclurcan ran deep.

•—•

They were amateurish and the sound was of low quality, but the 2CM Sunday music broadcasts caused a sensation in Sydney. Maclurcan's station was soon joined by others, such as Ray Allsop's 2YG in Coogee, while other stations commenced broadcasting across Australia. The only way to listen to these wireless stations was to get a licence and then build a wireless set. Most experimenters could not broadcast live voices and music as Maclurcan's 2CM could, but they could communicate with each other using Morse code.

Before long, the shop was as much as Violet could handle, so she stopped taking on new engineering contracts and began the process of slowly wrapping up her contracting business. She hired a full-time assistant, R.C. Marsden (whose first name was Ronald but, in keeping with the fashion of the time, he preferred to be known only by his given initials), who was an engineer and war veteran, and who, like Violet, was a wireless enthusiast. He even had a broadcasting licence and had installed an experimental radio station, 2JM, at his home.

Other wireless shops sprang up nearby, including in the Royal Arcade itself, but Violet's shop continued to dominate the local wireless-retail industry. The Wireless Shop was more than just a shop; it had become the unofficial meeting place for amateur wireless enthusiasts from around Sydney. According to one news report, Violet was 'known to almost every experimenter in the state'.[8]

She signed all receipts *Miss F.V. Wallace*, but with her customers went by the nickname 'Vera'. She sometimes gave free parts to regulars who were struggling financially. She also designed and built circuits that she would give away to customers, accompanied by the circuit's wiring diagram.[9]

4

THE METROPOLITAN RADIO CLUB

— ••••• • —— • — •—• ——— •——• ———— •—•• •• — •— —•
•—• •— —•• •• ——— —•—• •—•• •• — —•••

*Petite and frail to look upon, she has obviously bound-
less energy and an indomitable will.*

The Sun, 1922[1]

An event in January 1922 inspired Violet to take a formal
leadership role in the amateur wireless community.

The schooner *Helen B. Stirling* was crossing the Tasman
Sea from Auckland to Sydney when it was hit by a terrible
storm. Gale-force winds ripped off the mainmast, damaging
the ship so much that it started taking on water.

The ship's wireless operator, Raymond Shaw, was woken
at 5.30 a.m. and ordered to make a distress call. Luckily, the
ship's transmitter was intact and his distress call was detected
by another ship in the Tasman Sea, *Melbourne*, which changed

course to assist, but it would take twenty hours to get there. Australian onshore radio stations also picked up the transmissions, but were powerless to help.

As *Helen B. Stirling* lurched about in the churning sea, its generator's belt slipped off, causing the wireless transmitter to fail. Shaw clambered along to the engine room and remounted the belt; then he clawed his way back to his wireless set. The radio worked again until water flooded the engine room, stalling the generator. This time Shaw enlisted several other crew members to help dry out the cells and other electrical equipment so they could restart the generator.

The captain gave the order to abandon ship. So at 2 p.m., Shaw signed off by broadcasting in Morse code, 'Off to take my chances in the boat'. There was a period of radio silence before he again came on the air, transmitting an announcement that the life raft had smashed and therefore the order to abandon ship had been rescinded.

Shaw collected from each crew member a final message to their loved ones, which he transmitted later in the afternoon. He then sent one more urgent last-minute request to *Melbourne* for help: 'Please burn searchlights all night. Hurry. We may go down any minute now. Receiver is out of order. We are anxiously waiting for you.'

When *Melbourne* arrived in the vicinity, *Helen B. Stirling* was still afloat and everyone was alive. Shaw had repaired his receiver and was able to communicate with *Melbourne*'s wireless operator, from whom he learned that *Melbourne* could not locate *Helen B. Stirling* in the darkness. As a result, Shaw informed his captain, who sent up flares. *Melbourne* soon found them and rescued everyone on board *Helen B. Stirling*, which finally slid into the ocean. By then, Shaw had been transmitting without respite for over 24 hours.[2]

The rescue of the *Helen B. Stirling* crew caused great excitement in Australia and New Zealand. It was remarkable in part because, if a similar situation had occurred only a few years earlier, everyone on board would have perished. For merchant sailors, the high risk of death at sea had been a fact of life since time immemorial, but now wireless provided hope of survival where there had previously been none. Shaw was justifiably lauded as a hero, and his story reported in breathless detail by the local press.

When *Helen B. Stirling* sank to the bottom of the Tasman Sea, Shaw's job sank with it, and there were no vacancies for wireless operators with any ships currently in port. Violet learned of Shaw's plight and decided to help him. She arranged a reception in Shaw's honour at the Persian Gardens Tea Rooms on Pitt Street. Promoted heavily by Violet through her shop, the event was well-attended by people in the local wireless community. Her sales assistant, Ron Marsden, gave an address in which he praised Shaw's courage and technical expertise; he then handed over to Violet, who presented Shaw with a wallet full of cash that had been collected from members of the Wireless Institute of Australia.[3]

Violet had recently become a member of the New South Wales branch of the Wireless Institute of Australia, becoming the first woman to do so. She remained the only woman in the Institute for many years.[4]

She offered Shaw a job at her shop. He accepted, working there as a sales assistant for a few months until rival firm Electricity House poached him.[5]

Several customers told Violet how much fun they had had at the Shaw dinner, and suggested that she hold another one. Violet organised a second dinner, again at the Persian Gardens Tea Rooms. The agenda for this gathering, she told attendees in her speech on the night, was to create a new association for wireless enthusiasts. It would be called the Metropolitan Radio Club.

The club needed a committee, she told the audience, and nominations were hereby open. Who would like to be on the committee? By the end of the night, Ron Marsden was the president of the new club, and Violet was the treasurer. Journalist Albert Mitchell, who wrote a wireless column for *The Evening News* under the pen name Dot Dash, was secretary.[6]

The club held meetings every three weeks at a cafe in the Royal Arcade, with a roster of members providing lectures on various aspects of wireless. Violet gave a talk titled 'Primary batteries', Ron Marsden spoke on the topic 'Local potentials on crystals', while other members presented on a range of matters from earthing to valves to reception problems.[7]

The Metropolitan Radio Club was one of many wireless clubs that sprang up around the country. It was not the first, but within six months it was the largest amateur radio organisation in New South Wales.[8]

In July, the club held a dance. Charles Maclurcan agreed to provide the music for the dance by wireless broadcast, a plan that would have been impressive had it worked. However, while Maclurcan played music for them from his Strathfield studio, the receiving equipment constructed by the club members failed. The dancers therefore had no music. After a discussion, the club decided to send Maclurcan a sycophantic letter as a sort of apology, in which the committee members regretted that his broadcast 'did not function at the receiving end'. The letter concluded: 'We sincerely trust that your good work on behalf of amateurs and experimenters will long continue.'[9]

•—•

A club member named Oswald Mingay read in the news about a major Wireless Exhibition in Paris and a forthcoming one planned for later that year in London. He proposed that Sydney could host such an event as well, volunteering to organise the exhibition himself with help from the rest of the club.

Oswald Mingay and Violet, having both recently become members of the Wireless Institute of Australia, probably suggested their idea to the Institute before doing it under the auspices of their local, poorly resourced radio club. To the longstanding Institute members, their plan may have sounded like little more than the product of naive exuberance of two new members.

Held from 22 to 24 September 1922, Sydney's Wireless Exhibition was the second of its kind in the world. It pre-empted the London Wireless Exhibition by several weeks, although admittedly it was not quite on the same scale. In contrast to overseas events hosted at grand venues such as the Royal Agricultural Hall in London, Sydney's Wireless Exhibition was held in a church hall on Pitt Street.

The opening event occurred on Friday afternoon, with the NSW governor and his wife, Sir Walter and Lady Margaret Davidson, in attendance. They were welcomed enthusiastically on stage by Ron Marsden, Albert Mitchell and Oswald Mingay. Violet was offstage, among the general audience—a mysterious omission since she was the club's founder and treasurer. Perhaps Mingay had good reason for limiting the number of people to meet the governor, sadly necessitating Violet's exclusion.

At the completion of the opening ceremony, Sir Walter and Lady Margaret were given a tour by Mingay of the exhibits—arrays of homemade contraptions arranged on rows of trestle tables. Owners of local companies had been invited to hold commercial stalls as well, but few, other than Violet, had taken up the offer.

In total, around 2000 people attended the exhibition over the weekend. On Sunday afternoon, a judging panel led by Charles Maclurcan announced prizes for exhibits. The categories included best single-valve wireless set, best multi-valve set, best crystal set, best complete apparatus, best invention and best commercial exhibit, which was won by Violet's display.

Maclurcan then announced a 'special prize', which they had decided to award at short notice for an exhibit that did not win in any of the categories, but was so remarkable that they felt it deserved something. This was the Seashell Loud Speaker by Cecil Roland McKenzie, a man who in time would play an important role in Violet's life.[10]

A photograph of Cecil's invention was published in various magazines over the coming months and, because of its eye-catching eccentricity, it became a mainstay of news reports on the amateur wireless community. It has been described as 'surely one of the most frequently used illustrations ever in stories about early Australian wireless'.[11]

The club's exhibition had upstaged the Wireless Institute of Australia, which—as the nation's pre-eminent body—could have hosted such an event themselves. But the following year, the Institute did just that, and they hired Oswald Mingay for the task. Held at Sydney's Town Hall in December 1923, the Wireless Institute's event was billed, rather dishonestly, as 'the first exhibition of its kind in Australia'.[12]

Perhaps taking comfort in the adage that imitation is the sincerest form of flattery, Violet and her fellow club members attended in force, entering the competitions and submitting displays.

Bringing a rare touch of femininity to the occasion, Violet displayed a Woman's Dressing Table Radio Set, which—as the name suggests—looked just like a miniature model of a woman's dressing table. The coils and a buzzer were hidden in powder boxes, and the crystal was in a thimble. There was an elegant little 3-inch (7.6-centimetre) aerial attached to the table. Remarkably, it worked.[13]

Violet's Dressing Table Radio Set was described as 'very neat', and 'secures good results'. Attendees at the exhibition were astonished to discover that her stylish dressing table could pick up actual radio calls from nearby ships. But, despite the originality and craftsmanship of the Woman's Dressing Table Radio Set, it won no prizes at the exhibition.[14]

5

WIRELESS WEEKLY

•— — ••• •—••• •—•• • ••• ••• •— — •• —•— •—•• —•— —

*That bright little magazine, 'Wireless Weekly', the
pioneer radio paper of the commonwealth . . .*

Goulburn Evening Penny Post, 1924[1]

In the winter of 1922, about three months before the
Metropolitan Radio Club's Wireless Exhibition, the club's
three office holders had a conversation at The Wireless Shop
that would change the publishing landscape. Violet and Ron
Marsden were there because they worked at the shop. Albert
Mitchell had dropped in to chat about the latest goings-on.
The trio despaired at the dire state of news reporting about
wireless.

The only magazine on the landscape was the Wireless
Institute of Australia's monthly periodical *Sea, Land and Air*
(its title later changed to *Radio in Australia and New Zealand* to

better describe the contents). But they felt that it pandered too much to commercial interests and disregarded the amateur community. Sure, amateurs such as Charles Maclurcan had founded the Wireless Institute back in the day, but now it was aligned with big business and hostile to the 'little bloke'. It was no coincidence that the president of the Wireless Institute was Ernest Fisk, the managing director of Amalgamated Wireless Australia Ltd.

Fisk had emigrated from England in 1910 as a representative of the Marconi Company. He had wasted no time in getting down to business by filing lawsuits against the government and against Australia's one major wireless company, alleging infringements of Marconi Company patents. After subduing the locals, Fisk negotiated a series of deals with them that placed him in charge of a new private–public entity, Amalgamated Wireless Australia Ltd (AWA). From the day it came into being, AWA was a government-backed monopoly, and Fisk intended to keep it that way.

The Wireless Institute of Australia and its magazine relentlessly lobbied, often indirectly, for the interests of Ernest Fisk and his corporate monopoly. *Sea, Land and Air* kept up the appearance of being on the side of the amateurs—it would publish glowing feature articles about Charles Maclurcan, for example—but that hardly outweighed the hectoring tone it took towards the amateur community. The regulations favoured the cosy three-way relationship between the Wireless Institute, the government and Fisk's corporation; they squeezed the amateurs.

Fisk had little respect for the independent wireless clubs springing up around the place, and neither did *Sea, Land and Air*. It editorialised that there was no need for such clubs; everything would be much more orderly if they could all just be branches of the Wireless Institute of Australia, under its benign supervision.

Violet and Ron were already reform activists; they were representatives of a lobby group called the Radio Association of Australia, which wanted formal recognition for amateur clubs and more say for amateurs at the level of the Wireless Institute of Australia. But it looked like this effort was having little impact.[2]

The three of them—Violet Wallace, Ron Marsden and Albert Mitchell—decided that an alternative voice was needed. They hatched a plan to launch their own magazine— one that would rival *Sea, Land and Air,* and would focus on the interests of ordinary people involved in wireless, rather than on the interests of big business. Unlike its competitor, which was available by subscription only, their magazine would be sold in newsstands. They called it *Wireless Weekly.*

Mitchell approached a printer he knew, William M. Maclardy, with the proposal, asking him to get involved. William M. wasn't personally interested, but he introduced Mitchell to his brother, William J. Maclardy, who was also in the printing business and who happened to be an amateur wireless enthusiast with his own experimental radio station, 2HP. William J. Maclardy was keen to get involved, and joined as the fourth member of the *Wireless Weekly* team. Maclardy nurtured his own secret ambition to usurp Ernest Fisk's wireless monopoly and saw the magazine as a vehicle to achieving this dream.[3]

The four of them began to meet at Maclardy's printery, a dark basement off Castlereagh Street, in the evenings after work. There they compiled material and planned the launch. Violet promoted the forthcoming magazine heavily through her shop, which at first was the only place it could be purchased.

By August, they were ready to go. The first issue was printed with the date 5 August 1922 (a Saturday), and it was available for sale from Violet's shop on Friday, 4 August. The front cover featured a photograph of a regular visitor to The Wireless Shop, a local boy named Tom Featherstone, sitting in front of a crystal set while wearing headphones. It was captioned: 'They start young in Australia'.

Advertisements were solicited from local businesses and the amateur radio scene. One man submitted an ad for second-hand wireless equipment:

FOR SALE: One Tresco coupler, 20,000 metres. Brings in American stations on one valve.[4]

A wireless set that could pick up radio stations across the Pacific Ocean using just one valve? Not possible, the editors agreed, but when they confronted him about his implausible claim, he assured them that he had detected American broadcasts many times. Since he was well-known in the amateur community and 'a wireless man', they decided to take his word and his money.

There was a buzz of anticipation around the clubs about the forthcoming magazine, but, even so, the four creators were unsure of how much demand there really was. With an uncertain market and limited cash, they decided that the first issue would have a print run of 'a few hundred copies'.

The opening editorial was brash:

In stepping into the limelight of public opinion, the 'Wireless Weekly' is full of confidence.

It is not every publication that can start its strenuous life in this frame of mind, but this journal is justified in so doing.

In the first place, it is the first publication wholly devoted to wireless to be produced in Australasia.[5]

The pages were crammed full of do-it-yourself advice, including a column titled 'Make your own', and an article extolling the virtues of amateur experimenters titled 'The good they can do: The case for the amateur'. There were also radio-themed poems.

Years later, Violet confessed to having supplied all the poems in the early years of *Wireless Weekly*. A poem attributed to the pseudonymous 'Sister Sue' was titled 'Dah-da-dah-da-dah!'; it was about Morse code (*da* being a variant of *dit*).

Dah-da-dah-da-dah!

Dreaming, dreaming, dreaming, all the night I lie
Dreaming all of radio, till morning paints the sky,
And wakes me up from dreamland, and sends me out
    afar,
To dream again the same refrain
of Dah-da-dah-da-dah.

I hear the locusts singing on the gum trees by the way,
I never used to notice them, but now I hear them say,
With their shrill familiar music penetrating far,
Rising, swelling, most compelling,
Dah-da-dah-da-dah.

The trains and trams and ferries sing the same old song,
I think it has bewitched me, for as I go along,
The homeward track at nightfall, and gaze up at a star,
It seems to wink at me and say,
Dah-da-dah-da-dah![6]

The poem 'Paradise' captured the disappointment of staying up all night at a ham radio set without finding anyone else on the air. The message 'CQ'—transmitted as a two-letter burst of Morse code—was ham radio shorthand requesting conversation (CQ meaning 'seek you').

Paradise

'Tis three o'clock in the morning,
I've listened the whole night thru',
The sun will soon be shining,
And I haven't heard a CQ.[7]

When Violet opened the doors of the shop at 8 a.m. on Friday, 4 August, there was a queue of people outside waiting to buy the first issue of *Wireless Weekly*. The print run sold out by the end of the day. The second issue, released a week later, had a substantially larger print run, but it also sold out quickly, leaving many would-be buyers empty-handed.[8]

The team behind the venture met every week in Maclardy's printery to plan the next issue. Mitchell was the editor; Maclardy was responsible for typesetting and printing; Marsden was responsible for technical articles; and Violet provided industry news and brief technical notes, as well as radio-themed short stories and poems.[9]

The magazine effused about the virtues of wireless amateurs, urging them to get politically active. '"Wireless Weekly's" advice to the experimenter can be summed up in one word—Organise!' implored one editorial. 'Officialdom is certainly not the happy hunting ground of progress,' claimed another.[10] The cover of another issue was emblazoned with the slogan 'Experimental broadcasting will not be stopped!'[11]

The magazine warned of a looming monopoly and

criticised Prime Minister Billy Hughes for his cosy relationship with Ernest Fisk's corporation, AWA. An editorial
thundered:

> Mr. Hughes announced during last session that he would not
> grant a monopoly to any one firm or combine in respect to the
> Radio business in Australia, yet there are indications that such
> a monopoly is being sought. How can the Prime Minister be
> a director on the Amalgamated Wireless Ltd., and yet be the
> ministerial head of the Radio Service?[12]

It was a good question from *Wireless Weekly*. Why indeed was
the prime minister also a director of a large corporation?

Every issue of *Wireless Weekly* sold more copies than the
one before it. Within a few months, the magazine had attained
national distribution; circulation was in the thousands—and
climbing.

•—•

Wireless Weekly's suspicions about the cosy relationship
between the politicians and the big end of town soon turned
out to be well founded. The federal government hosted a
conference in 1923, supposedly to seek public consensus
about radio broadcasting. The whole thing was a sham, a
fig leaf of coverage for a scheme designed to benefit Ernest
Fisk and his corporation, Amalgamated Wireless Australia
Ltd. The conference was declared a success, and the Hughes
government passed their legislation, ushering in a law that
was as absurd as it was short-lived.

The so-called Sealed Set Scheme prohibited the sale
of radios with frequency dials or with any tuning mechanism at all. Every radio set was permanently tuned to a
single station. So, for example, if you wanted to listen to

Fisk's forthcoming station, 2FC, you would have to buy a 2FC radio set. Tampering with your 2FC radio set—for example, so you could pick up another station—was illegal. It was *sealed* shut, not to be opened by anyone but a licensed repairer. Building your own was also illegal.

Clearly the whole point of the Sealed Set Scheme was to entrench a monopoly. An entrepreneur who wanted to launch a new independent radio station would find it too hard, because the public would not hear their broadcasts until they bought a new radio.

Wireless Weekly first took a wait-and-see approach, but within a few months it was launching full-throated denunciations with editorials such as 'The iniquitous sealed set':

> The sealed set is an attempt to create a monopoly and stifle competition.
> THE SEALED SET MUST GO.[13]

Meanwhile, they continued to publish do-it-yourself advice to help people break the law, peppered with admonitions that readers must never break the law. Naturally, this benefited Violet's business, as she was the leading retailer in components for do-it-yourself experimenters. Not that she needed much in the way of publicity: her retail business, like her publishing business, was making a killing.

•—•

The first commercial radio broadcasting licence was issued to the department store Farmer and Co. for station 2FC, an entity controlled by Ernest Fisk (the station broadcast from a studio located on the city store's roof garden, with its transmitter at Willoughby on Sydney's north shore). The culmination of years of planning, 2FC's launch was planned for the end of

1923 and would give Fisk a stranglehold on the Australian broadcasting industry from its inception.

William J. Maclardy—Violet's business partner and printer—put together a consortium of small businesses that he called Sydney Broadcasters Limited, and obtained a licence for a station named 2SB. (He later changed the name to Broadcasters Limited, and likewise changed the name of his station to 2BL.) While 2FC was still in its final preparations for launch, 2SB started broadcasting, becoming the first commercial station on the air in Australia.

Several years later, both stations were nationalised, along with other commercial stations around the country. 2FC became Radio National, while 2BL became the ABC's local AM station in Sydney.

The Sealed Set Scheme did not share the longevity of those first radio stations. Within a year, even the scheme's most ardent supporters had to admit that it had failed, with only 1400 sealed radio sets sold nationwide, rendering the commercial radio stations unviable. It was rescinded in 1924.[14]

•—•

The ever-expanding *Wireless Weekly* needed more capital investment than its creators could raise. Maclardy had financed successive hikes in its print runs; however, within three years—with the magazine now a major national publication—he could no longer continue to do so, particularly as he was investing more and more time and money into his radio station, 2SB, renamed 2BL in 1924.

Like the others, Violet was ready to move on. While Maclardy focused on building his media empire, her energy went into managing her large retail business.

In late 1923, the shop relocated to a larger, more prominent location. A piano store at 6–8 Royal Arcade—a double space on the ground floor—had gone bust in September of that year. Violet took over its premises while retaining the upstairs location as a workshop, where she employed women in a small manu- facturing operation to make electrical parts such as solenoids.[15]

Wireless Weekly was sold to a publishing consortium called Publicity Press in 1924, with the four founders going their separate ways. It had been a wild journey: in just two years, their magazine had become a major publication. It would continue into the next century, eventually becoming the magazine *Electronics Australia*.

We do not know how much money Violet made from *Wireless Weekly* and its sale to Publicity Press. Her payout must have been substantial, though, because she went on an extended overseas holiday soon after the transfer of funds.

6

LOVE AND LOSS

•—•• — — — •••— • •— —• —•• •—•• — — — ••• •••

I am satisfied that there is a large demand in business
for qualified women, possibly because of their capacity
for loyalty to their firm, their enthusiasm, and their
attention to detail.

Florence Violet McKenzie[1]

The Sun newspaper ran a feature article about Violet in
September 1923 under the heading 'The Radio Girl':

Her card introduced her as 'Miss F. V. Wallace, Electrical
Engineer', and to get a chat with her it was necessary to step
high over small mountains of shavings and packings, as she
was unearthing from huge cases a new stock of electrical and
wireless gear from England.

Miss Wallace was the first woman to get a diploma of

electrical engineering at the Sydney Technical College, and no other woman has been impelled to do likewise since. 'Yet, I cannot understand why,' said this efficient person, 'because wireless and electricity are fascinating. I've got two stations—one at my home in Burwood and one in town, and really, I don't know what mother—let alone myself—would do if she couldn't listen in occasionally. Last Saturday I climbed on the roof and fixed a new mast for my aerials. It was great fun. I haven't been on a roof for some years now, although it was a pretty common occurrence when I was working at electrical wiring. Now I devote all my time to wireless.

'Wireless is real woman's work, I think. There is no manual labour, and a woman has a natural aptitude for all the little bits of fiddling which are connected with much of the gear. Another thing, women seem to know by instinct what is wrong with a set, whereas a man will spend an hour or so testing to find out. I've noticed that frequently. Yes, there are about a dozen women I know who are very interested in wireless. Soon there will have to be a wireless women's club.'

Miss Wallace has already had proof of the value of wireless for women, outback, and invalids.

'It brings those who are otherwise isolated from the world of affairs into touch with what is happening abroad,' she said.

'A little boy—an invalid—has found fresh interest in life since his parents installed a wireless set for him; he can listen in on concerts, pick up messages from ships, get the time of day, and other messages. Think what that means to him!'[2]

●—●

Violet finished her engineering coursework in 1922 and was awarded the diploma the following year, becoming

Australia's first woman electrical engineer. In doing so, she was also the first woman to become an Associate of Sydney Technical College.[3] In a story about Violet, *The Bulletin* magazine said of her: 'She weaves her magic spell over boys from 7 to 70 in her wireless rooms in Imperial Arcade [*sic*]. Boys and their radio experiments make her world.'[4]

Violet was queen of the amateur radio world, but by 1923 the amateur radio craze had peaked. The public's appetite for radio was growing, but—with cheap mass-produced sets coming onto the market—there was less need to make your own. With commercial stations on the air, the do-it-yourself approach lost much of its shine.

In early 1924, Violet gave a demonstration of 'radio telephony' to 750 male students at the technical college from which she had recently graduated. The following week, she departed on a holiday to Mudgee, telling the papers that she would be completely incommunicado and would not even be taking a wireless set. She explained that 'wireless is a great thing, but it is possible to have too much of it'.[5]

●—●

The young inventor of the Seashell Loud Speaker, Cecil Roland McKenzie, was an active member of the Metropolitan Radio Club and a regular customer of Violet's. One day early in 1924, he placed an order for an expensive valve from America (valve sets were an electrically powered—and superior—alternative to crystal sets). After picking it up from the shop with great excitement, he took it home to install in his wireless set; however, he put it down near the edge of a table, where it rolled off and smashed on the floor.

He returned to the shop to tell Violet of his misfortune. Violet recalled, 'He looked so miserable that I burst into tears!'[6]

Cecil told her later that, when she cried for his broken

valve, this was the moment he decided that he wanted to marry her.

•—•

Like Violet, Cecil had studied Engineering at the Sydney Technical College, but his study had been interrupted by a two-year gap.

After enlisting in the army in 1917, he was sent to France with the Australian Army's 26th Battalion. There his unit engaged German forces and was attacked with mustard gas. Used by both sides during World War I, gas weapons were later banned under the Geneva Convention and today their employment is considered a war crime.

Immediately after the gas shell exploded, Cecil seemed unharmed; however, within a few hours he had abdominal pains, he was coughing violently, and he had a hoarse voice. Within a few days he could not speak at all. He convalesced for several days in a medical camp in France before being sent to England, where he was deemed no longer medically fit to serve and discharged from the army.

His voice eventually returned, and he believed for a while that the gas attack had left him with no long-term issues. On returning to Australia, he resumed his engineering apprenticeship with Sydney City Council.[7]

•—•

Cecil and Violet courted through the autumn and winter of 1924. He made his feelings clear, but she stalled. There were things she wanted to do before settling down into marriage. After the sale of *Wireless Weekly*, for the first time in her life Violet had an opportunity to travel. In particular, she wanted to go to the Radio World's Fair, to be held in late September in New York. So at midday on 11 September, she departed

Sydney Harbour on board the passenger ship *Maunganui*, bound for the United States.[8]

The Radio World's Fair at Madison Square Garden was a dizzying panoply of all the latest developments in radio. It was like nothing Violet had seen before. The opening night of the exhibition included a demonstration of moving pictures transmitted by radio waves, an early prototype of what futurists called 'television'. Over the next several days, she saw the latest wireless products, prototypes and handmade gadgets from around the world, and she met international luminaries of the radio industry.[9]

On her return journey she stayed in San Francisco, where she met up with Charles Maclurcan, her friend and fellow wireless enthusiast, who happened to be on a world trip himself.[10]

American station KGO had been operating from San Francisco since February, with transmitters so powerful that broadcasts could often be picked up in Australia. When Violet stopped in San Francisco in preparation for her journey home, she visited the station's studios. She was greeted enthusiastically and invited to speak on air.

After a series of musical items, the presenter announced, 'Miss Wallace, an electrical engineer from Australia, will now talk from the studio.' Violet talked mainly about her impressions of the United States and about the differences between it and Australia. She used the example of the tram system in San Francisco and how it differed from the system in Sydney to illustrate the point.[11]

Two employees of the Sydney-based Wireless Electric Company, Mr Sexton and Mr Green, were listening to KGO while on an assignment in the NSW town of Tenterfield, and were surprised to hear a woman on air speaking with an Australian accent. When they returned to Sydney a few weeks later, they reported this to their employer, who explained that the woman's voice they had heard was that of well-known Sydney identity Violet Wallace. As reported in *Radio in Australia and New Zealand* magazine:

> Mr. Green, not realising that Miss Wallace was a well-known personality in local radio circles, did not appreciate the importance of the reception of this particular item, or otherwise he would have notified the company much earlier.[12]

The significance of Violet's broadcast was not lost on Dr Cutler of Moruya, who transcribed the entire interview, although he later downplayed this accomplishment as being no big deal. Dr Cutler, incidentally, could pick up KGO broadcasts because of his powerful five-valve set, which also allowed him to listen to the racing results from 2BL as soon as they came in. On Melbourne Cup day, the whole population of Moruya gathered outside his residence, waiting to learn which horse had won.[13]

In November, Violet arrived home in Sydney and returned to work immediately, announcing that for her it was 'business as usual'.

Cecil again asked Violet to marry him, and this time she said yes. Their age difference was rather scandalous, as Violet was nine years older than Cecil; so, too, was the speed with which they tied the knot after announcing their engagement. The small, low-key ceremony took place at Auburn's St Philip's Church of England on New Year's Eve, less than two months after Violet's return from America.

Her father George was there, but her mother Annie could not make it because she was seriously unwell, dampening everyone's mood.[14] The next day, the couple travelled to Gulgong in the state's central west for their honeymoon.[15]

●—●

A feature article on Violet appeared in the *Australian Woman's Mirror* magazine in July 1925, titled 'The Radio Girl' (not to be confused with a feature article about her two years earlier with the same title). This provided a vivid snapshot of Violet six months after her marriage, building her dream home with Cecil and operating her radio station, 2GA.

The Radio Girl

Australia's first certified amateur woman radio telegraphist, and only woman member of the Wireless Institute of Australia, Violet Wallace, is a tiny handful of a woman—she looks about seven stone [44 kilograms]—with a big smile that crinkles up her face until the bright-blue eyes behind her glasses disappear in a humorous maze . . .

'When I began selling wireless necessities I didn't know a thing about it,' she chuckled. 'The laddies coming into the shop gave me my first lessons, and I began to be ashamed of my ignorance, so I determined that I would help my customers instead of always filching information from them. I got interested and enthusiastic, and worked until I was qualified to get my certificate. I simply love my little shop; all my customers are genuinely interested, most of them are experimenters— there are such a lot of women experimenters that I would like to form a Women's Wireless Club.

'My customers are so interesting—they range from the black-shirted workmen to the black-coated clergyman—and each is as keen as the other over radio. The black-shirted band are my favorites—their courtesy goes to my heart.'

But wireless does not gobble up all Miss Wallace's enthusiasm. At present she is most enthusiastic about matrimony. She is rather delighted to find that she grows happier the longer she is married. The fact that her husband is an electrical engineer and a wireless enthusiast may be a contributing factor to her increasing bliss—they certainly have interests in common.

'We are building our little house of dreams.' She is musingly tender. Then her bright eyes dance before they disappear in that crinkly smile. 'But we're building it to suit wireless—with gables and an attic. An attic is ideal for a wireless room.'

This busy little lady does all her own housework, despite the fact that she lives in an outer suburb and is in her shop at 8 a.m. daily. She loves cooking, and is as enthusiastic about trying new recipes as she is about wireless.

'When the boys asked me the latest circuit to-day, I astonished them by replying with a new way of doing vegetable marrow.'

Miss Wallace is also a collector of china (Wedgewood being the favorite) and antique furniture.

Melbourne has the honor of being the birth place of our first woman electrical engineer and radio expert, who is now busy conversing with America through the ether, and whose main ambition, for the moment, is to talk further East than Texas. She was educated at the Sydney Girls' High School.

It seems that there must be a particular thrill in talking to some one on the earth, so the little Radio Lady gives the sum total of conversation at her end with perhaps half a world between:

'What station are you on?'

'What wave length?'

'Are my signals clear?'

Well, at the station in Texas the listener-in will miss the best part when 2GA gets him—for he won't be able to see Miss Wallace's fascinating crinkly smile.[16]

●—●

The 'house of dreams' that Violet referred to was built on a block of land overlooking Sydney Harbour at 26 George Street, Greenwich Point. Violet's radio station, 2GA, was installed in the attic, with its aerial and transmitter attached to the roof. They put a fish pond in the front yard, as Cecil liked to breed fish; it was a hobby that Violet soon picked up. Naturally, they did all of the electrical installation themselves; Cecil also installed an automatic switch for the porch light, so that it came on whenever someone opened the front gate.[17]

It was a short walk from their house to the point, where a steep set of stairs led down to the water's edge and a ferry wharf. No more train trips for them: each morning, they strolled down to the wharf and caught the ferry to Circular Quay, and from there they walked to their workplaces—Violet to her shop, and Cecil to the Sydney City Council chambers.

Inspired by what she had seen in New York, Violet turned her attention from radio to television, constructing her own apparatus to transmit pictures using radio waves. Her early investigations filled her with optimism, leading her to announce in late 1925:

> We hope shortly to place on the market a small sealed apparatus, costing not more than £5, which can be attached to any three-valve set for the reception of pictures from any theatre.[18]

But it was not to be. She had profitably designed and manufactured radio sets and other electrical gadgets, but television eluded her. Violet's timing—in business and in activism—was usually impeccable, but when it came to television she was too far ahead of the curve. Its time had not yet come.

Violet fell pregnant in the spring. Preparing for motherhood, she divested all her business interests, selling The

Wireless Shop in February 1926 to Alan Burrows, a journalist and amateur wireless enthusiast. Under Burrows, the shop kept its reputation for personalised service and expert advice—and it also kept its title. Because Burrows retained not only the store name 'The Wireless Shop' but also the business trading name 'F.V. Wallace', this caused confusion in the minds of some about whether Violet was somehow still involved.[19]

•—•

In April 1926, around nine months after the 'Radio Girl' feature article came out, a musical comedy called *The Radio Girl* by Australian composer Rex Shaw opened at the Sydney Conservatorium of Music.

The plot, such as it was, revolved around the love affair of a young couple obsessed with radio, in a large house right next to Sydney Harbour. In a futuristic twist, the stage backdrop depicted the Sydney Harbour Bridge, which was still under construction and would not be completed for another six years.

In the musical number 'Ring Me Round with Radio', the female lead (played by Nelle McGee) sang:

Ring me round with radio, to me a pal indeed.
When I am feeling out of sorts, it's just the thing I need.
Let me have my radio, wherever I may go.
It's grave, it's gay, it's hip-hooray!
My ra-di-o![20]

A reviewer from *The Sydney Morning Herald* dismissed the show's lyrics as 'very undistinguished, either in the way of sentiment or wit', but noted sarcastically that 'audiences do not trouble too much whether the words of a song are inspired or not, so the defect is not a serious one'.[21] The show received a standing ovation on opening night. Violet was then six months pregnant.

Alas, the future that Violet imagined for her 'house of dreams' never came to be. On 9 July 1926 she gave birth to a daughter, but the baby was stillborn.[22]

She never had any other children.

7

THE PHILLIP STREET
RADIO SCHOOL

— ••••• • •—••• •••• •• •—•• •—•• •• •——• ••• — •—• •• • —
•—• •— —•• •• ——— ••• —•—• •••• ——— ——— •—••

Scores of thousands of Australian men, women, and children are hardly getting enough to keep body and soul together.

Ben Chifley, 1934[1]

Each morning, Cecil caught the ferry from Greenwich Point wharf into the city for work, leaving Violet to spend her days in the house alone. She had never had so much free time in her life.

She would climb to the attic and talk to people across the ocean on her radio station 2GA; she cooked and cleaned; and she stocked the pond with fish, catching live specimens from the harbour's edge at the bottom of the sandstone bluff.

None of it was enough, so she got a job in the radio retail section of the David Jones store on the corner of George Street and Barrack Street. Taking the job meant that at least she was again commuting across the water with her husband in the mornings, and was again involved in the Sydney radio industry, but the shine soon wore off.

Having run her own successful retail business, Violet soon grew tired of working as a sales assistant for others. In November 1927, David Jones moved into a new nine-storey building that had been built on the site of Violet's old school—Sydney Girls High School. The buildings where she had studied as a teen had been demolished, and the school had relocated to a new campus in the eastern suburbs.

Around the time of the opening of David Jones's grand new store, Violet quit her position there with the idea of going back into business. After all, she had done it before and surely could do it again.[2]

She opened a new radio shop in 1928 on Phillip Street, on the ground floor of Chancery Chambers, an office building full of lawyers and accountants near Martin Place. Branding was complicated. She could not trade as 'Miss F.V. Wallace', because that was the name of her former business, now in other hands, and the new owner was getting as much mileage from it as he could. Although she had not been involved in it for two years, the name 'F.V. Wallace' was emblazoned in huge lettering above The Wireless Shop in Royal Arcade, allowing them to continue to trade off her reputation, and giving customers the mistaken impression that she still owned the place.

It ultimately didn't matter, since she wasn't Miss F.V. Wallace anymore: she was Mrs F.V. McKenzie. She simply named her new shop The Radio Shop.

The Radio Shop was never as successful as The Wireless Shop, partly because there were by then already several large retailers that were now well established (including The Wireless Shop itself) and partly because of the economic collapse that became known as the Great Depression.

After the crash of the New York Stock Exchange, beginning in late October 1929, Australia was hit hard. Its principal exports, wheat and wool, were hurt by the dramatic drop in international prices; in the cities, factories closed and workers were laid off.

A few hundred yards from The Radio Shop was the Domain, a grassy expanse of parkland where thousands of people lived in a makeshift tent city. Thousands more lived in similar tent cities around the city's fringes and in Salvation Army centres. Unemployment climbed to a peak of 32 per cent in 1932.[3]

Violet was not selling a lot of radios, so she broadened her wares to include tropical fish. She advertised them as 'splendid, healthy specimens' that had been locally bred.[4]

She wrote an article about fish that was published in the American journal *Aquariana* in January 1933. Titled 'Some interesting inhabitants of Sydney's seashores', her article began:

In Sydney Harbour and Botany Bay are all kinds of gorgeously coloured fish, sea horses, crabs and sea anemones of extraordinary delicacy. The sea horses, looking as if they had just stepped from a fairy tale, are quite numerous around the foreshores, and may be caught quite easily by sweeping a small net fixed to a long pole, among the kelp beside the rocks. They are most humorous little fellows, and are quite sufficient justification for keeping a saltwater aquarium, in themselves.

She also provided advice on breeding native Australian fish.[5]

Violet came across a second-hand wooden statue of a dog for sale. With its glassy eyes and rabbit-like ears, it was grotesque. Maybe its otherworldly eeriness appealed to her, because she bought it and placed it outside the door each day as the shop's mascot. In keeping with the electrical theme, she named the dog Plug-In.[6]

•—•

Violet soon made enquiries about getting involved in the local radio-broadcasting scene. The industry had changed since the heady days of 1923, when Fisk and Maclardy had been racing to be first on the air. In 1929, the Australian government had nationalised the broadcasting infrastructure—all the transmitters that the stations had deployed—and had appointed an entity known as the Australian Broadcasting Company to be in charge of all content coming from so-called A-class stations: those stations originally under the Sealed Set Scheme.

The two A-class Sydney stations were the original broadcasters, 2FC and 2BL. For three years they remained nominally independent, but under the supervision of the government-appointed controlling body. Then in 1932, the government took control of the Australian Broadcasting Company, renaming it the Australian Broadcasting Commission (people just called it the 'ABC'), and also nationalised the A-class stations, placing them under the umbrella of the ABC.

The owners changed, but it was the same people running the stations as before, and Violet had known many of them since the early 1920s. Everyone was keen to get her on board, with the idea that she could provide a woman's perspective on local radio.

In the early 1930s, her voice could be heard on a range of Sydney radio stations, sometimes on one station in the morning and another that same afternoon. She hosted a regular show on 2BL about breeding fish, and another regular show on 2GB called *Electrical Fittings*. She did features from time to time on 2FC and 2UW on topics such as 'How to use your vacuum cleaner' and 'Careers for women'.[7]

One evening, Violet and a friend were dining at a restaurant on Bathurst Street, talking loudly. The proprietor came over to their table and asked them to please be quiet.

Violet replied, 'Yes, I'm sorry. What's the trouble?'

Indicating the radio set, he explained, 'I want to listen to the session coming on: on tropical fish.' The show he wanted to hear was Violet's show, which had been pre-recorded.[8]

Meanwhile, she remained active in the amateur radio community through her station 2GA, and even dabbled in experiments to broadcast television.[9]

•—•

Eight years after graduating, Violet was still the only female electrical engineer in Australia, and no other women had even enrolled as students or apprentices. She campaigned to get more women involved in electricity and radio. To persuade women to take an interest, she made the case that radio was actually better suited to women than men. In an interview with a journalist from *The Sun*, she said:

> I just wish more parents knew of the splendid opportunities there are for girls with a general knowledge of radio. There are heads of radio shops and departments in Sydney today who would be delighted to secure a bright, intelligent demonstrator and saleswoman with some sort of knowledge of the goods, but they are not to be had.

There's more instinct about radio—a tremendous lot of guesswork. You've just got to feel what's wrong. And this is where women excel. Men work by rule, and there are no rules in radio. Women's fingers, used to doing fine work, also seem to me more adaptable to the fine parts of a radio outfit. I know lots of my women clients who wouldn't let a man touch their sets.[10]

Violet decided to open a private college in Phillip Street, the Women's Radio College, with the aim of educating women in technical skills related to radio. She placed the following ad in *The Sydney Morning Herald* in February 1930:

Ladies—Radio as a profession. Private lessons, postal course. Qualify for waiting positions. Experienced teacher, Mrs F.V. McKenzie, electrical engineer. 158 Phillip St, Sydney. [11]

A total of eight women enrolled in her course that year. Two of them completed it as a correspondence course. One was a 72-year-old woman who wanted to understand how her new radio set worked, and who to Violet's delight 'showed an amazing amount of intelligent interest'.[12]

Only two of her eight students, both of whom were teenagers, showed any interest in entering the industry. Once they had completed their course, she lined up jobs for both of them with Airzone, a radio-manufacturing company in Camperdown whose directors she knew. Interest increased when it was reported that two of her students got jobs from doing the course.[13]

She kept the Women's Radio College running the following year, advertising in the city papers:

Women's Radio College—Evening Class,
commencing after Easter.
Enrol now. Learn to make your own Radio Set.
Mrs F.V. McKenzie, 158 Phillip St, Sydney. [14]

Enrolments picked up. Violet wanted them to love radio the way she did, but for young women in the Great Depression, the lure of a job weighed more heavily than learning a new hobby. They wanted work, and they hoped that she could help.

In that respect, she delivered. The jobs she lined up for her graduates were nothing special, being for the most part jobs in repair rooms and on factory floors, but at least the women were in paid work, which was a better situation than many other women found themselves in. Before long, thanks to Violet's efforts, large numbers of women were employed in radio and electrical companies around Sydney.

An engineer commencing work at the AWV wireless factory in Ashfield was surprised by how many women were there:

> It was fascinating to watch their deft fingers—from afar—positioning the tiny nickel parts and securing them in place with the tap-tap-tapping of the pedal-operated spot welders. This was without apparent effort, while listening to background music and/or engaging in small talk with their neighbours on the bench.[15]

Many women who signed up for Violet's course were enthusiastic about their new-found skills. Violet was pleased to be able to bring in a faulty radio for them to repair and see them converge on it, ready to solve the problem. 'They're like a pack of wolves,' she observed approvingly.[16]

•—•

Violet's brother, Walter, who had been living in Melbourne for several years, got in contact. He was getting by with odd jobs as a handyman and roustabout between long spells of unemployment; he was estranged from his wife and close to destitute. The bottom line was that he could not afford to keep his two sons anymore, and hoped that Violet might take them in for a while. Of course she could.

Merton and Lindsay Wallace arrived in Sydney, and moved in with Violet and Cecil. The two boys became, in many ways, the children that she had never had herself. Exactly how long they lived there is unknown, but they seem to have stayed for some years.

In summer they would play at the harbour's edge, swimming at Greenwich Baths, a netted beach to the east of the ferry wharf. Luna Park opened in 1935, an amusement park next to the northern piers of Sydney Harbour Bridge, not far from Greenwich Point. On hot days, Merton and Lindsay would take a short cut to Luna Park by swimming across the small bay to Wollstonecraft and then walking the rest of the way. Violet put a stop to this practice after a man swimming in the harbour was killed by a shark.[17]

They took a great interest in Violet's radio station and The Radio Shop. Years later, having returned to Melbourne, Merton and Lindsay Wallace opened a radio shop of their own on Chapel Street, Prahran.[18]

8

THE ELECTRICAL ASSOCIATION
FOR WOMEN

— ••••• • • •—•• • —•—• — •—• •• —•—• •— •—•• •— ••• ••• — — —
—•—• •• •— — •• — — — —• ••—• — — — •—• •—— — — — —— • —•

> *Think of the fatalities that would be averted if women*
> *had a general knowledge of electricity and electrical*
> *appliances.*

Florence Violet McKenzie[1]

In August 1931, a Sydney cleaner was found dead on the floor of a Point Piper house, having been electrocuted when a screw on her vacuum cleaner came loose.[2] Another woman had recently been killed by her vacuum cleaner in Wagga Wagga when she touched an uninsulated wire. And vacuum cleaners were not the only appliances that could be deadly: a woman in Maryborough, Queensland, was electrocuted when using a faulty iron. Electrocutions were increasingly common in the workplace, too, such that the Sydney City Coroner recommended a full inquiry by the Department of Labour and Industry.

Violet was a regular speaker around Sydney on the topic of electrical safety. *The Sun* reported her daily lectures at Anthony Hordern's department store:

> Going right through the day—beginning with the electric comb and shaving mug, and continuing to the hot breakfast plates, jugs, cookers, and then on to washing machines, vacuum cleaners, floor polishers (Mrs. McKenzie thinks the last one of these is the most interesting and helpful of the new inventions), she will show women how to use these safely, explaining the principle at work behind each.[3]

In September 1931, she spoke at a meeting of the Housewives' Association, a prominent women's group founded by the artist Portia Geach in 1918. With a focus on consumer activism, they had organised boycotts of potatoes in 1923 and 1929, and of eggs in 1926, in campaigns against food price gouging.

Violet was there to educate them about the benefits of electrical appliances. She told them that in her seventeen years of electrical engineering, by observing safety rules, she had never experienced an electric shock. She also gave an hour-long address to Sydney's Forum Club, where she advised women using electrical appliances to, above all, 'keep an eye on the cord'.[4]

She was on a mission to dispel fear, believing that the dangers of appliances—both real and perceived—were an impediment to women's progress. If the fear was removed, then the technology could liberate Australian housewives from their lives of drudgery.

The appliance with the most profound impact on day-to-day life was the electric washing machine, because it automated a long, arduous task that was almost universally performed by women. A news item from 1925 described how it used to be:

> In the days of the tub, the wash boiler, and the hand clothes wringer, the week's washing was a formidable task, consuming the entire day, leaving no time, and little energy or spirit, for anything else.[5]

With an electric washing machine in the home, an Australian housewife had up to an entire extra day in her week, freed up by not having to boil items of clothing, then grind them against a washboard one by one. As labour savers, ovens and ranges were also miracles. No longer would a fire have to be stoked and maintained before a meal could be cooked. Vacuum cleaners replaced brooms. Refrigerators enabled food to be stored, allowing women (for it was mostly women who had to do it) to make fewer trips to buy groceries, and keeping food fresh for longer periods of time.

New appliances were appearing on store shelves each year, giving modern women of the 1920s and 1930s opportunities that their mothers never had—there were devices that would save them time and free them to do other things. Some quickly grasped the opportunity, but many Australians were suspicious of the new gadgets and wary of their cost. Some of the resistance to change may have been because women were the primary beneficiaries of such appliances, and yet the primary earners and financial decision-makers in most households were the men.

•—•

In 1924, a group of women in England had formed the Electrical Association for Women (EAW), in order to educate English women about the liberating power of electricity. Seven years after its formation, the EAW had 7000 members in branches across Britain. The leading light and driving force was Caroline Haslett, who travelled around Britain giving lectures to women on electrical appliances.[6]

With Violet taking on a similar role in Australia, it was only natural that the press would call her 'Australia's Caroline Haslett'. *The Sun* reported:

> Sydney women have a potential Caroline Haslett in their midst in the person of Mrs. F.V. McKenzie, the city's only woman electrician, who for a long time has advocated a course of simple lectures on electricity in schools and through women's clubs and organisations.
>
> At the moment, Mrs. McKenzie is initiating fifteen women pupils into the mysteries of radio for which she has held a transmitting licence since 1921. Among them is an elderly lady who is building her own radio set to present to her husband for his birthday. Some of the others are hoping to turn their knowledge to material advantage.[7]

The comparison was well intentioned, but it didn't do either woman justice. Certainly, Violet was educating women—just as Haslett was—but, unlike Haslett, she had not built an association with thousands of members. On the other hand, Violet had singular achievements not matched by her English counterpart—such as being Australia's first (and only) woman electrical engineer, a pioneer of Australian amateur radio and a successful entrepreneur.

Sydney's Feminist Club hosted a dinner in 1933 at the Wentworth Hotel ballroom for 100 prominent women in

Australian society. Violet, still the only woman electrical engineer in Australia, was one of the women honoured at the event.[8]

The Electrical Association for Women in Britain was in the news around that time as they had moved into new clubrooms in London's West End, with a modern electrical kitchen. Perhaps it was Violet's Sydney peers who suggested that, if she was indeed 'Australia's Caroline Haslett', maybe she ought to go all the way and create an Australian version of the EAW. Or maybe she came up with the idea on her own, after reading inspirational stories of Caroline Haslett's achievements in the morning newspaper.

Violet wrote to Haslett in October 1933, telling her that she planned to form an Australian organisation along the same lines as the EAW, and asking if she could do so as an affiliate of the British organisation. She received Haslett's reply, sent by cablegram, while she was visiting a friend in Brisbane. Haslett told her that the EAW would be delighted by the formation of an Australian EAW, and of course it could be affiliated.[9]

Ernest Fisk's company, Amalgamated Wireless Australia Ltd, provided sponsorship, as did the Trades Hall Council. The Society of Electrical Engineers provided her with temporary office space while she searched for a more permanent venue.[10] The Sydney City Council eventually provided her with space at Halsbury House, 170 King Street—only a minute's walk from her radio shop—and fitted out the new premises as clubrooms, providing modern electrical cookware.[11]

The Radio and Electrical Exhibition, a successor to the Wireless Exhibition organised by Violet and her colleagues twelve years previously, was now an annual event at Sydney Town Hall. Other states were holding them, too: Melbourne's first radio exhibition took place in 1926, and by 1934 such events were held regularly in all of the nation's capital cities. The organisers of the Sydney exhibition in 1934 provided Violet with free space to set up a stall to promote her new organisation, and to sign up members.[12]

The stall attracted a lot of public interest, with hundreds of membership enquiries. Violet was flat out throughout the event, although there were other displays attracting far more attention. Visitors to the exhibition could see the latest technological developments, including car radios, new domestic appliances and demonstrations of wireless transmission. The Town Hall was packed, with such large throngs of visitors jostling past the displays that the police at various times were forced to cordon off the entrance until the crowd inside had dwindled to a manageable level.

The exhibit that garnered the most interest was a device called the Pashometer, which claimed to provide a scientifically accurate measurement of a person's attractiveness. A group of men loitered near the machine to watch women take the test, until the police forced their way in and evicted them.

This did nothing to dampen the enthusiasm of throngs of young women eager to take the test, and to learn from the machine how attractive they were. Women crowded around the Pashometer until the crush became so dangerous that the police had to intervene and impose crowd control.[13]

Now that she had a book full of membership applications, Violet was ready to launch. The opening ceremony was held at her new premises on the evening of 22 March 1934, less than two weeks after the exhibition closed. Five hundred women arrived, far too many for the small rooms that the council had generously provided. Women stood shoulder-to-shoulder in the rooms, outside the door and even on the stairs up from the street while the event took place.[14]

Violet extolled the virtues of electricity. As she had recently said: 'Every home should be equipped, at least, with its vacuum cleaner, its toaster, and its electric iron.'[15]

The line-up of speakers that evening was impressive. Ellice Nosworthy was a notable Sydney architect; Caroline Martha David was the former president of the Women's National Movement, a vegetarian, an advocate of sex education and a proponent of weight training; and Linda Littlejohn was a prominent feminist active in both the Feminist Club and the National Council of Women, who in 1928 had launched the League of Women Voters. Other prominent women in Sydney society, including Dr Mary Booth and Dr Frances McKay (who was a close friend of Violet and Cecil's), attended the launch but did not speak.[16] The enterprise also had the enthusiastic support of Portia Geach, the activist founder of the Housewives' Association.[17]

In reporting the launch, *The Bulletin* magazine commented:

Mrs F.V. McKenzie is going to have her hands full teaching by word and demonstration the safe handling of electrical domestic appliances and arranging about the training of girls wishing to qualify in the science that most nearly touches the pleasant sides of modern life . . .

And here's a tip for homemakers—the curtains of the clubrooms are made of blue check oilcloth, similar to that which covers pantry shelves. It's cool-looking, stays in its folds, and when it gets dusty all it needs is a rub down with a damp cloth.[18]

Violet formally lodged the establishment documents for the Electrical Association for Women (Australia) in May 1934. Its stated goal was the 'instruction of women in electrical matters'[19] and its formal aims were:

1. To have centrally-situated premises, where women will be encouraged to come at all times for advice and instruction on all electrical matters and the proper and safe use of all electrical appliances.
2. To collect and distribute information on the uses of electricity, and to have regular lectures and demonstrations on the premises.
3. To have special courses of lectures and classes for different groups, such as for training girls who wish to take up electrical work as a career; for issuing certificates of competency to those who wish to take up household work (as far as the use of electrical appliances is concerned), and for women generally who are progressive enough to wish to know the best and most economical methods of eliminating household drudgery.
4. To arrange for lectures in schools, colleges, and broadcasts on safe handling, and the advantages of electrical appliances.
5. To arrange visits to factories, show rooms, broadcasting stations, etc., and to promote the social side to stimulate and maintain interest.
6. To test for safety, any domestic electrical appliances, without charge, brought in by members.
7. To endeavour to reduce the present charges for electricity by educating women to its advantages and thus promoting the consumption of current.
8. To have all women who come into contact with electricity, as members of the association, the only necessary qualification for membership being the obtaining of a membership ticket at 5/ per annum or an associate membership ticket at 2/ per annum.[20]

Four weeks after the launch, Violet McKenzie swept into the electrical section of Anthony Hordern's department store, followed by 200 women. She stopped, turned and asked the women of the EAW to gather around before giving them an impromptu speech on the benefits that the science of electricity was providing to the women of the world. She then gave them a tour of the various appliances on display, explaining each in turn.[21]

Anthony Hordern's staff members were ready and waiting for Violet's tour. They gave the women demonstrations of cakes and pastries being cooked using electrical appliances, they washed some clothes with an electric washing machine, and they even showed them an electric heater in operation.[22]

Over the next few weeks, the women of the EAW criss-crossed the city, visiting stores, factories, government buildings and electrical sites. They visited the Sydney City Council's electricity department (where Violet's husband, Cecil, happened to work) and were again provided with demonstrations of electric cooking, using the council's facilities. The general manager, Forbes McKay, greeted the women—no doubt wearing his smartest suit—and spoke about his department. He explained that electricity could save Australian households a lot of money. In fact, his engineers had done calculations on the matter, and had found that the cost of cooking ten breakfasts with electricity was a mere one penny! That was a saving nobody could ignore. He reassured the women that the council priced electricity as low as it could, because 'the object of the department was not to make money but to provide a service'.[23]

Returning from a visit to the Associated General Electric Company's works at Auburn, the two buses transporting the women stopped in traffic. Two men by the side of the road mistook the buses for standard public transport and jumped on board one of them. As the men entered the bus, the eyes of every passenger fixed upon them. Violet introduced herself and explained that these were not public buses. They asked her to allow them to catch a ride into the city. She relented, but only on the condition that they pay her two pence each, which she would donate to The Smith Family charity.[24]

At the King Street clubrooms, Violet arranged a program of lectures, appliance demonstrations, cooking lessons for electric kitchens, and social events. If a woman was concerned about the safety of an appliance, she could bring it to the EAW, where Violet would test it for her and issue a certificate of safety. All the while she continued her broadcasting commitments on multiple radio stations.[25]

Violet was the guest speaker at the October 1934 meeting of the United Associations of Women. There she spoke (as she often did) about the liberating power of technology. 'Women today have so many opportunities for spending their leisure in interesting ways, such as club work, that they should aim at obtaining this leisure, and one way is using labour-saving devices.'[26]

Her audience was probably less enthusiastic than other recent audiences. The United Associations of Women was a radical feminist group formed in 1929 by activists disenchanted with the existing women's associations, such as the Feminist Club and the National Council of Women, which these activists felt had evolved into little more than social clubs. The United Associations of Women had a sharp focus on political activism. Regardless of their differences, Violet wanted to tell them about her project, and they in turn were willing to listen.[27]

As Christmas neared, Violet's opinions were sought on electrical cooking. *The Sydney Morning Herald* published her advice on Christmas cakes:

A cake of about 12 lb should be put into the oven at a temperature of about 400 degrees. The top element should then be switched off immediately, and the bottom element left on 'low'. For the last half hour, switch off entirely. There is absolutely no need to open the oven door.[28]

In December, the EAW held a Christmas luncheon, and each guest received a small gift from Violet. There was also a lucky door prize, which was a chromium electric torch.[29] The guest speaker was Dr Frances McKay. After proposing a toast to the king (a standard formality), McKay praised Violet for her achievement in starting and running the organisation with energy and efficiency.[30]

Another speech was given by May Mathieson, an active member of the EAW. She said: 'Women are no longer satisfied to stop in the old groove of household drudgery. They are becoming electrically-minded, and will not be satisfied until they have electricity as a handmaid in the home.'[31] She then presented Violet with an electric table lamp as a gift on behalf of all the members of the association.

But while McKay and Mathieson sang Violet's praises in front of the EAW members, Violet was uncharacteristically quiet. Something had happened—something terrible—that had shaken her and undermined her role as a champion of electrical safety. And it was all because she and Cecil were so damned busy.

9

THE BODY ON THE LAWN

— •••• • — ••• — — — — •• — • — —
— — — — • — •••• • •— •• •— •— •

If an electric switch leaks—if, when turning it on, you
feel a tiny shock—have it repaired without delay.

Mary Tallis, syndicated advice columnist, 1935[1]

On a wet spring morning in November 1934, when Violet walked out of the front door of her home at Greenwich Point to collect the newspaper, she made a terrible discovery. There was a dead boy on the ground near her gate. She hurried inside, called for Cecil, and phoned for an ambulance. But it was too late, because the boy had died during the night.[2]

Thirteen-year-old Harold Navy Hinks lived in Mitchell Street, Greenwich Point, around the corner from Violet and Cecil. Maybe he intended to pilfer something from the McKenzies' house—things had gone missing from the yard recently—but, while opening the gate, he was electrocuted by the circuit that Cecil had installed to turn on the porch light.

It was a tragic combination of faulty wiring, wet grass and bare feet, turning Harold Hinks into an electrical conduit between the gate's latch and the ground. If he had been wearing shoes, or if the ground had been dry, he would have got nothing more than a sharp zap to the hand.[3]

The boy's father, Leslie Hinks, was a businessman with investments in mining and property projects around Australia, owning (among other assets) the Greenknowe apartment block in Potts Point, which was estimated to be worth about £750,000. He was in Kalgoorlie on goldmining business when he learned of his son's death. Hinks immediately chartered an aircraft to return to Sydney in time for the funeral on Thursday of that week.[4]

The first leg of his trip was on a mail plane that would take him as far as Ceduna, where he boarded a private aircraft that had come from Sydney to collect him. In the late afternoon, the aircraft stopped in Mildura to refuel. The pilot, Oliver Bythe Hall (known to everyone as 'Pat'), suggested to Hinks that they stay in Mildura overnight and depart early the next morning, but Hinks was having none of that and insisted that they press on to Sydney.[5]

During the final leg of the journey, the aircraft encountered an enormous cloud of grasshoppers, towering 8000 feet (2400 metres) above the ground. Seeing the swarm in front of him, Hall told Hinks that he wanted to turn the aircraft around, return to Mildura and stay there overnight, as he had suggested earlier. Hinks instructed him, 'Push on. I must be in Sydney tonight.'[6]

The grasshopper cloud was too high to detour around, so Hall went up and over it, taking his plane to a very high altitude, where he lost his bearings. It was dark when he returned to a lower altitude, and the eastern seaboard was covered by a blanket of low clouds that Hall mistook to be the ocean. Believing that he had overshot Sydney, the pilot wheeled the plane around to head west again, with an almost empty fuel tank. This error took them directly into the Blue Mountains at low altitude at night.[7]

Hall glimpsed some trees through a break in the clouds below and realised his mistake, but it was too late. A rock wall appeared ahead of them. Hall swung the aircraft around in the hope of 'pancaking' the plane onto the canopy below, but one of the wings clipped the top of a tree. The plane flipped over and crashed into the mountainside.[8]

Hall was thrown from the plane but, although seriously injured, he survived. Hinks, trapped in the wreckage, was alive when a rescue team found him, but died at the scene later in the night. His last words were 'Goodbye, my darling wife'.[9]

The next day, as mourners gathered outside St Giles Anglican Church for the funeral of Harold Hinks, news spread through the crowd that Harold's father, Leslie, had died the night before on his way back to Sydney. Harold's mother dropped to the ground, wailing with grief. The funeral for the boy transformed into a sort of double funeral for both father and son.[10]

A coronial inquest was held into Harold Hinks's death. Violet and Cecil hired legal representation for the hearings.

Following the death, the police had asked an electrician named Ivor Mitchell to inspect the scene. Called as a witness, he said that when he first touched the gate, he received an electric shock. Mitchell added that, upon examining the gate, he realised that the circuit had no earth wire, which it should have had.

Cecil took the stand where, under questioning, he admitted

that he had received a complaint from a milkman earlier in the year about getting a shock from the gate. However, Cecil stated that he had personally never received a shock from it, despite using it daily.[11]

The coroner concluded that Cecil and Violet were not responsible for the boy's death, declaring it to be an accident. In his report, however, he recommended that a law be introduced mandating that all electrical circuits be inspected annually for defects.[12]

Two weeks after Harold Hinks's death, a nine-year-old girl was electrocuted in Hobart when she climbed onto the roof of her home. The following week, a man and women died of electrocution from a high-voltage wire on a farm near Mackay, in the state's north. And in January in Manilla, also in the state's north, an eight-year-old boy was electrocuted when he climbed onto the roof of his home so he could jump into the backyard swimming pool. Electricity wires were lying on the roof and were in his way, and he was killed when he tried to move them. In New South Wales alone, eighteen people, including Harold Hinks, had died from electrocution during 1934.[13]

A coroner overseeing the inquest of another electrocuted child twelve months later blasted the government authorities for inaction, particularly on their failure to crack down on older installations that had been done before the current safety regulations had been introduced.[14]

•—•

How did Violet deal with the discovery of a dead boy on her lawn? How would anyone respond to the grief and self-recrimination that such an event would bring on?

We don't know how she responded in private to the death of Harold Hinks, or what conversations she and Cecil had about it. We know that she didn't stop her frenetic public activities. Violet's response to adversity, as always, was to keep moving forward. The EAW was now steaming along, and she—as the central driving force—was needed there.

Just before Christmas 1934, a major personality in the British Electrical Association for Women arrived in Australia and was the guest of honour at an event held by Violet's Australian EAW. Lady Gladys Swaythling was the treasurer of the British organisation as well as an active patron and supporter of charities and causes including refugees, Girl Guides and various women's organisations. Her visit to Australia was part of an extensive around-the-world tour.[15]

Later that month, Violet held a public lecture on the dangers of electricity, providing lessons on how to assist in the case of electric shock. Maybe, if she educated the public about responding to electric shock, someone else's life could be saved in the future.[16]

At the EAW Christmas luncheon the following December, the guest speaker was the NSW Minister for Local Government, Eric Spooner. He used the occasion to rail against the dangers of faulty electrical installations. If Violet felt that his speech was, even in part, directed at her, she gave no indication of it.

During 1935, she had ceased her broadcasting activities and closed her Phillip Street retail business. She had continued in her role as president of the EAW and had spent more time at home, exploring and developing a skill that previously had not interested her in the slightest: cooking. This new hobby would become her next major enterprise.

10

COOKING WITH ELECTRICITY

—•—• — —— ——— —•— •• —• ——• •—— •• — ••••
• •—••• •—•—• — •—• •• —•—• •• — —•— —

The progress in the knowledge of food and its prepara-
tion is one of the wonders of today!

Dr Frances McKay, 1936[1]

When a representative of [this newspaper] called at
the council chambers to find out how long the blackout
would last, he noticed on the counter a copy of the All
Electric Cookery Book!

Cootamundra Herald, 1952[2]

Within two years, Violet's Electrical Association for
Women had attracted over 1000 members, and within
three years it was approaching 2000 members. It also had a

theme song, 'Electrical Girls', written and composed by Violet (the lyrics of which have sadly evaded this author).

At its heart, the EAW was about encouraging women to embrace modernity, in the hope that technology would liberate them from the drudgery of manual housework. However, despite Violet's enthusiasm, the science of electricity held little interest for most members. One thing they *were* interested in was cooking.[3]

But while she was styled as a champion of the modern electric home, Violet's shortcomings in this area were quickly apparent, certainly to herself. As an engineer, publisher, entrepreneur and radio broadcaster, she had always been too busy to bother with homecraft. The media had portrayed her as a sort of superwoman who did it all—managed a career while lovingly doting on her husband at home—but that image was not entirely accurate.

Now, however, having enlisted hundreds of women—soon to be thousands—into an association that in part promised to help make cooking easier for them, the time had come to take homecraft more seriously. She invested in a few cookery books to get started but soon discovered that there were none devoted entirely to electricity, other than some thin booklets produced by Westinghouse and General Electric.

She explained later, 'I found I couldn't get a good, plain, honest book with plain cooking. You could get fancy things, American ones, with things that you and I don't bother making, as a rule.'[4] Since no cookbook existed with standard home recipes in electric kitchens, Violet decided to write one.[5]

She bought or borrowed every cookery book she could find and piled them all onto a trestle table in her kitchen. Then she worked through each one, trying the recipes and attempting to adapt gas-cooking and fire-cooking recipes to electricity.

She ignored anything fancy, unusual or that sounded too difficult. Sticking only to 'good, sensible ideas',[6] she attempted to update each recipe, cooked each one in her expensive new electric kitchen as best she could, and served the outcome to Cecil that evening.

Two major brands—Westinghouse and General Electric—allowed her to incorporate recipes they had distributed in their booklets into her cookery book.

Many councils employed 'demonstrators' to teach the public how to use electrical appliances. As Violet was well known to the demonstrators around Sydney, they proved to be a great source of knowledge on electric cooking and provided her with many recipes.

Her published cookbook contained over 600 recipes. It included the staples of Australian dinners, such as tomato soup, minestrone, curried prawns, roast chicken (which included instructions for plucking the chicken) and roast leg of lamb. There were two pages of rabbit recipes, including baked rabbit, steamed rabbit, fricasseed rabbit, curried rabbit, rabbit pie and rabbit casserole, along with the suggestion: 'It is always advisable to cook bacon with rabbit to supply the deficiency in fat.'[7] Always scrupulous in giving credit where credit was due, Violet titled one recipe 'Mrs Nickson's Indian Curry'.[8]

Breakfast dishes included fried bananas and bacon, cheese soufflé, mock pigeon pie, potato sausages and porridge pancakes. The desserts—then more commonly called puddings—were a collection of dishes well known to Australians growing up in the 1930s, 1940s, 1950s and 1960s, such as tapioca pudding, lemon pudding, lemon sago, stewed fruit, stewed rhubarb, and trifle. The cake section included (among many others) apple teacake, coffee cake, coconut fingers and four recipes for fruit cake.

She included a section at the back called 'Safety First Hints', where she impressed upon readers the need to be careful with electrical appliances and to always be mindful of the dangers. She implored, 'Impress on children the danger of touching any overhead or dangling wires, especially when standing on an iron roof, or on the ground.'[9]

Violet financed and managed the publication of the *Electrical Association for Women's Cookery Book*, which was released in June 1936. Her friend, Dr Frances McKay, wrote the foreword, which concluded, 'I hope that every electric cook will get both help and pleasure from this book, and that the book will have the success it deserves.'[10]

Later renamed the *All Electric Cookery Book*, it was an instant bestseller, quickly establishing itself as a mainstay reference in kitchens around Australia. It ran to four editions, sold innumerable thousands of copies, and remained constantly in print for eighteen years.[11]

The Electrical Association for Women suddenly had sufficient funds to acquire the larger clubrooms they had been talking about for more than two years, and moved into new premises at 9 Clarence Street. There were several rooms behind the main showroom, including a library, a bridge room, and a kitchen with a primrose and blue colour scheme. One reporter described the kitchen as 'every woman's dream of a kitchen combining utility and beauty'.[12]

The kitchen alone cost over £100—equivalent to more than $10,000 in today's Australian currency—and it was an extravagance during the Great Depression. The showroom was for educational purposes only: nothing was sold at the EAW except the *All Electric Cookery Book*.[13]

The opening of the new clubrooms on 18 November 1936 was attended by 250 people, with live music playing for three hours. Violet dispensed with the usual speeches and ribbon-cutting ceremony. The music was enough.[14]

•—•

In August 1936, a representative of the NSW Department of Education approached Violet and invited her to be on its electrical safety advisory committee, and she accepted.

The first meeting she attended was unpleasant. Perhaps referring to her small stature (she was only a little over 150 centimetres tall), one of the men on the committee joked that she was clearly well suited to the role because she was 'half-way between a man and a child'.[15] Recalling the incident 40 years later, Violet said, 'Luckily, I have a sense of humour. Nothing like that could possibly upset me.'[16]

Being on a government advisory committee was tedious and unsatisfying, with only the vague possibility of effecting long-term social change. Violet suggested that, as a member of the committee, she should write articles on electrical safety for *The School Magazine*, a publication distributed to schools around the state. This meant that, instead of sitting in a boardroom, she was at least doing something to get the message out to children.

Her articles described electricity as being carried out by mischievous little creatures called electric imps that could do good work, but were dangerous if released from the powerlines:

Do you know where electricity comes from? Well, millions and millions of tiny Electric Imps are sent out from a power station, and they come along one of the copper wires you can see high up along the street, and they go back to the power station again, along another of the copper wires. Here they come!

91

Now you know what is meant when wires are said to be Alive! They are just crowded with Electric Imps!

These little imps are very powerful and are ready and willing to do all kinds of work for us, but they can be mischievous too, so the copper wires along which they run are put high up on poles, right out of reach. The men who sometimes work on these poles are very careful not to touch any bare wires carrying the Electric Imps for fear of being killed, so all boys and girls should keep right away from them whether the wires are very high or on the ground.[17]

The editor of Sydney's *The Sun*, having seen the articles in *The School Magazine*, contacted Violet and asked if he could reproduce 'The Electric Imps' as a newspaper series. Violet asked how much he was prepared to offer.

'You wouldn't expect me to pay for them!' he retorted.

She was more interested in getting the message out than making money, so she relented—but she offered him a deal. He could publish the articles, as long as he gave her the lithograph plates used to print them after each publication.[18]

Once all the articles had appeared in *The Sun*, Violet obtained the plates from the newspaper as agreed. She used the plates to compile the articles into a small children's book, which she self-published with the title *The Electric Imps*. She never sold any copies of *The Electric Imps*, but merely gave them to anyone who wanted one.

In early 1937, she posted two copies to Buckingham Palace, in the hope that Queen Elizabeth would read them to her daughters, eleven-year-old Princess Elizabeth (the future Queen Elizabeth II) and her six-year-old sister, Princess Margaret. She did not receive a response, so she never knew whether or not Queen Elizabeth ever received her copies of *The Electric Imps*.

The *All Electric Cookery Book*—Violet's second successful publishing venture (*Wireless Weekly* being the first)—grew in reputation and scope with each passing year. By contrast, her children's electrical safety book—although it mattered greatly to her—was not of the same quality and, despite her adept marketing skills, it didn't gain traction with the public. There was only ever one print run of *The Electric Imps*.

11

THE AUSTRALIAN WOMEN'S FLYING CLUB

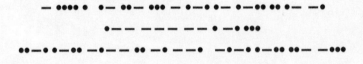

*We will have a well trained and perfectly fit army of women
which no government could refuse in a time of war.*

Betty Mullins, 1938[1]

On a cold and windy winter evening in 1938, Violet
McKenzie walked across the city through heavy rain to
the Feminist Club on King Street, where a meeting was being
held for women interested in forming a flying club. Violet
was one of the organisers of this first general meeting; her
EAW clubrooms on Clarence Street had been used for planning meetings.[2]

Around 200 women took their seats to hear Betty Mullins—the driving force behind this new club—outline her plan. Her speech unfortunately was not recorded, but it was in the same vein as one she had given earlier in the day to the Farmers' Business Girls Luncheon, as reported in *The Sydney Morning Herald* on 24 August 1938:

> The formation of the Australian Women's Flying Club has as its basis the desire to see Australian girls able to obtain thorough training in all branches of aviation at a reasonable cost. It has been suggested that this movement may become an association of 'flying Amazons', but the primary objects are associated with the benefits to be derived from the advancement of aviation for women ... It is essential that we all become increasingly air-minded, and it is a necessary service to the community that girls from the earliest age be given the opportunity of understanding the marvellous possibilities of aviation, and if they so desire, become proficient in the piloting of a machine.[3]

Mullins had been agitating for the formation of the club since June. She had given interviews to journalists, held town hall meetings and had even become embroiled in a war of words with the federal Minister for Defence.

The news from abroad was ominous. Twenty years after the end of World War I, there was a fear that it could all happen again. Fascism was ascendant, with fascist leaders in Spain, Hungary, Austria, Italy and, most notably, Germany, where Adolf Hitler's Nazi party had reignited nationalist resentment and was turning Germany again into a military superpower.

If war broke out in Europe, Australia would be involved. That was simply a given. The only question was whether there would be another European war. With the situation overseas in mind, Betty Mullins's 'flying club' looked a lot like an attempt to create a women's air militia.

Mullins took great pains to emphasise that her club would *not* be military in nature. She told a journalist from *The Sun*:

> The Women's Flying Corps will not be a lip-serving, flag-waving patriotic organisation . . . Those who join will be fully occupied learning the technical side of flying through lectures and study, first aid, and other subjects that will make the corps a valuable asset to Australia. They will be able to progress to the stage at which they may qualify for the pilot's licence if they so desire. In no sense will we be anything suggestive of a military organisation, but in the event of trouble threatening Australia's shores we shall be available to the authorities if needed.[4]

Those final words—'we shall be available . . . if needed'—were all the journalist needed to completely undo everything else Mullins had said. The news article about Mullins later that week was emblazoned with the headline: *WOMEN AS WAR BIRDS IF WANTED.*

Mullins had meanwhile written to the Minister for Defence, Harold Thorby, outlining her plans for a women's flying club and asking if he would endorse it. But Thorby made political hay out of her letter and publicly excoriated Mullins for it:

> Flying for defence or commercial purposes by women is neither advisable nor desirable. My government does not consider women as suitable for such occupations, and has no intention of encouraging them to participate . . .
>
> Some women flyers, such as Jean Batten and Amy Johnson, have done very well—performed remarkable feats, in fact.

I am satisfied they can be as capable in the air as men, but I do not consider commercial or defence flying a suitable sphere for their activities.

We don't have women as railway engineers or tram drivers, and we don't want them as pilots.[5]

Others piled on. The Melbourne gossip magazine *Table Talk* published a column by the pseudonymous William Hazlitt Jr titled 'Why must women butt in?' The column mocked Mullins, every word dripping with sarcastic contempt:

O, why must women butt in? Man cannot enter any sphere of endeavor or succeed in any exploit demanding those peculiar qualities which make him man, without some woman or other trying to imitate his dexterity . . .

[W]hat a woeful change is here! Woman no longer is satisfied to be queen—she wants to be king also . . . But the dear creature was never built for strenuous competition, prodigious mental effort, sheer physical strength . . .

All this sounds like the disgruntlings of a liver the morning after. But nay, my pretties. It is inspired by the news that Miss Betty Mullins is asking Minister for Defence Thorby to support her scheme for creation of an Australian women's flying corps to be trained in aviation, nursing and first aid. Miss Mullins adds glibly that her corps would not be a military organisation, but 'in the event of trouble threatening Australia it would be available to the authorities.'

I suppose most women will think Mr Thorby should be grateful for such a gallant gesture. His only comment, however, is that he does not believe there is any lasting place for women in either defence or commercial aviation, which take them out of their natural environment—the home and the training of a family.[6]

The irony of all the outrage was that many Australian women already had civilian and commercial pilot's licences and had been flying aircraft for more than a decade. The first had been Millicent Bryant, who performed a ten-minute solo flight at Mascot in 1927. Bryant drowned in a ferry accident later that year. The pilots of the NSW Aero Club paid their respects with a formation flyover of the church during her funeral, followed later by a single low-flying plane that dropped a wreath at her grave.[7]

In 1930, Bobby Terry—a farmer's wife living near Gunnedah—became the first Australian woman to obtain a commercial pilot's licence, which she used to carry out farm work as well as participate in flying races.[8]

When English aviator Amy Johnson flew into Sydney in 1930, completing her renowned solo flight from London, her aircraft was escorted to the airport at Mascot by six planes, all flown by Australian female pilots: Margaret Skelton, Bobby Terry, Evelyn Follett (who had actually started her pilot training in 1926—before Bryant), Una Upfold, Jean Arnott and Freda Deaton.[9]

So, despite the denunciations, Betty Mullins's proposal for a women's flying club was not particularly radical. As Mullins explained, the objective was really just forming a club, encouraging women to take up flying and helping them develop what she called 'air-mindedness'.[10]

She might have taken some satisfaction from the fortunes of her detractors. *Table Talk* went out of business twelve months later. Thorby was voted out of office two years later and never succeeded in winning back his seat.

●—●

Two of Australia's most reputable aviators—Nancy Bird and Margaret Adams—attended the August 1938 meeting.

They had previously been planning to form some kind of women's flying club themselves, but Betty Mullins (whom they had never heard of) had come out of nowhere and beaten them to it, disrupting their own plans. Since Mullins was such a mover and shaker, they decided to get on board.[11]

At the general meeting on that rainy Sydney night, Margaret Adams was elected president of the club, Violet the treasurer and Betty Mullins the secretary.

Betty Mullins was not a pilot. Nor, it turned out, was she a 'twenty-two-year-old office worker', as initially reported— she was only seventeen years old. She and her friend, Yvonne Wurth, had wanted to learn to fly, but they couldn't afford the lessons—so they came up with the idea of starting a flying club, which would subsidise them.[12]

•—•

The flying club was temporarily headquartered at the clubrooms of Violet's Electrical Association for Women. Later in the year, it relocated to Young Street, and then to more permanent premises on Phillip Street.[13]

The club organised a program of courses for its members on aviation-related skills and attributes, including instrumentation, aerodynamics, first aid and physical fitness. Members paid a nominal fee. A bursary system was established to subsidise a comprehensive pilot-training course for members who showed a high level of aptitude. This was exactly what Betty Mullins had hoped would happen.[14]

Morse code was a necessary skill for pilots. Since Violet was proficient in Morse code, she held courses in it for the club's members. She and Cecil installed Morse keys with circuits and headphones at the EAW clubroom so that the women could get hands-on practice.

Her Morse code lessons were featured in an issue of *The Australian Women's Weekly*:

In their airforce-blue uniforms these girls, whose average age is 21, are attractive as well as alert. Two hundred and thirty members are learning the theory of all branches of aviation, and bursaries are being made available so that outstanding girls may have practical flying instruction. The organisers hope to extend the scheme to all States.

In her section Mrs. McKenzie conducts extra classes for advanced pupils. She has been interested in radio for many years, and holds a transmitter's licence.

'I think everybody should understand Morse,' she says. 'Apart from its everyday use, there have been innumerable cases—such as that of the fisherman in distress on the N.S.W. coast recently, who flashed an S.O.S. call from his boat to the shore—where it has saved lives.'[15]

In January 1939, Violet gave an examination to her Morse code students, and presented certificates to the students who had attained proficiency (which was most of them). In the flying club curriculum, the Morse code classes had been a standout success.[16]

In February, Betty Mullins resigned her position as secretary of the Australian Women's Flying Club and was replaced in the role by Barbara Hitchins. Mullins was appointed as 'Honorary Secretary', a title she retained until the next general meeting, after which she left the club entirely. The reason for her resignation is not known. Maybe she was asked to resign the position because of her age, or maybe she clashed with other committee members.

It may be no coincidence that Violet left the flying club at around the same time. Unlike Mullins, she did not resign, staying on as treasurer until the next annual general meeting later that year; however, she reduced her involvement, and by the end of the year she was not involved at all.

Around March or early April, Violet informed the Australian Women's Flying Club that she would no longer train girls in Morse code for the club, but would establish her own school. She explained the situation to the current crop of students, reassuring them that she intended to keep running classes but not as part of the flying club. Instead, they would be part of something entirely new.

Violet was about to create the Women's Emergency Signalling Corps, which would be dedicated to teaching Morse code to women.[17] This was to become her greatest achievement.

12

THE WOMEN'S EMERGENCY
SIGNALLING CORPS

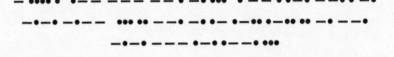

*Even before the declaration of war, Mrs McKenzie had
gathered about her a group of young women willing to
give up their spare time for an ideal.*

Margaret Curtis-Otter, W.R.A.N.S.[1]

The threat of war hung like a dark cloud over Australia,
infiltrating the collective consciousness through news
reports, around barbecues, at pubs and social clubs, and in
hushed conferences in the meeting rooms of generals and
politicians. Despite Germany being crushed by the Allies
in World War I twenty years earlier, the country's military

resurgence—and the extremism of its leader, Adolf Hitler—was frightening.

Optimists hoped that some kind of peace deal could be sorted out and everything would calm down. Those of a more pessimistic nature believed that Hitler was interested in conquest, not peace; that he could not be trusted; and that war was coming, whether the Allied nations wanted it or not. Violet subscribed to the pessimistic point of view, which morphed into gloomy certainty in late 1938, when British Prime Minister Neville Chamberlain struck a deal with Hitler.

Hitler had been raising the temperature with strident claims that the Sudetenland, a region in Czechoslovakia, rightfully belonged to the German people. Chamberlain was on a mission to avert war from happening, no matter what. He travelled to Germany several times to find some kind of compromise with Hitler. On returning home after his final negotiation, Chamberlain praised Hitler. 'Here was a man who could be relied upon when he had given his word,' he said. Chamberlain boasted that, by doing a deal with the German leader, he had prevented the world from plunging into a second world war: 'My good friends, this is the second time in our history that there has come back from Germany to Downing Street peace with honour. I believe it is peace for our time.'[2]

The peace deal came with a big price tag, though. The entire population of the Sudetenland, who had been citizens of Czechoslovakia only a day before, instantly became—with the stroke of a pen—a part of the Third Reich under the iron rule of Adolf Hitler.

Predictably, responses to the deal in Australia were split down the optimist–pessimist divide. Newspapers applauded Chamberlain as the man who had prevented a second world war, while sombre voices muttered that Hitler was a dangerous man who could not be trusted. A Sydney history professor, Stephen Roberts, denounced Chamberlain's dangerous naivety. He made the cynical (but sadly accurate) observation that if the Allies wanted peace at any price, then Germany and the other fascist nations would demand an ever-higher price. Hitler had manufactured the entire crisis, Roberts said, and the compromise solution gave the German chancellor exactly what he wanted.[3]

Violet was appalled by Chamberlain's naivety, and thought that his capitulation to Hitler now made war a certainty. She described her reaction to the news: 'When Neville Chamberlain came back from Munich and said, "Peace in our time", I began preparing for war.'[4]

As she later explained, 'I realised that one of the most important parts of the war would be communication, so I decided to open a school to train girls in Morse code and radio.'[5]

•—•

Morse code was a vital part of the public communication system, used for transmitting telegrams and cablegrams (coordinated by the Postmaster General). The military services also used Morse code in their radio signals. If war broke out—and Violet was sure that it was coming—the military would grab as many civilians employed in communications as they could, leaving the country with a shortage of expertise . . . particularly in Morse code.

But if women were trained in Morse code, they could fill all those vacant positions left by men who had gone to fight in the war. Women could do the jobs that the men had left behind, if they were trained and ready in time.

At the start of May 1939, Violet established the Women's Emergency Signalling Corps (WESC) at the clubrooms in Clarence Street, under the auspices of the Electrical

Association for Women. Fifty women joined immediately; most of them had been involved in the Australian Women's Flying Club.[6]

She made public appeals to other Sydney women to attend. 'There is no age limit, and the only distinction we make is to ask members whether they are under or over 40 years of age. We just put a small O or U on the form.'[7]

The lessons were free, and anyone could join as long as they had attended school at some point, and were willing to learn. A news item outlined the requirements:

> Sound education in English and spelling and geography, concentration and perseverance are the qualifications. No age limit. Procedure will be part of the course, including accepted signs, abbreviations, hand signalling, and transmitting formulas.[8]

Within six months, the membership had tripled to 150 women.

Anyone can join, Violet had said publicly, with no age limit. Yet her classes swelled with young women in their teens and early twenties, full of enthusiasm, and much, much younger than her. At 49 years old, she was in many cases older than their mothers.

They called her *Mrs Mac*. She called them *My Girls*.

•—•

Violet explained to the newcomers that when talking about dots and dashes, they're called *dits* and *dahs*. She told them, 'The first letter we will learn is E, the most used letter in the alphabet. It's just one *dit*.'[9]

Violet provided tea and coffee. Some would bring sandwiches and other homemade snacks to share. Classes began at 7 p.m., covering a range of topics well beyond Morse code.

After all, if her students were really going to step into men's civilian jobs, they needed to know more than just how to tap a Morse key.

She taught them circuit theory, the physics of electromagnetic radiation, how to install an antenna and how to troubleshoot a faulty portable radio. She taught them about call signs and their usage, common abbreviations, and other conventions they would need to know. She taught them about dry batteries, buzzers and loudspeakers.

She also taught semaphore—the nautical system of communicating with flags—as well as hand-signalling systems and visual signalling, which was basically Morse code using a light known as an Aldis lamp. She would give a lecture, followed by a practical demonstration and practice session.[10]

Violet created a puppetry model of an arm and hand, with a string attached to the wrist so that she could show the correct wrist movement for using a Morse key.[11] She was quoted in *The Sydney Morning Herald* praising the progress of her students. 'The girls are picking up the work very quickly, and of course in a job like this, they are just as competent as the men.'[12]

The former flying club members had enjoyed wearing that club's smart blue uniform, and asked if their new club (which they called Sigs) could have a uniform. Violet designed two uniforms, one for summer and one for winter. The summer outfit consisted of a forest-green skirt with white blouse, a jacket, and a badge with the WESC logo. The winter uniform was in the same green-and-white colour scheme, but with overalls instead of a skirt.

Violet could see how keen her students were to get their uniforms, so she used that as a way to motivate them to learn. 'You can't just join up and get a uniform right away,' she told them. In order to qualify for the right to wear a WESC uniform, they had to pass a ten-words-per-minute Morse code test, administered by her. They had to buy their winter uniform from Violet (at cost—she did not want to make a profit from her girls), and they had to make the summer uniform themselves.[13]

Violet told her students that they were welcome to come along at any time during the day to practise their Morse code. The Morse stations at the EAW clubrooms were soon filled each day with eager young women tapping their keys. Lunchtime Morse sessions at Sigs became a regular part of life for many Sydney women.

One group of eight women employed near Haymarket would share the cost of two taxis in their lunch breaks to ride to Clarence Street, put in some Morse code practice while eating sandwiches, then share two taxis back to work for the afternoon shift.[14] Two friends employed at a nearby law firm had previously eaten lunch and had a smoke at a city restaurant before Sigs came along, but now they gave up that routine and would walk each lunchtime to 9 Clarence Street, eating their sandwiches as they walked.[15]

One student explained her love of Sigs in a newspaper article: 'I like the idea of women doing something, and this telegraphy seems practical to me.'[16]

When anyone proudly turned up in their WESC uniform for the first time, Violet would send them off to a nearby photographer: 'Go around to Julia Leslie, who will take a photograph for me.' Leslie had offered to photograph without charge every uniformed WESC member, as her way of supporting Violet's endeavour. She would give Violet two photographs of each subject: a large one to put on the wall, and a small one to put into a photograph album.[17]

As a result of this charitable gesture, Leslie ended up making a lot of money from the pictures, because the women would return and ask to purchase additional copies for themselves, which they would give to aunts, grandmothers and so on. Leslie would charge standard rates for these photographs.[18]

Violet, who loved to play the piano and enjoyed writing songs, composed a song for the WESC. The melody is unknown, but the words remain:

The WESC Song

Signallers keen are we
Our dits and ours dahs are in harmony
Dah-di-di-dah di-di-dah
We can get a message through,
A buzzer, flag or lamp will do.
So here's a message straight to you,
We're ready to serve our King and our country.
Dah-di-di-dah di-di-dah
Signallers keen are we.[19]

Because rhythm is so intrinsic to Morse code, Violet was sure that music would help people learn it. She purchased an Audiophone, an early sort of jukebox that played vinyl records. While her students were practising Morse, she would play tracks including 'The Teddy Bears' Picnic' so that they could tap their messages in time with the music.[20]

A beginner would have a paper copy of the Morse alphabet on the table in front of her. She could consult the page when she was sending or receiving at very slow speeds, but as the pace picked up the page was of no use. There was simply no time to consult the chart to look up each letter. The Morse code simply had to be memorised.[21]

Her girls struggled to learn those dots and dashes, so Violet invented memory tricks to assist them. For example, in

Morse code the letter Q is — —•— or, as Morse practitioners would say, *dah-dah-dit-dah*. That's the exact same rhythm as the wedding-day tune 'Here Comes the Bride'. As Violet transmitted a Q to any of her learners, she would sing (or sometimes hum), 'Here comes the bride!' That was all it took to implant it in someone's memory. Nobody at Sigs would ever forget how to send Q in Morse code.[22]

The letter V (which happens to be the number five in Roman numerals) in Morse is *dit-dit-dit-dah*. This sounds just like the opening notes from Beethoven's Fifth Symphony. Violet would transmit a V to the students, and simultaneously hum Beethoven's Fifth.[23]

Some of her other mnemonics for learning Morse code were:

- The letter A (*dit-dah*) sounded like the start of a magic show: 'ta-dah!'
- The letter B (*dah-dit-dit-dit*) sounded like 'beef essences'.
- The letter D (*dah-dit-dit*) was 'dog did it'.
- The letter L (*dit-dah-dit-dit*) was 'to hell with it'[24] (to 'L' with it).
- The letter P (*dit-dah-dah-dit*) was 'a pork sausage'.[25]
- The letter X (*dah-dit-dit-dah*) was 'look at the king' (the word for king in Latin is *rex*).
- The letter Y (*dah-dit-dah-dah*) was 'happy birthday'.

A lot of people struggled to learn the code for the number three (which was *dit-dit-dit-dah-dah*). With a twinkle in her eye, Violet would sympathise with them, and say, 'Yes, this is a hard one.'

This is a hard one. *Dit-dit-dit-dah-dah*. That was the mnemonic for the number three.[26]

•—•

The devotion and zeal of the young women were extraordinary. They sat attentive and wide-eyed in Violet's lectures; they proudly wore the uniforms she had designed for them; and many purchased a Morse key set so they could practise at home. But Violet became aware that they were not actually interested in doing civilian jobs. If—or when—the war began, they wanted to enlist.

With some rare exceptions, throughout human history warfare had been a male endeavour, although World War I had seen a major shift, with women actively participating in several countries. Australian women had served as nurses and other medical staff, while in Britain they could join a women's army service and women's royal naval service to take on non-combat roles such as cooks, mechanics, ambulance drivers and telegraphists. Britain discontinued these services as soon as the war finished. Russia had gone further than any other modern nation in forming fifteen all-women combat battalions. But these measures were seen as being a singular response to a unique situation, not as part of a global trend towards the enlistment of women.

•—•

World War II began in September 1939, when German troops crossed the Polish border on the orders of Adolf Hitler. Poland's allies—Britain and France—immediately declared war on Germany, and nations within the British Commonwealth, including Australia, followed suit. The second world war had started, and Australia was in it.

13

A SENSE OF RHYTHM

•—　•••• • —• ••• •　— — — ••—•
•—• •••• —•— — — •••• — —

It is funny with Morse, you are better at it if you are not too imaginative. And it helps if you have a good sense of rhythm.

Florence Violet McKenzie[1]

Young Australian men enlisted in droves, just as an earlier generation had done 25 years before. At this stage, the war was primarily a fight between European powers (Japan and the United States were not yet involved), but even at the beginning it was startlingly close to home for Australia, because those European powers had territories in Asia and the Pacific. The German navy was active near Australian shores, and it was a German raider that sank HMAS *Sydney* off the Western Australian coast in 1941.

Violet's school continued to expand, with membership hitting 300 by the end of 1939. *Wireless Weekly* helped to promote it, running an article titled 'Women's signal corps invites volunteers', which stated that the only requirements for joining were 'a fair education and an ability to concentrate'.[2]

For the WESC end-of-year function, Violet booked the ballroom in the NSW State Theatre, with various dignitaries in attendance, including Florence Parkhill (the wife of former Minister for Defence Archdale Parkhill), who handed out proficiency certificates to 73 WESC members. Lieutenant Colonel Rupert Smith, the officer in charge of the second-division signallers, also attended as a representative of the army and gave a speech.

In the days prior to the event, Smith had visited the WESC classes at Clarence Street, where he had been surprised and impressed by their rigour and the technical competence of the women. He was particularly struck by the achievement of Myrtle Reeves, who could send Morse code at a rate of ten words a minute after a mere sixteen days of practice. Smith spelled out why this was such an astonishing achievement: 'The average army man is lucky if he can send ten words a minute after two months' training.'[3]

Violet thought that Myrtle Reeves' talent might be due to her learning ballet when she was younger. 'As a result, she has rhythm, which may be responsible for her speed in sending Morse.'[4] Another standout pupil was Ena Stewart, who could send and receive Morse code at 25 words per minute.[5]

In his address at the WESC end-of-year function, Smith praised Violet's teaching methods and raised the possibility of the women being employed by the army in signals (in a civilian capacity, he hastened to add):

I don't see why girls shouldn't be employed as signal operators in the army. After having seen the corps, I am convinced Australian girls make better operators than men. Your training system is the same as in the army, but your results are better. Girls either have more brains or some other attribute, perhaps a sense of rhythm, that men lack.

As chief signal officer of this district I need 400 operators, and I have no more than 130 now. I am going to see if some avenue can be found, in the army or connected with it, for the employment of women operators.

Women have no place in an army on active service, but they might be of great value as operators in Australia, if we have to send a large force overseas.

However, if a bevy of beautiful girls were introduced into the signalling corps, I am afraid communications would be completely upset![6]

The next day, Smith followed up on his comments at the event in the ballroom. 'I was impressed by the teaching methods used by the principal (Mrs F.V. McKenzie), and probably will use it in my division. I will have to study them more closely first, but even if they are not fully adopted by my division, I can certainly benefit from them.'[7]

Lieutenant Colonel Smith had tried to walk a fine line. On the one hand, he assured Mrs Mac's girls that they would be assets to the military if they ever joined, but then he added that they couldn't actually join. Why not? He didn't have the authority to talk about policy, so he explained that they were all just too beautiful! The army was not equipped to deal with such chaos.

His balancing act didn't quite work. Violet was deluged by calls from young Australian women excited by the prospect of joining the army, and she had 50 new membership inquiries by the end of the day.

The army moved into damage control and issued a media statement from Victoria Barracks in the afternoon, stating that a corps of women signallers would be 'impracticable'. A spokesman for the army said that women 'would disturb the whole construction and establishment of signal units, who did all signal work both in action and behind the line', and that 'even to put the women to work behind the lines would disorganise signal units'. The women's collective beauty—earlier noted by Lieutenant Colonel Smith—was used again as the excuse. Apparently their seductive appeal was too powerful for the army to handle.[8]

The air force contacted Violet. With the surge in recruitment, they simply did not have enough instructors who could teach Morse code, and they hoped that she would help by training their recruits. She replied that unfortunately she was not personally available, but that many of her 'girls' were highly proficient and would be able to help. Sixteen of her best Morse operators attended the nearby air force training grounds where they commenced duty as Morse code instructors on a voluntary basis.[9]

●—●

On a Tuesday evening in late January 1940, all the members of the Women's Emergency Signalling Corps assembled at 9 Clarence Street in their uniforms. From there, Violet led them on a parade across the Sydney Harbour Bridge, walking in formation on the pedestrian walkway, and stopping to pose for a news photographer along the way. When they reached the other side, she led them through the streets of North Sydney to a cinema, which the owner had provided to them for the evening. They entered the cinema for free, took their seats and watched a special movie that Violet had arranged for their enjoyment, a documentary about wireless telegraphy.[10]

With the recent pushback from the army—and with the heat that the flying club had received still fresh in her memory—Violet, in her public statements in early 1940, was careful to say that she was not training women to join the military. But while she was skirting that particular minefield, there was another raging social debate that she also wanted to avoid—the issue of women taking men's jobs.

As thousands of men enlisted and departed for Europe and Africa in crowded troopships, some feared that their jobs would not be waiting for them when they came home. Australia had been slowly recovering from the Great Depression's peak in 1932, but at the outbreak of war the unemployment rate was still around 8 per cent. Having a job was not taken for granted. The anxiety was exacerbated by women's pay rates being lower than men's. When the men returned at the end of the war (whenever that was going to be), employers might not want them back, and might instead choose to keep the 'temporary' women doing the same jobs for less money.

The unions campaigned for equal pay for women, motivated not by noble comradeship with feminists but by the self-interest of their male members. The president of the Trades Hall Council declared: 'The employment of women at lower rates than those payable to men, particularly in clerical work, makes it imperative that the government should take more drastic steps than in the last war to safeguard the positions of men on military service.' In Perth, the Country Water Supply Department was forced to deny 'wild rumours' that women were filling the jobs of men gone to war.[11]

The WESC was *absolutely* about training women to fill

men's jobs. After all, Violet had spent the past ten years doing exactly that—encouraging women to enter tradition-ally male domains, such as engineering, radio and aviation, and providing them with the skills to do so. But her current priority was simply training as many women as she could. She wasn't going to stumble into that political brawl until she had to, and in the meantime she cultivated a feel-good public image to which nobody could object.

She gave soothing reassurances. 'We are not after men's jobs, we are not aping men, and we are not competing with them,' she said on one occasion. On another: 'They have no intention of replacing men; they are simply becoming more efficient so that in an emergency they could do the work of men on active service.'[12] A Sigs member at the North Sydney movie night told a reporter, 'We don't want the men's jobs, but it is wonderful to know that we could give a real service if we are needed.'[13]

One of the fun activities at Sigs was putting together comfort parcels for soldiers, a common activity around the country during both world wars. These were gifts for men fighting on the front lines to enjoy, to make life more toler-able and to boost their spirits. A comfort parcel from Sigs included two pairs of socks, two packets of cigarettes, some tubes of shaving cream, books, handkerchiefs and any other treats that the girls wanted to include. Violet obtained from Lieutenant Colonel Smith a list of Australian signals units serving overseas and would draw one randomly from a hat. This was the unit that would receive their comfort parcels that week.[14]

Violet held regular outdoor drills and exercises in Centennial Park. There they practised semaphore across long distances and transmitting Morse code using nautical sound horns, honking their messages from one end of the park to the other.[15] She also taught them to set up an outdoor wireless station from scratch, getting them to rig aerials and to wire up portable radio equipment.[16]

The Bulletin reported with bemusement on these outdoor sessions:

> Some day when you are strolling through Centennial Park you may have the luck to see crisp young women, their trig suits of forest green belted with brown, topped by jaunty forage caps, engaged in mysterious rites amid sward and boskage.
>
> You won't be seeing fairies at the bottom of the garden, or even daughters of the leprechaun. The busy ones will be members of the Women's Emergency Signalling Corps running wires and telephone buzzers, and indulging in outbursts of Morse.
>
> Before they can do this they must give many nights and afternoons, or, if they are business girls, their lunch hours, to attending lectures and acquiring practical knowledge of the electrical and radio apparatus necessary.[17]

One weekend, a regimental sergeant major attended one of the field days. Violet had invited him to run the day's drill, and he did so with gusto, shouting orders at the women such as 'Spring to it!' and 'At the double!' After a gruelling two hours, the women were relieved when he finally said, 'Fall out and dismiss.'[18]

Violet—always with a talent for publicity—had also happened to invite a journalist from *The Sun* along to observe the sergeant major giving the drill. The journalist interviewed him afterwards, and—since the 'distracting beauty' of the women had been a contentious issue lately—asked him if he had, in fact, been distracted by their beauty.

He had not: 'Those faces may be pretty, but they don't

mean a thing to me. All I see is a sea of hands and feet.' He then added how impressed he was with their discipline. 'They're a pretty fine bunch. They've learned more in two hours than most men learn in a week of drill. That's because women pick things up more quickly, I suppose.'[19]

In March 1940, Violet administered her proficiency test to 100 members that included a Morse rate of ten words per minute, with only two women failing the test. All the others had earned the right to wear the WESC uniform. She attributed the high success rate to women's natural aptitude for Morse code: 'I believe the average percentage of failures with RAAF candidates is about 25 per cent, so girls must have an ear for rhythm.'[20]

14

WOMEN IN UNIFORM

●— — —— — —— ● —● ●● —● ●●— —●●● ●●—● ——— ●—● ——

We must be 100 per cent efficient to be 100 per cent useful.

Florence Violet McKenzie[1]

In March 1940, on the Thursday afternoon before Easter, 150 women arrived at the Castle Hill showground west of Sydney, ready for a four-day camp over the long weekend with the Women's Emergency Signalling Corps. Each of them wore the winter WESC uniform, consisting of green overalls, brown belt, brown shoes and a white blouse, and each carried her own small bag with toiletries and extra clothing.

Violet showed them where they would be living for the next four days, on stretcher beds side by side in the pavilions. She also revealed that they would be eating in style, because—in preparation for the camp—she had installed two modern electric kitchens in two of the pavilions. She was taking the opportunity to educate the campers in electric cooking as well as signals.[2]

Not all the campers were pleased with the sparse, military-style camp accommodation. Two women complained that the stretchers did not have mattresses. One of them described it as 'like sleeping on a hedge', and her friend added, 'The Foreign Legion must sleep like we did.'[3]

A woman doctor (probably Violet's friend, Dr Frances McKay) visited the camp each day, giving lectures on first aid and consulting with anyone who had medical conditions.

The camp had been planned with the assistance of Lieutenant Colonel Rupert Smith, the man who had given the speech at their end-of-year dinner, and who was the officer in charge of second-division signallers. Violet announced in the lead-up to Easter, 'The strictest discipline will be maintained. Only under special circumstances will leave be granted.' She added, 'However, that does not mean we will lose our identity as women. We intend to preserve our femininity.'[4]

The lessons of the flying club had been learned: Violet successfully managed the two faces of Sigs' public image. It was a serious business that contributed to the war effort, *yet also* a perfectly respectable, feminine activity that was suitable for your daughters. It was a clever media strategy. Unlike the women's flying club, there was no backlash against Sigs; there was no snarky commentary about 'amazons', and Sigs continued to grow in popularity.

The camp was run according to military routine. Every day at 6.15 a.m., the women woke to the sound of one of their number playing reveille on a bugle, after which they quickly put on their uniforms and gathered outside for morning parade. At the end of the day, after a long program of activities, they bedded down on their stretchers with a strict 'lights out' at 10 p.m. Outside, there was a 24-hour roster of women guards armed only with whistles.[5]

Just one man stayed at the showgrounds for the duration of the camp, an Aboriginal man who was responsible for various tasks such as maintaining the fire.[6]

Never one to let a media opportunity go to waste, Violet ensured that there was a steady flow of journalists visiting the camp. In an interview with one journalist, she said, 'The majority of the girls are already trained for emergency jobs such as are likely to be available in post offices and ambu- lance stations. And one girl, who has had only six months training in Morse, can transcribe thirty words a minute.' (The woman was Pat Ross, known as 'Sparks'.)[7]

To another journalist, she boasted that any WESC woman would be a great catch for a man: 'Even if their services as signallers are never needed, their training will be useful when married. Such pretty girls are sure to get married. They will be able to mend the wireless or the iron, fit up extra lights, and understand the workings of electric stoves.'[8] She also noted that 'We are women first, and wireless operators second. If we remember that, we will be better wireless operators.'[9]

Some army officers visited from a nearby camp at Wallgrove, and were highly complimentary. The visiting quartermaster said, 'The camp is run on almost the same line as ours. The discipline is every bit as good!'[10]

•—•

That same Easter long weekend, the Australian Women's Flying Club also held a camp, theirs being at St Ives show-ground on Sydney's north shore. Their camp was run by Gwen Stark, a schoolteacher and Girl Guides leader who had recently obtained her pilot's licence through the club, and who had become—after Violet's departure—the club's 'commandant' (as she called herself). Gwen Stark's leadership style was rather different to Violet's.

A reporter who visited both camps highlighted the differences:

> There was a military air about the camp . . . at St. Ives. Orders were barked out and obeyed at the double. 'Smith, Jones, Brown, and Robinson' were summoned and dismissed by surnames alone—and it seemed a long cry from the daily city life of these girls, where perhaps Miss Smith is a typist, Miss Jones a florist, Miss Brown a shopgirl, and Miss Robinson a schoolteacher . . .
>
> The Women's Emergency Signalling Corps camp was run on more happy-go-lucky lines. 'Smith' and 'Jones' were not told 'to get into line there' and expected to do it on the double. When lined up for inspection it was a case of, 'Mary dear, you're a little too close to Jean. Would you move back a little? Thank you, dear.'
>
> But otherwise their camp was run on much the same lines . . .[11]

•—•

Early hopes of a quick peace deal in Europe soon proved to be forlorn. When Prime Minister Robert Menzies announced Australia's entry into the war, the nation's armed forces were in a pathetic state, having been starved of funds through the Great Depression. Political leaders justified the atrophy with the perhaps naively optimistic belief that if there were a crisis, then surely Britain—our strongest ally and a military superpower—would ride in to save us.

The army consisted of a paltry 3000 full-time soldiers, although there was a reserve militia force numbering 80,000. The navy had a handful of ships, and the air force had fewer than 250 operational aircraft. Menzies announced that Australia's army would build a new imperial force—the 'Second Australian Imperial Force'—and a massive enlistment drive began, such that within six months, one in six Australian men of service age had enlisted. The nation's attention turned entirely to gearing up for war, both fighting abroad and preparing defences at home.

By the time it was all over, which would not be for another five years, a million Australians would have served, with 27,000 being killed on active service and another 8000 dying in prisoner-of-war camps.[12] But for most of 1940, the focus was on readiness.

With the aim of helping the war effort in various ways, women's groups sprang up around the country, many of them inspired by similar groups in Britain. The Women's Land Army, modelled on a British group of the same name, prepared to run the farms of Australia while the men were away at war. The Women's Transport Corps learned to drive trucks, buses, lorries and all manner of heavy vehicles, to ensure the transport system kept functioning. The Women's Voluntary Services ran canteens and put together comfort packages.[13]

The Australian Red Cross Voluntary Aid Detachments (VAD)—comprising mostly women—had such an influx of members that by June their membership exceeded 4000, and they had to cease taking on new members. Violet McKenzie's lifelong friend, Dr Frances McKay, who had written the introduction to her *All Electric Cookery Book* and who had been an early and enthusiastic supporter of the Electrical Association for Women, became the NSW state director of the VAD during the war.[14]

Other women's groups included the National Defence League, the National Emergency Services Ambulance

Drivers, the Australian Comforts Fund, the Women's National Emergency Legion, the RAAF welfare group, the Women's Naval War Auxiliary, the Methodist Women's Emergency Group, Women's Australian National Service, and the Ladies Harbour Lights Guild. Women even joined rifle clubs to learn to shoot 'just in case'.[15]

Long-established groups—such as the Girl Guides, the Country Women's Association and various church auxiliary groups—swelled in numbers, refocusing and ratcheting up their activities to help with the national crisis.[16]

There were mixed responses to this surge in activity by Australian women. *The Australian Women's Weekly* quoted an anonymous 'leader':

> Some women think that the further they get away from their homes the more assistance they can give, and the more exciting will be their tasks. To those women we say: STAY at home . . . Learn to knit, study first aid, give small gifts of money or goods to the local comforts fund depot, and you will be playing a helpful part.[17]

Momentum was building within the wartime women's movement to allow women to join the armed forces directly. In Britain, each of the three services—the navy, army and air force—had a women's auxiliary service. These were the Women's Royal Naval Service (WRNS, commonly known as the *wrens*), the Auxiliary Territorial Service (ATS), and the Women's Auxiliary Air Force (WAAF). Australian women questioned why the same system couldn't be introduced for them. Ten thousand women rallied at Sydney Town Hall in June 1940, calling for the right for women to enlist in the armed services—just as they could in Britain.

By this time, Violet's curriculum was fully aligned with

the army corps of signals, thanks to the help of Lieutenant Colonel Rupert Smith. Her girls were even practising Morse code with messages encrypted in numbers and letter–number ciphers, in line with military procedures.[18]

The volume of new applicants to join the Women's Emergency Signalling Corps was so great that Violet was forced to temporarily close the books to new members in June. The clubrooms of the Electrical Association for Women were now at capacity, bursting at the seams with young women practising Morse code and other signalling methods; if the corps grew any larger, Violet would need a bigger venue. As Violet told *The Australian Women's Weekly*:

> We have 500 trained women signallers, and I have had to turn away 200 volunteers in the last two days. Our girls could be sent to any post or telegraph office to relieve men in key positions, or do wireless work. We are helping the Air Force recruits who are waiting to be called up, by training them in Morse code and signalling. We have sufficient trained women to be able to train 1000 men at a time. The enthusiasm of the women is outstanding, and all are volunteers.[19]

15

THE WOOLSHED

— •••• • •— — ——— ——— •—•• ••• •••• • —••

She was just the most amazing woman. And I went
there voluntarily every day after work, Saturday morn-
ings, because there was a need.

Patrice Dow[1]

The Women's Emergency Signalling Corps needed larger
premises. The clubrooms of the Electrical Association for
Women were now devoted entirely to the activities of the
WESC, with no room to grow. In June 1940, Violet obtained a
lease on two floors of a large old three-storey woolshed across
the road at 10 Clarence Street.[2]

The lower storey was above street level, accessible only
by a long, steep, narrow flight of stairs; the floor above it
was accessible only by a second staircase that was just as
forbidding. With its massive brick arches and high ceilings

vaulted by wooden beams, the cavernous space had a gothic air about it.[3]

The walls and floors were filthy, and the place had a lingering stench, but it was enormous, conveniently located and inexpensive. The cheap rent was the deciding factor.[4]

Weekend 'working bees' were held to get the woolshed ready for the move, with hundreds of enthusiastic volunteers. They scrubbed the floors and laid linoleum over them; they draped hessian to hide the dirty walls; and they arranged a motley collection of second-hand tables and chairs that had been donated by family, friends and the public.[5]

Cecil installed dozens of Morse stations, each consisting of a transmitting key and headphones; he ran transmission wires between them and installed power throughout the woolshed.

There were twelve zones on the main floor, each designated as a classroom with a specific purpose. Zones for learning to receive Morse code consisted of a long table with several Morse stations in rows along it, and a station from which an instructor would send Morse code at a particular speed. Cecil provided various configurations, so that sometimes the instructor would be right in front of the students and some-times on the floor above. There were also Morse transmission zones, an area for practising semaphore and a darkened area for practising Morse with an Aldis lamp. For an additional ten shillings, the women could buy their own Morse key, buzzer and Aldis lamp, so they could practise at home.[6]

Violet's Irish terrier, Ginger, was often seen at the woolshed, befriending all the visitors. Ginger was jokingly assigned the role of mascot until she was superseded by a doll dressed in a WESC uniform named Winnie the War Winner.[7]

•—•

Not long after the woolshed had been set up, a young man appeared at the top of the stairs and inquired as to whether Mrs Mac could help him. His application to join the air force would not be accepted unless he knew Morse code, so he wanted to learn it—but there was nowhere for him to do so.

The man's predicament was caused by a crisis in recruitment. Despite being desperately short of personnel, the air force was picky about the applications it accepted: of 200,000 applications for voluntary service between 1939 and 1941, they accepted only a quarter. Applicants were told to go and learn various skills that they would need to master before being called up. There was a training bottleneck in Morse code, because the men with expertise in it were either on active duty or were overwhelmed by the tidal wave of recruits.[8]

This young man was certainly *not* allowed to join the WESC, which was exclusively for women and was going to stay that way; however, Violet told him that yes, she would help him learn Morse code. She recalled later that, as they talked, 'a whole world opened up before me. Then I knew what we could do. We could train girls to train the men.'[9]

•—•

The qualification of *instructor* was introduced at Sigs. Its requirement was a Morse rate of twenty words per minute, which was double the speed of the basic entry test for the WESC.[10]

Sixty women immediately qualified and were keen to help train the air force recruits. Within weeks, Violet had 50 male air force trainees learning Morse code. They attended the old premises, the EAW clubrooms across the road at 9 Clarence Street, where rows of Morse stations that Cecil had wired up were still operational. Meanwhile, unless they were instructing men, the women continued to attend the new Sigs premises in the woolshed at number 10 Clarence Street.[11]

Violet wrote to the Minister for Air, Jim Fairbairn, in June, offering the services of the WESC to formally instruct air force recruits in signalling and Morse code. She noted:

We are already unofficially training 50 R.A.A.F. recruits who came to us of their own accord. Over 60 members of the Corps are qualified to act as instructors. By officially making use of their voluntary services, instruction of recruits could be facilitated, especially in the case of men who are waiting to be called up.[12]

The instructors started a fund, with each woman donating one shilling per week, so that they could provide tea and coffee to the men across the road, just as Violet had provided free tea and coffee to them in the same situation. Some were even more enthusiastic, making use of the electric kitchen to prepare lunchtime meals for the men. Others knitted clothing for them to take when they were called away to war.[13]

Myrtle Reeves, the fast-learning former ballerina, organised a mid-year revue at the Roxy Theatre in North Sydney, to raise money for their Signals Comfort Fund. Fifty women participated. The instructors told their male students about the upcoming concert and asked if they wanted to be involved. Several did participate, performing a comedic ballet on stage.[14]

Keen to entertain the troops, Myrtle organised a series of concerts at air force training grounds. Violet attended the first of these concerts, which was held at the Ultimo base in February 1941 and starred 25 WESC members.[15]

Violet's husband, Cecil, was active in the Australian Air League, a club for boys and young men interested in learning to fly. As with Sigs, interest had surged in the Air League. With its membership at now over 10,000 nationwide, the resources in this volunteer-run organisation were stretched. Cecil, as the education officer, asked Violet if some of her girls could attend the Air League as signalling instructors, which they did with enthusiasm.

The instructors needed a daily supply of material to send in Morse code; Violet had often used the newspapers for material, but men's tastes differed from those of the women. The men's preferred material for practising Morse code was the *Popeye* comic strip, closely followed by *Tarzan*. Created around a decade earlier, Popeye was a hugely popular comic-strip character, particularly with men; a new story was published each day in *The Sun*.

The instructors tapped out dialogue between Popeye, his friend J. Wellington Wimpy, and his girlfriend Olive Oyl; this included idiosyncratic words such as 'lobsterburger' (a hamburger with lobster), 'lemingade' (lemonade) and 'Neutopia' (a fictitious country that Popeye often talked about). After a visit from a journalist to the clubrooms, *The Sun* ran a story with the headline: *GIRLS TRAIN BOY SIGNALLERS: 'LOBSTERBURGER' IS GOOD WORD FOR CODE.*[16]

Violet insisted that she was teaching the men, and the women, the bare minimum: 'There's a war on. It is no use cluttering up your brain with unnecessary details. It is, however, necessary that you should understand the instruments used in signalling enough to diagnose any trouble should they go wrong and rectify it.' Although she had trimmed the curriculum, the 'bare minimum' was substantial, including lessons on electrical circuit theory as well as Morse code.[17]

Just as for the women, the men were trained free of charge. Violet's only stipulation was that they provide a photograph of themselves. The photos were pinned onto the woolshed's hessian wall covers in a montage of portraits that she called her 'rogue's gallery'.[18]

The RAAF started advising applicants to attend signals classes at WESC while they were waiting for call-up, resulting in droves of young men arriving at 9 Clarence Street wanting to be trained. By September 1940, Violet was coordinating activities across Sydney, including air force recruitment proficiency tests; the training of air league members, air force recruits and reservists; and even providing staff as volunteer telegraphists (in a civilian capacity) at Victoria Barracks in eastern Sydney. She acquired some motorbikes, gave a handful of women the role of dispatch rider, and assigned the motorbikes to them to facilitate fast, secure communication between the various locations.[19]

Branches of the Women's Emergency Signalling Corps started outside Sydney. The Wollongong branch was formed in mid-1940 and met three times a week in a basement below a newsagency. It soon had thirty members, nineteen of whom had qualified for the WESC uniform. Branches also opened in Wagga Wagga, Taree, Inverell and Brisbane.[20]

The neat demarcation between men's and women's training—with men attending 9 Clarence Street and the women attending 10 Clarence Street—no longer worked. The clubrooms at number 9 were just not big enough, and so around September 1940 Violet consolidated all training of men and women in the woolshed, vacating the original premises at 9 Clarence Street. A by-product of this decision was that the Electrical Association for Women ceased to exist other than as a legal instrument for running WESC.[21]

A party of 50 air force men based at Ultimo would march from their base to the woolshed each day for lessons. Merchant sailors started attending, too, in preparation for their master mariner exam. The army, in dire need of training, made use of WESC; 90 of their men camped at Sydney showground in the army's signals division and received daily lessons.[22]

By Christmas 1940, 100 women were volunteer instructors for WESC, and they had trained over 1000 air force reservists as well as an unknown number of army signals personnel, merchant marine and Air League members. It was reported that WESC instructors had trained more than 90 per cent of the ground crew at Sydney Airport.[23]

That Christmas, the women held a concert at the woolshed, donating the money raised from ticket sales to the Signals Comfort Fund. The opening act was a choir that several of the women had formed called the Choir of Limericks (the reason for their choice of name is a mystery). Following the opening number was a variety of performances. Marion Stevens sang 'The Pipes of Pan', Denise Owen recited poetry, and several women performed comedy skits. The final event of the evening was a performance of the national anthem. When it started, the entire audience stood up and joined in.[24]

Around Christmas time, a letter arrived for Violet from one of the first men she had trained:

Dear Mrs Mac,
   Just a note of thanks for your assistance in improving my Morse. I managed my final with full marks, thanks wholly and solely to your organisation. Wishing you a happy new year, and thanking you once again for your many kindnesses.[25]

Patrice Dow, one of the instructors at Sigs, later recalled that, when she arrived each day, Mrs Mac would assign her where she was needed:

She would stand at the top of the stairs . . . and she'd say good morning or good afternoon. She'd have a cup of tea in her hand and she'd say, 'Bay number 3', so you went straight to bay number 3, and you sent Morse all the time you were able to spend there to the people that wanted to learn it.[26]

16

WOMEN FOR THE AIR FORCE

•— — —— — — —— • —• ••—• —— — •—• — ••••• •
•— ••• •—• ••—• ——— •—• —•—••

What part shall women play in war? Shall they sit at
home and knit, or shall they go out and fight with their
men?

Geoffrey Hutton, *The Argus*[1]

On 3 September 1940, about 10,000 residents of Sydney
watched a military parade in the city centre, marking
one year since the war began. A hundred men each from the
army, navy and air force marched to Martin Place, accompanied by representatives from eleven voluntary women's
associations, with four armoured cars bringing up the rear.
The 500 uniformed women outnumbered the servicemen.
Included among them was a large contingent from the
Women's Emergency Signalling Corps led by Violet McKenzie,
described in the media as its 'commandant' or 'director'.[2]

The WESC summer uniform turned out to be ill-suited to a burst of unseasonably cold weather. The *Sun* reported:

> A keen wind whistled from the south-west and the girls in cotton frocks, some with low necks and hatless, were so frozen that after the proceedings they had to thaw out before they could answer the order, 'Quick march.'
>
> Women's services so far have not been organised long enough for them to march well and if they did not move along out of step, many of them did so with arms swinging at different angles. But, what they lacked in efficiency they made up for in enthusiasm and representatives from eleven women's movements took part.[3]

Similar parades were held in Adelaide and Brisbane, with the one at Brisbane Exhibition Grounds attracting an estimated 20,000 people.

•—•

The news from Europe was dire. A week before the Sydney parade, Hitler had ordered a naval blockade of Britain, and air raids across Britain had commenced. The day before the parade, news arrived from London that the German Luftwaffe had carried out a series of nine air attacks on the London area in the space of 24 hours, in addition to raids on industrial centres further north. Luftwaffe aircraft strafed crowds at a shopping centre where the air-raid siren had failed to go off; the sound of their approach had been masked by the noise of nearby traffic.[4]

The situation on the European continent was even worse. The Axis powers now comprised Germany, Italy and Austria (the original signatories); they controlled the Netherlands, Belgium, Denmark, Norway, Luxembourg, France, the Baltic states, Czechoslovakia and Poland. In short, Hitler was winning.

The trickle of news reaching Australia from nations under Nazi occupation was horrific. In one Polish town, the German Gestapo had executed all the members of the Boy Scouts who, on realising their imminent fate, had knelt and prayed, then stood and sang the Polish national anthem at the soldiers, before the machine guns opened fire. Jews were being persecuted most of all, particularly in Poland, but across all Nazi-held territory there were stories emerging of Jews being victims of mass killings while many others were sent to concentration camps.[5]

The full impact of the war was yet to be felt in Australia. A number of Australians serving in British forces had already been killed, but the Australian forces had yet to suffer the thousands of casualties that they would incur in the coming years. The armed forces were being rapidly rebuilt, most notably the Second Australian Imperial Force, which was to experience its first combat engagement of the war in Egypt in December 1940.

Violet now openly campaigned for the right of women to enlist in the armed forces, which many of those in her organisation wanted to do. Gone were the bland reassurances that her girls simply wanted to fill in while the men were away, and had no intention of serving themselves. They wanted to serve, and they had the skills to do it.

In June 1940, two influential people had written to Prime Minister Robert Menzies about allowing women into the armed forces. They were NSW Premier Alexander Mair, and Lady Wakehurst, wife of the NSW governor and a friend of Violet McKenzie. Menzies informed the war cabinet of the correspondence and asked them to investigate the possibility.[6]

The chief of air staff was keen on the idea, having seen firsthand the successful enlistment of women in his home country. Sir Charles Burnett had arrived from Britain in February, having been appointed the new chief of Australia's air force. He was joined three months later by two of his daughters, Joan and Sybil (who was known as 'Bunty'), both of whom had been in the British Women's Auxiliary Air Force (WAAF). Joan had been in charge of 190 women at England's coastal air force headquarters, while Bunty had had a more junior role. Burnett was proud of his daughters' achievements, and from the moment he arrived in Australia he was publicly advocating for the creation of a women's air force along the same lines as the one in Britain.

The Australian air force was suffering shortages in several key areas of expertise, and this situation was only going to get worse. For telegraphists in particular, a shortfall was expected of up to 500 by the end of the year. To Burnett, the solution was obvious and simple. Thousands of women were training themselves for the air force around Australia through the Women's Air Training Corps, and in New South Wales hundreds of women had been trained as telegraphists by Violet McKenzie. He ordered that the air force prepare for the creation of a women's air force.[7]

But the air chief's enthusiasm met a brick wall of resistance from the Minister for Air, Jim Fairbairn, who told the war cabinet that there was no need to enlist women because there was such a plentiful supply of young men clamouring to join.[8]

In August 1940, an aircraft carrying three cabinet ministers and the chief of the general staff crashed on its descent into Canberra, killing everyone on board. Minister for Air Jim Fairbairn and Minister for Army Geoffrey Street were among the dead.[9]

Prime Minister Menzies—who was deeply affected by the death of several of his senior colleagues—appointed Arthur Fadden as the Minister for Air, as a temporary replacement for Fairbairn. When Sir Charles Burnett pressed the case for a women's air force to his new minister, he found that Fadden was more receptive to the idea. He explained to Fadden that Mrs McKenzie had 150 trained telegraphists who met the standards required by the air force and were therefore ready to start immediately; there were also another 200 women whose training was close to completion. The Women's Air Training Corps also claimed to have large numbers of women telegraphists ready to go (these had largely been trained by Violet McKenzie when she was still involved in the women's flying club).

Fadden was persuaded, and in October he tabled a proposal to the war cabinet to create a women's air force. But he discovered that his colleagues opposed it. Fadden appealed to their hip pocket, noting that, because the women's rate of pay would be around two-thirds that of the men, the government could save around £25,000 if they recruited women. But his colleagues could not be persuaded: letting women join the air force was just asking too much.

The war cabinet would not agree to Fadden's proposal, but they couldn't exactly say no, either, given the crisis in expertise that the air force was facing. So they shunted the proposal off for consideration by a committee called the Advisory War Council. As for his claim that the plan would cut costs, they referred that to Treasury to look into.[10]

By the time the council reported back to the war cabinet in November, Fadden was no longer the Minister for Air, having been promoted to Treasurer in a cabinet reshuffle. His replacement, John McEwen, was dead against allowing women to serve in the air force. McEwen acknowledged the sad fact that they might have to enlist women . . . but only if all else failed.

The Advisory War Council came up with a plan to avoid the need to enlist women: how about one more try at finding male telegraphists? They could run an advertising campaign, and relax restrictions such as medical fitness and age. The council also requested a report from Burnett on whether the air force could solve the problem by speeding up its training courses.[11]

Burnett told them that their recruitment plan and their training plan were both destined to fail. There was no hidden reservoir of telegraphists, and there was no way to accelerate the training systems that were currently in place.

Someone proposed another solution: there must be large numbers of *retired* male telegraphists who could surely be brought into the services if needed. If they could be found and enlisted, there would be no need to bring in women.

The committee sent inquiries to the unions, requesting estimates of the number of retired male telegraphists in Australia. By mid-December, the unions had responded, bluntly telling cabinet that they did not know. But at that time there were many other important issues to deal with, so the council postponed any decision until January.

They considered the issue again on 8 January 1941. According to the minutes of the meeting, 'the feeling of the council was against the enlistment of women in the fighting forces, particularly for duties which in civil life are performed by men'.[12] Burnett was in attendance, and he argued strenuously with the council members, retorting that in civilian life women were already being employed as wireless telegraphists.[13]

The war council was out of options and had exhausted all its excuses. The Minister for Air finally conceded that he had no choice but to allow the air force to enlist women. Oh, but there was a caveat.

Before they could start enlisting women, numerous issues had to first be resolved. Things such as conditions of employment, how much to pay the women, and all the procedural stuff. These things seemed like trivial administrative issues, but the council was adamant that procedure must be followed, even in this time of national crisis.[14]

Moreover, those decisions could not be made by the war council but had to be made by the war cabinet. So the council duly shunted the issue back across to the war cabinet (from where it had come in the first place) for consideration. The war cabinet, in turn, gave consideration to this extremely pressing issue, and decided to send a letter to the Minister for Defence Coordination (i.e. Robert Menzies, who was also the prime minister) for 'consideration of this matter'. On receiving the letter, Menzies approved the plan, sending it back to the war cabinet, which finally approved the enlistment of women. But again, there was a caveat. Cabinet stipulated that the air force could not recruit any women until they had first established a women's training depot. Sir Charles Burnett was on it. Six weeks later, the training depot was up and running, and the first intake of women entered the Women's Auxiliary Australian Air Force (WAAAF) on 17 March 1941.[15] This was quick, considering the politicians had stalled for a full six months.

Meanwhile, Burnett's colleagues on the air board and their subordinates were busy undermining the plan. Violet was told by representatives of the air board that her women were wasting their time, because the air force would never need them. Mary Bell, head of the Women's Air Training Corps and another advocate for the enlistment of women, was told the same thing.[16]

Fed up with the stalling and mixed messages, Violet had given up on the air force and made inquiries elsewhere. She had contacted the navy, again offering the service of her women as telegraphists, with much better results.

17

THE ARMS OF THE NAVY

— •••• • •— •—• —— ••• ——— ••—•
— •••• • —• •— •••— —•— —

With sheer determination and lobbying of Government officials and the RAN by WESC founder Florence McKenzie, the WRANS was eventually inaugurated.

Lieutenant Commander Andrew Stackpole, *Navy News*, 2011[1]

Around Christmas 1940, Frances Provan and Joan McLeod—smartly dressed in the green uniforms of the Women's Emergency Signalling Corps—entered the recruitment centre at the naval base at Rushcutters Bay in Sydney. Two of Violet McKenzie's top students, they explained to the staff officer that they were responding to an appeal for telegraphists and wished to apply.

The navy, like the air force, was suffering a critical shortage of telegraphists, and Minister for the Navy Billy Hughes had appealed to the public for help. The minister's appeal had been reported widely in the news:

'Now is the time for radio amateurs to put their enthusiasm to practical use in defence of their country,' [Mr Hughes] said. 'Young men between the ages of 18 and 35 who are able to transmit and receive Morse at about 20 words a minute are wanted.

'Volunteers will be enlisted for service in Australia and overseas, either in seagoing ships or in the naval wireless stations. They will be employed on naval duties immediately on conclusion of a three months' special course in naval procedures, coding, and organisation. The next special course will begin in January and personal applications should be made now to the Naval Officer, Rushcutters Bay, Sydney.'[2]

But the staff officer informed the women that they were not eligible to apply, to which Provan and McLeod protested, 'You're appealing for wireless telegraphists!'

The officer replied, 'But *male* wireless telegraphists.'[3]

Violet McKenzie wrote about the issue to the minister, Billy Hughes:

I would like to offer the services of our signalling corps, if not acceptable as telegraphists, then at least as instructors. We have more than 100 girls capable of sending and receiving Morse at 20 words a minute.[4]

The minister notified the naval board of her offer.

The naval board, based in Melbourne, sent the director of signals and communications, Jack Newman, to Sydney to investigate Mrs McKenzie's school and to find out whether there was any merit in her offer. Arriving at the woolshed in Clarence Street on 9 January 1941, Newman was greeted by Violet McKenzie, who was wearing the green, brown and white uniform that she had designed. Newman was dressed in his naval officer's 'summer whites'. Violet ushered him upstairs, introduced him to a group of her best students and gave him a tour of the woolshed.[5]

What Newman wanted to find out most of all was how good these women actually were at sending and receiving Morse code, and to this end Violet had arranged for him to administer a test using the Morse equipment that Cecil had installed. Newman had come prepared, setting printed copies of coded messages on the table next to the Morse key as he sat at the Morse station.

The women sat with headphones, side by side at Morse receiving stations, ready to receive. Highly skilled in Morse code himself, Newman effortlessly tapped out his messages at a rapid canter of 22 words per minute.

The initial confidence of the women collapsed into confusion. They struggled to pick up the rhythm. The commander seemed to be leaving no pause between each word, and was randomly hesitating in the middle of words. Then one of the women realised the problem. These were groups of five letters and numbers—not four, as they were used to!

This group of women were Violet's best; she had not only trained them to be proficient in Morse code, but also in all manner of military and civilian procedures. She had even trained them to send and receive letter–number combinations to simulate the encrypted message systems usually employed by the military. When encoded, the strings of letters and numbers were always sent in groups of four (such as A78C and 9235), which was the style that the air force used; but the navy's ciphers used groups of five. These women had never been exposed to navy ciphers.

Newman's messages for decryption looked somewhat like this: RT9T2 H5331 3JJ0K M576E LIP66. Someone figured out what was going on, and there was a whisper along the Morse table: 'These are groups of five!' Very quickly, everyone adjusted to the novel system.

After the test, Newman was pleased to inform them that they had all passed. When the problem with groups of five was explained to him, he was even more impressed that they had adapted to a message structure that they had never previously encountered.[6]

In his report to the naval board, Newman spoke highly of Mrs McKenzie and the women telegraphists that she had trained, recommending that the navy make full use of them. The board wrote:

> Consideration was given to the minutes of the Director of Naval Communication and the Second Naval Member, relative to the question of employing women in naval establishments as telegraphists to release male telegraphists for seagoing service.
>
> Mrs F.V. McKenzie of the Electrical Association for Women (Australia) had written to the Minister on 27th December 1940, offering the services of women signallers from her Association.
>
> In view of the shortage of trained telegraphists and having regard to the employment of women in naval establishments in England, the Naval Board decided to approve the proposal in principle, but instructed that the matter be further investigated, having regard to the existing amenities and air force proposals along similar lines.
>
> The board desires particularly information on whether an organisation could be established similar to the

W.R.E.N.S. in England, providing for ranks and the enlistment of ratings, uniform, discipline, pay, etc., and that the question of additional accommodation be addressed.[7]

The 'further investigation' they had in mind also involved a meeting with Mrs McKenzie herself. They invited her to appear before the board to explain what she was doing and to answer a few questions.[8]

Violet arrived by train in Melbourne. Newman met her and escorted her to the naval board meeting at Victoria Barracks, where she sat face to face with, as she described it, 'a ring of Admirals'. She said later, 'I had to talk hard to persuade the Navy Board to accept the girls.'[9] She outlined the history and purpose of the Women's Emergency Signalling Corps, what kind of training was being given, and why she was qualified to do it.

The board members were worried that if men and women served side by side, all sorts of shenanigans could take place. 'What about sex?' one of them asked.

Violet reassured them that there was no risk of that happening. She replied, 'I've had hundreds of men and women working together, and there have never been any goings on.'[10]

Persuaded that the benefits of employing women outweighed the risks, the naval board ordered the creation of the Women's Royal Australian Naval Service (WRANS), to be activated once the conditions of service were finalised and the minister had approved them. Newman ensured that Violet was kept informed of the developments, and assured her that, as soon as the service was active, her women would be needed. He told her that he would need her twelve best telegraphists, ready to start right away.

•—•

The Australian Women's Flying Club, which Violet had helped found more than two years earlier, had since been absorbed into a national organisation, the Women's Air Training Corps. And while Violet had given up on the air force, the Women's Air Training Corps had not. After all, they had no choice.

Because Violet was providing training in skills that could be employed by any of the military services, as well as in civilian jobs, she had the option of switching her attention to the navy when she hit a brick wall with the air force. By contrast, for those in the Women's Air Training Corps, the only realistic option for serving was in the air force. The name of the organisation said it all: they were betting all their chips on the air force.

The head of their Sydney branch, Gwen Stark—the schoolteacher who had commanded the flying club's camp a year earlier—declared that the corps had 2000 women ready to join the air force at a moment's notice. She pointed out that many of them were already doing voluntary work for the air force. Stark said:

> But we are capable of undertaking much more numerous duties. We could supply in New South Wales alone more than 50 girls who have been trained as signallers and radio operators. Numbers of girls have been trained as air force cooks and stewardesses.[11]

After months of wrangling and arguments with politicians, the air force finally got around to creating the Women's Auxiliary Australian Air Force (WAAAF) in March 1941. When the local headquarters contacted Violet about bringing in her girls for testing and possible enlistment, she told them that that was no longer possible. She explained that, having been informed by the air board that her girls would never be allowed into the air force, she had now promised them to the navy instead. She was finished with the air force.

Opposition to the air force's plan came from multiple directions. A feminist group called the Council for Action on Equal Pay protested against the pay differential for men and women in the air force.

Norman Makin, one of the ALP's three members on the Advisory War Council, railed against the plan in parliament:

> We contend that it cuts across certain fundamental principles that should be safeguarded jealously; we should not permit even wartime emergency to influence us to approve a system the full consequences of which cannot be foreseen at the present time. We object strongly to women being called into the actual fighting services until the full strength of the country's manhood has been canvassed completely.[12]

Makin used the pay issue as a wedge against the government, attacking them for the pay gap between men and women:

> The members of the opposition are insistent that, in the event of women being recruited, they shall receive the same rate of pay as are applied to men. I am not satisfied that the Government has exhausted all the possibilities of recruiting for the particular service described by the Minister the man-power that should be available. It is true, as the Minister stated, that this matter was considered by the Advisory War Council, but the honourable gentleman will admit that I opposed the proposal from its inception.[13]

A young Violet Wallace with a cat, near her family home in Austinmer, circa 1900. (Ex-WRANS Association)

Violet as a young woman, reading a book. (Ex-WRANS Association)

Portrait of Violet as a young woman. (Ex-WRANS Association)

Rawson Chambers, a sprawling business complex in Haymarket, where
Violet ran her engineering firm.

An advertisement for The Wireless Shop in *The Sydney Evening News Wireless
Handbook,* 1924.

Violet at her radio set in 1922. (Ex-WRANS Association)

People queuing outside The Wireless Shop for the first issue of *Wireless Weekly*, August 1922. (Ex-WRANS Association)

The cover of *Wireless Weekly*, vol. 1, no. 16, 1922.

Violet with The Radio Shop mascot, Plug-In, 1929. (Fairfax archive of plate-glass negatives held at the National Library of Australia)

A family in their living room listening to a radio broadcast, New South Wales, circa 1930. (Fairfax archive of plate-glass negatives held at the National Library of Australia)

Violet at the Electrical Association for Women's clubrooms, sitting at the piano. (Ex-WRANS Association)

The entrance of the Electrical Association for Women in Clarence Street, Sydney. (Ex-WRANS Association)

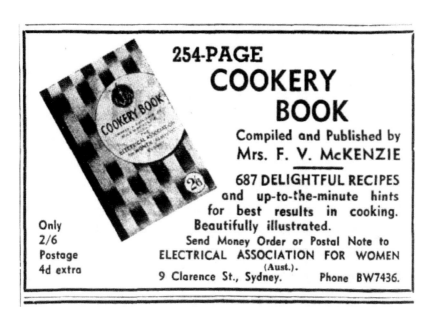

An advertisement for Violet's *All Electric Cookery Book*, 1938. (*The Daily Telegraph*)

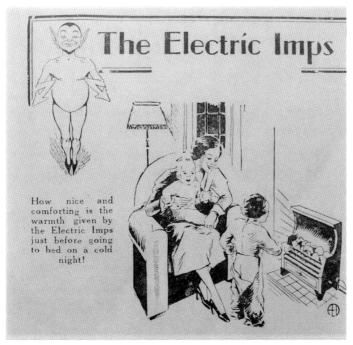

An excerpt from Violet's book *The Electric Imps*, 1937.

TOP LEFT: Violet McKenzie in the uniform of the Women's Emergency Signalling Corps, 1940. (Australian War Memorial)

TOP RIGHT: Cecil McKenzie in the uniform of the Australian Air League, circa 1937. (Ex-WRANS Association)

LEFT: Violet McKenzie in 1935. (Ex-WRANS Association)

Members of the Australian Women's Flying Club learning Morse code, 1939.
(Argus Newspaper Collection of Photographs, State Library of Victoria)

A member of the Australian Women's Flying Club working on an aircraft
engine. (Argus Newspaper Collection of Photographs, State Library of Victoria)

Three members of the Women's Emergency
Signalling Corps practising semaphore signalling,
1940. (Australian War Memorial)

Violet McKenzie inspecting a parade of members of the Women's Emergency
Signalling Corps, 1940. (Australian War Memorial)

Four members of the Australian Women's Flying Club. (Australian War Memorial P03221.002)

Members of the Women's Emergency Signalling Corps practising Morse code, 1940. (Australian War Memorial)

Five women at a Women's Emergency Signalling Corps camp, 1940.
(Australian War Memorial)

Josephine 'Jo' Miller. (Argus
Newspaper Collection of Photographs,
State Library of Victoria)

Joan Cowie turned eighteen while
on a training course in Melbourne
in 1941. She and her colleagues from
WESC celebrated with a cake in a
nearby park. (Australian War Memorial)

Members of the WRANS at drill practice at Harman in 1941. (Australian War Memorial P01262.307)

WRANS on parade during World War II. (Argus Newspaper Collection of Photographs, State Library of Victoria)

ABOVE: A shoulder badge with the emblem of the Women's Emergency Signalling Corps. (Australian War Memorial)

LEFT: WRANS S. Flower and M. Walker sending messages by Aldis lamp. (Argus Newspaper Collection of Photographs, State Library of Victoria)

Drummers at a Women's Emergency Signalling Corps camp, 1940. (Australian War Memorial)

WRANS holding their hats while visiting the flight deck of a ship.
(Argus Newspaper Collection of Photographs, State Library of Victoria)

WRANS member Gwenda Cornwallis, trained by Violet McKenzie, at the Bradleys Head degaussing station on Sydney Harbour. (Australian War Memorial P02632.001)

Violet McKenzie in her air force Flight Officer uniform. (Ex-WRANS Association)

'Stand easy' mail being distributed at Harman's post office. (Australian War Memorial P00784.042)

Violet McKenzie testing a man's Morse code proficiency. (Australian War Memorial)

Sailors entering the Women's Emergency Signalling Corps rooms at the woolshed at 10 Clarence Street. (Ex-WRANS Association)

Violet posing at the Royal Botanic Garden in Sydney with members of the Royal Indian Navy in 1942. (Australian War Memorial)

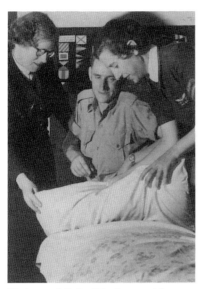

Violet and Ruby Hughes making up a bed for a merchant mariner who slept overnight at the Clarence Street woolshed in order to attend Morse code lessons there the next day, 1944. (Australian War Memorial)

Violet instructing American naval personnel in semaphore. (Australian War Memorial)

WRANS at Harman taking a stroll in 1941. From left to right: Frances Provan, Joan Furley, Bea Ogilvie and Marion Stevens. (Australian War Memorial 009214)

Violet McKenzie with Squadron Leader A.G. Pither, head of air force training, in 1940. (Australian War Memorial)

Noreen Dudgeon instructing American naval personnel in visual signalling, 1944. (Australian War Memorial 017674)

Members of the Women's Emergency Signalling Corps instructing Australian service personnel in Morse code in 1944. (Australian War Memorial 017675)

A line of WRANS receiving instruction on how to put on a gas mask. (Argus Newspaper Collection of Photographs, State Library of Victoria)

Violet McKenzie with some of her students in her post-war training school. (Australian War Memorial)

Violet and Cecil McKenzie at a social function, circa 1950. (Ex-WRANS Association)

Violet at a plaque-unveiling ceremony in her honour at The Mission to Seafarers, 1980. (Ex-WRANS Association)

Violet McKenzie on her birthday in 1980 with former members of the Women's Emergency Signalling Corps. (Ex-WRANS Association)

Makin thus skewered the government's plans from two directions in a brilliantly calculated manoeuvre that appealed to both conservative voters and progressive voters at the same time, over the same issue. He was personally against women in the military (appeal to the right), but *if* women were allowed into the military then they should get paid the same as men (appeal to the left). It was a win-win situation for Makin.

Recruiting commenced on 19 March, with the air force seeking women as cooks, mess stewards, mess women, teleprinter operators and wireless operators. The last two categories, being the highest-skilled occupations, were the crucial ones. The Women's Air Training Corps hyped the event with media photo shoots in Sydney and Brisbane depicting women being trained as telegraphists. Fifty members of the old Australian Women's Flying Club, who had been trained by Violet in Morse code, lodged their applications to join the air force.

The recruitment drive was sabotaged by the recruiting office being hostile to the whole idea. Of the fifty women who applied to be telegraphists, the recruiters rejected twenty right away on medical grounds. That left only thirty to sit for the Morse aptitude test, which would be supervised and scored by the recruiting office staff. They failed all but five of the women. It made headlines:

TRAINEES FOR WAAAF
SMALL SYDNEY QUOTA
ONLY FIVE PASS[14]

Two of those five successful women were from the Women's Emergency Signalling Corps, despite Violet instructing her girls not to apply to the air force.

The state commander of the Women's Air Training Corps, Nancy Bird (now referred to as 'Mrs Charles Walton'), blamed the situation on a lack of equipment. 'Because military orders must take precedence, we are unable to obtain oscillators. We ordered one last November but have not received it.'[15]

When interviewed about her opinions on the air force debacle, Violet gave a shrug of disinterest. She noted:

> Many of our girls are trained to the WAAAF standard, but the best of them are instructors, and they feel that they are doing a better job instructing men of the services than they would be if they volunteered for service in the WAAAF.
>
> Apart from these instructors, fifty of our best girls have been reserved for another service. I arranged this after I had been told, three days before the minister for air Mr McEwen made his announcement about the WAAAF, that wireless operators were not likely to be wanted for some time.[16]

The navy had been keeping quiet about their plans for a women's service, but Violet's slip about keeping her girls for 'another service' gave a hint of what was coming. Later that week, she let the cat out of the bag completely, telling *The Sun* that the navy would be taking 50 of her best signallers.

The headline on Sunday was:

Girl Signallers to Join Navy, Says Director

Fifty members of the Women's Emergency Signalling Corps are to be appointed to shore jobs with the Royal Australian Navy, said the organiser of the corps, Mrs. F.V. McKenzie, yesterday.

'I received official confirmation through the Women's Voluntary National Register that 50 of the girls, who have been specially trained in anticipation of the call-up, may be enlisted at any moment for work under the Navy Department,' Mrs. McKenzie stated.

At present only telegraphists will be called up, their speed must equal 25 words per minute.

Many of the girls, who will do a special training course lasting three months, in Sydney, will give up excellent posts to serve their country.

The signallers may abandon their present uniform of sage green to don uniforms of navy blue worn by the Wrens in England, of which the Duchess of Kent is commandant.

The Wrens wear the feminine counterpart of the naval 'square rig' and in place of the peaked officers' caps, wear the now familiar tricorne hat.[17]

When parliament resumed in Canberra on Tuesday, the Opposition pounced. Makin asked the minister responsible, Billy Hughes, about the news report:

Will the Minister for the Navy state whether the press report is correct that the Department of the Navy intends to recruit 50 women for the Signalling Service? If the report be true, will these women receive pay equal to that of male signallers? Before a final decision is reached, will the Advisory War Council be given an opportunity to review the principle involved in the appointment of women to this service?[18]

Hughes replied, 'I have heard of no such proposal as that to which the honourable member has referred.'[19]

He was lying. As he knew perfectly well, the navy was

planning to post telegraphists to Harman in the near future. He knew it because he had personally instructed the navy board to pursue Violet McKenzie's offer to provide the navy with trained women.

18

HARMAN

•••• •— •—• —— •— —•

*HMAS HARMAN will always stand for something
special in the memories of the WRANS, for it was to
this station, on 28 April 1941, that fourteen appre-
hensive young women in the uniform of the Women's
Emergency Signalling Corps came as the vanguard of
the new service.*

Margaret Curtis-Otter, *W.R.A.N.S.*[1]

On Friday, 18 April 1941, the war cabinet approved the
creation of a women's auxiliary to the Royal Australian
Navy. Three days later, the navy office informed the commodore in charge of Sydney Harbour, Rear Admiral Gerard
Muirhead-Gould, of the decision, thus giving him the tacit
go-ahead to recruit Violet McKenzie's telegraphists.[2]

The rear admiral notified Violet, who in turn notified the

fourteen young women she had chosen: Judy Alley, Joan Code, Elsie Colless, Shirley Drew, Joan Furley, Joan Hodges, Jess Prain, June McLeod, Denise Owen, Frances Provan, Pat Ross, Marion Stevens, Sylvia Thompson and Daphne Wright.[3] The news did not come as a surprise. She had quietly talked to each of them during the preceding weeks, explaining that they had been hand-picked to be the first women in the Royal Australian Navy, and seeking assurances from each that they were serious about wanting to do it.

Marion Stevens later recalled that Violet was so excited for them that she was 'like a clucky old hen'. Stevens, like the rest, had become completely immersed in the world of Sigs. She attended evening classes at first, going in after finishing her day's work at radio station 2UE. Once she qualified to become an instructor, she quit her job so that she could be at Sigs all day, every day—from about 10 a.m. until about 5 p.m.[4]

Violet accompanied the fourteen women to the Loftus Street medical centre, where they were given a quick examination and were signed off as medically fit for service. She told them to meet her at Central Station by 8 a.m. Monday morning, dressed in their WESC uniforms.

One by one, the fourteen women arrived at Central Station on the morning of 28 April 1941, accompanied by their tearful parents. They were all in uniform as instructed, and they all brought with them a suitcase of personal effects, since the one thing they knew was that they were likely to be gone for a long time.[5]

When they were all present, Violet issued them with their tickets and informed them that she and they would be departing on the 8.30 a.m. train to Queanbeyan, a small town east of Canberra—just over the border from the Australian Capital Territory in New South Wales. A few miles from

Queanbeyan's railway station was the navy signals base known as Harman, their ultimate destination.

Several hours later, Violet and the girls stepped off the carriage onto the platform at Queanbeyan Station. They were greeted by a naval officer, who led them to the street where several automobiles were waiting to chauffeur them to Harman. After the drivers had loaded their suitcases into the vehicles (it was inconceivable that the men would let the women do that themselves), they transported the women out of town to the signals base.[6]

Two senior officers stood waiting to meet them. They were Commander Jack Newman, who had travelled from Melbourne for the occasion, and the head of Harman, Commander Archibald D. McLachlan. The officers walked with them across the grounds.

There were no trees or gardens or shrubs on Harman's barren landscape, only a cluster of navy-constructed cottages on a grassy field. As Newman led them across the grounds, no other human could be seen ('not even a dog', commented Marion Stevens), giving the eerie sense that they had entered a ghost town. But as they neared some of the buildings, they saw glimpses of people inside, young men with their faces pressed against windowpanes, looking out.[7]

It turned out that Commander McLachlan had ordered all the men to stay confined to their huts when the women arrived. The men had done as instructed, but they were curious and wanted to get a glimpse of their new colleagues. They did not need to have the historical importance of the event explained to them. Until that moment, the Royal Australian Navy had been an exclusively male domain. That age-old demarcation was being obliterated in front of them by fifteen pairs of shoes crunching across the dusty grounds of Harman.

Newman and McLachlan led the women to the recreation hall, where Newman gave a speech. He said sternly, 'I'm told there are two kinds of women doing war work: ones that sit around and drink tea, and ones that work. I hope you are the latter.'[8]

This was a modified version of his standard new-recruit speech, but he had more reason than usual to hope that they were the 'right kind' of woman. He had personally fast-tracked their enlistment; he was the reason that they were on the grounds of Harman, rather than waiting at home for the wheels of bureaucracy to turn.

The WRANS existed in the sense that the war cabinet had given its approval, but it had not actually been set up. There was no director, nor even any officers of the WRANS, no headquarters, no uniform and no administrative structure of any kind. But all those things would soon be sorted out, so Newman had brought the fourteen women (and Violet McKenzie) to Harman. In the meantime, he suggested that they wear the smart WESC uniforms designed by Violet, which they were wearing that day, and that—until there was some kind of WRANS leadership appointed—they report directly to Commander McLachlan.

They learned that of the fourteen of them, twelve would be wireless telegraphists while two would be required to be cooks. This was because the navy board wanted them to be a completely independent unit, and that included not being dependent on the male navy cooks. Their living quarters consisted of four cottages, three of which were accommodation for the telegraphists, and the fourth was their mess hall as well as the cooks' accommodation.[9] McLachlan told them that, if they needed anything at all, they should ask Petty Officer Grieve Pennyquick for help.[10]

The navy allocated them to their huts based on Mrs Mac's

instructions. Some of the girls were in 'pairs'—they had particularly close friendships with each other—and were allocated to the same hut as each other.[11]

The weather turned cold that evening. There was a log fireplace, which they got going; they then gathered around it, drinking tea and toasting bread on the flames.

The hot-water system was fuelled by a chip heater, which they were not confident about starting, so they fetched the petty officer to help. The petty officer came with them as far as he dared, but he refused to enter the hut.

The boundary between the women's huts and the rest of the base, delineated by markings where a hedge would one day be planted, was a barrier that the men were forbidden to cross. The women learned that Commander McLachlan had told the men, 'If any man is found with one foot inside the hedge—the line where the hedge will be—he is drafted to sea forthwith.'[12] To get around this prohibition, the women opened the window. The petty officer stood outside it, on the far side of the imaginary hedge, shouting instructions to them about the chip heater.

Once they had hot water, Denise Owen disappeared to have a bath. The others soon heard an ear-splitting scream from the bathroom, causing two of the women to run to her aid. She had accidentally turned on one of the shower taps and been deluged with ice-cold water.[13]

In the morning, they reported to the recreation hall for a training session with Petty Officer Grieve Pennyquick in Morse techniques and naval communication standards. Nobody had briefed him on their skill level, so he commenced the session with some practice, sending them messages in Morse code at ten words per minute. For these women—the best Morse operators that Violet McKenzie had produced—it was absurdly slow, but they dutifully transcribed groups of five letters as he tapped them out. After completing his transmission, Pennyquick tested their accuracy by asking them to report the first group of letters that he had sent. They gave him the answer while trying not to roll their eyes.

He noticed the bemused looks passing among them, so he asked, 'What's the second group?' They gave him the answer to that, too, telling him that his test was too easy.

He then sent them Morse code at fifteen words per minute, and tested their answers. Again it was too easy: they got it all correct. He sped up to eighteen words per minute, but the women continued to keep pace as if at a slow canter.[14]

Eventually, the frustrated Pennyquick snapped at them, 'Well, get this!' He then fired off a string of encrypted Morse groups as fast as he could, his hand and wrist almost a blur as his Morse key issued a staccato hum. Finally, he stopped to find out how they had fared. Everyone had successfully captured most of it, and some of them had successfully captured the entire message.

Pennyquick sat back in his chair, looking at them. Then, with a broad smile, he said, 'Well, that's a good morning's work.' He spent the rest of the morning regaling them with stories of life in the navy.

After lunch, he had planned a lesson on single-letter procedures, important codes in which a single letter could be used to relay a key piece of information. Single-letter codes could be used in situations where a full message was not possible. For instance, W (or rather a string of Ws) meant 'being attacked by a warship'; Q (or a string of Qs) was 'being attacked by a raider'; R was 'being attacked by a submarine'; A was 'being attacked by an aircraft'; and M was 'being attacked by a mine'.

He started with A, the single-letter code for 'being attacked by an aircraft'. The girls responded by chanting the meanings of the next letters in the alphabet: 'B is "more to follow"; C is "correct"; D is "deferred" . . .'[15]

Pennyquick turned to them and demanded to know where they had learned these procedures.

'The air force taught us,' someone said.

Pennyquick was sceptical, because he was sure that the single-letter system he was teaching them was specific to the navy. 'They couldn't know it,' he replied.

He subsequently learned that the girls had been taught the procedure by Mrs Mac in their classes at the Women's Emergency Signalling Corps. Whether she really got the single-letter codes from the air force, or whether she was covering for Newman, who in revealing them might have been breaking protocol, nobody knew.[16]

Violet stayed with them at Harman for two nights. When she was satisfied that they were settled in and comfortable, she returned by train to Sydney alone.[17]

About a month later, a piano was delivered to Harman, where it was placed in the recreation hut. It had been donated by Violet McKenzie, who had been worried about the lack of recreational activities for her girls. She believed that a piano would help them pass the time.

•—•

Training for the women lasted a week. As it turned out, they were already familiar not only with Morse code but also with the full range of navy signalling protocols, so most of their training consisted of drills. After that, they were assigned to watches and commenced duty.

As a self-contained unit on base, they had to do everything for themselves: maintaining their chip heaters, cleaning their huts, washing their own clothes (a novelty for the younger women, who had never lived away from home before) and even chopping their own wood. After several injuries, including gashed faces requiring stitches, male sailors were assigned to chop their wood, but all the other duties remained theirs.[18]

The men were unsure about them at first—sometimes checking in a panic that an important message had been taken correctly—but they quickly adapted to having the women around. According to Marion Stevens, 'We got on all right and they were good to us.' But if the men were impressed with their ability, they did not let on—compliments were few and far between.

Stevens got a pleasant surprise at another station later in the war when she encountered the man who had been the base's lead telegraphist at that time. Recalling the arrival of the first women at Harman, he said, 'Gee, those women were good.'[19]

Since they had no military uniform, they continued to wear the WESC uniform, as did subsequent intakes. When the navy eventually recruited more widely than through Sigs, some women arrived from Melbourne who had never been in the WESC and did not have the WESC uniform, so they wore their Girl Guides uniforms instead.

Harman was the largest wireless station in Australia, one of a network of Allied stations across the Asia-Pacific region. Like the men, the women worked around the clock in eight-hour shifts, taking messages from ships as well as from distant transmitting stations, including one in Rugby, England.[20]

Despite McLachlan's best efforts, relationships did blossom between some of the men and women. Occasionally, the relationships led to marriages.

•—•

On 19 November 1941, an Australian cruiser named HMAS *Sydney* was patrolling the Indian Ocean off the Western Australian coast when it encountered a German raider,

Kormoran, which was disguised as a Dutch merchant ship. Both ships opened fire on each other—*Kormoran* firing first—and both were destroyed.

Sydney sank so quickly that nobody could get to the life rafts. Everyone on board—a crew of 645 Australians—died. *Sydney* had sunk so rapidly that it did not even send a distress signal. A British ship picked up the 345 survivors from *Kormoran* four days later.

Rumours of a cover-up spread. A signal from *Sydney* had been heard at Harman, they said. Some claimed that there had been a Q message ('under attack by a raider'); others claimed that a voice message had been sent saying, 'We're about to open fire!' (or, in some versions, 'We are under fire'). Most damning were the rumours that the WRANS woman on duty at Harman had missed it, because she was away from her station making a cup of tea.

The woman on duty when *Sydney* was sunk was Marion Stevens. In her submission to a government inquiry into the circumstances of the sinking, she stated (using capital letters to emphasise her point): 'NOTHING WAS RECEIVED.'[21] Two men had been on duty with her. Stevens explained that the wireless room was small, and that therefore 'if any signal had been received, we'd all have known about it'.

She derided the claims that someone on *Sydney* had broadcast in voice, 'We're about to open fire!' For one thing, she told the parliamentary inquiry, no commander who is about to open fire and is in his right mind would broadcast a radio message about it beforehand. Furthermore, the only communication system installed on *Sydney* was a Morse transmitter: it was simply impossible for someone on that ship to send a voice message, even if they had wanted to.[22]

It turned out that the source of many of the rumours was a sailor whom Commander McLachlan had confined to barracks after he was caught sneaking around near the women's huts. He had reason to resent the women as well as the commander, and to slander the efficiency of his station.

The inquiry vindicated Stevens, concluding: '*Sydney* sent no signals immediately before, during or after the engagement with *Kormoran*.'

Nonetheless, Jess Prain recalled that in the days following the sinking, some naval officers arrived at Harman announcing, 'The *Sydney* has been lost with all hands. I hope one of those damned women hasn't missed the message.'[23]

19

AN SOS FROM MARY BELL

•— —• ••• — — — ••• ••—• •—• —— — ——
— — •— •—• —•— — —••• • •—•• •—••

The formation of the WAAAF was eventually approved by cabinet in February 1941 ... This approval was only given because it had been found to be impossible to get enough male signal personnel.

Mary Bell, WAAAF commanding officer, 1941

Violet's stance against the air force was softened by a desperate call for help from the newly appointed director of the WAAAF in April.

Mary Bell had held a pilot's licence since 1926 and had an intimate knowledge of the air force through her marriage to Group Captain J.T. Bell. Since forming the Women's Air Training Corps in Brisbane in 1939 she had been lobbying the air force for the enlistment of women, with considerable success. Chief of air staff (CAS) Charles Burnett had invited her in 1940 to provide a report on the possibility of a women's auxiliary air force. As a result of this work, Bell became the obvious choice to lead the service, if it was ever to come into existence.[1]

In January 1941, the Advisory War Council approved the creation of the WAAAF, but cautioned that numbers should be kept as low as possible—'the minimum number for the minimum period'. Mary Bell was made acting director in February, the minister making the whole thing public in March.[2]

Her dream of a women's air force had become a reality and she was running it, but Bell's troubles were only just beginning. She later described her brief time as head of the WAAAF:

> I was given an office containing two tables, one chair, one form, one telephone and nothing else and told to get on with it. Luckily I had been associated with the R.A.A.F. since its formation when my husband was one of the original officers, so knew most of the senior officers and my way about generally. This made it possible for me to cope with a situation that to anyone not used to the air force and its ways would have been virtually impossible.[3]

She was allocated a building, which later became the first WAAAF barracks. In an act of petty hostility, the southern area command immediately began using the building as a dumping ground for pots, pans, beds and so on. Bell had no staff, so she called on her friends in the Women's Air Training Corps, several of whom came to the rescue, working for her on a voluntary basis until the WAAAF was up and running. When given the chance, she appointed them as her senior officers.

Her recruitment drive for women telegraphists had been sabotaged, and the Advisory War Council was entertaining the possibility of reversing direction and closing the WAAAF down completely, only weeks after its formation. After all, the rationale for creating it was that there was a ready supply of women who could work as telegraphists.

Violet told Bell that she was 'fed up' with the air force and had no intention of helping them out of their predicament. But Bell replied that the entire enterprise was at risk. There was talk in the corridors of power that, if the WAAAF was axed, plans for a women's navy and women's army would be scrapped, too.

Violet caught the next available train to Melbourne. She met with Mary Bell and her boss, Air Vice-Marshal Henry N. Wrigley, to plan how to fill the cohort of telegraphists before the next council meeting.

Wrigley was an ally of Bell's and a strong advocate of the formation of the WAAAF, but he was facing stiff opposition. He had to report at the next meeting about whether the courses for women's telegraphists had been filled. If they had not, then it was likely that the WAAAF would be closed down.

Violet returned to Sydney, and Mary Bell came as well. They had two days before the meeting to find enough women to fill the cohort. Violet was able to quickly recruit enough of her girls to fill one course. There were dozens of others whom she knew would be keen to join the air force, but with only two days she was not able to make contact with them— mostly it was a matter of waiting until they next turned up at Sigs. Many would not be in until after the critical war council meeting.

With the first training course filled, Violet confirmed to Mary Bell that the second and third courses would easily be filled also, but that this could not be done in two days. They just needed to let the air vice-marshal know the good news before he went to the meeting. He was somewhere in Sydney, so Violet sent one of her women out as a dispatch rider to find him and deliver the message.

The rider found Wrigley, who was able to report that the WAAAF had filled its training cohorts for telegraphists. Of course, this was not actually true. Having filled the first training course, Mary Bell was trusting Violet's word that, with a bit more time, she could fill the later courses (which she did).[4]

In gratitude for her help, Wrigley gave Violet McKenzie the rank of Honorary Flight Officer. She was issued with a uniform, but her appointment was never gazetted or otherwise formalised.[5]

•—•

Mary Bell's tenure as director of the WAAAF was brief. Sir Charles Burnett was a supporter of the WAAAF, but he had hoped that his older daughter Joan could become the director.[6]

Wrigley, an Australian with a nose for what could cause trouble, demurred. 'There was enough public outcry in Australia in certain directions against your appointment as CAS,' he told Burnett. 'There's going to be a further public outcry if a woman other than an Australian is brought out as the director of Australian WAAAFs. So your daughter's out of the question.'[7]

With Joan eliminated from contention, Burnett lost interest in the WAAAF from then on, other than to insist that his younger daughter, Bunty, should at least be an officer.

Bunty proved to be a headache for Mary Bell. She did not get along with Bell or the others at the WAAAF headquarters, often expressing disapproval of the decisions they made. If things were not changed to conform to her ideas, then Bell would receive an instruction from the chief of air staff to implement his daughter's views.[8]

The tension between Bell and Burnett meant that Bell's days in the job were numbered. She learned later in May that Wrigley—under instructions from Charles Burnett—was seeking applicants to replace her as director of the WAAAF. Her replacement was a Sydney businesswoman, Clare Stevenson, who had previously been an executive of Berlei Australia, the well-known lingerie manufacturer.

Bell was appalled at her replacement's lack of relevant qualifications. 'I had never heard of her and all I could find out was that she was some sort of senior instructor at the Berlei corset factory responsible for training corset fitters,' she complained later, although her depiction undersold Stevenson's standing and ability. Bell was offered the chance to be an advisor to Stevenson, but the thought of being the same rank as—and in competition with—Bunty Burnett was too much. Bell resigned from her position.[9]

Stevenson took over and remained the director of the WAAAF until the end of the war.

20

THE NEXT EIGHT

– ••••• – –• • –•• – – • •• – –• •••• –

*To Mrs McKenzie must go much of the credit for
the early success of the service. It was she who made
it possible for patriotic young women to train as
wireless telegraphists. It was she who pleaded their
cause and when they, and those who followed, were
accepted as part of the Senior Service, she remained
their friend.*

Margaret Curtis-Otter, W.R.A.N.S.[1]

Sometime in May 1941, Commander Jack Newman made
contact with Violet, asking her to choose another eight
women for a second intake of naval telegraphists. He told her
that there was no need to select fast *senders* of Morse code,
because these women would only ever be *receiving* messages.
Newman had a rather special project in mind for them. He

was planning to assign them to listen to enemy frequencies and transcribe enemy radio messages, which would then be passed to his code-breaking unit in Melbourne.

Violet chose Bea Ogilvie, Betty Cleburne, Bobby Chatterton, Dorothy Johnstone, Heather Dunshea, Joan Cowie, Joan Senior and Josephine ('Jo') Miller, all of whom were willing and ready to join the navy. Once they were selected, Newman instructed Violet to bring them to Melbourne.

Commodore Gerard Muirhead-Gould, the commanding officer of the Sydney navy establishment, ensured that Violet was issued with nine rail vouchers for third-class travel from Sydney to Melbourne (the cheapest tickets it was possible to get). Violet was informed that, on arrival, she and the eight telegraphists were to check into the Melbourne YWCA (Young Women's Christian Association) housing, where accommodation had been booked for them.[2]

It was dawn on 2 June 1941 when the train pulled out of Central Station in Sydney, and evening when they stepped onto the platform of Spencer Street Station in Melbourne. They carried their suitcases through steadily increasing rain to the YWCA. The receptionist had no record of any booking for them and could not provide them with rooms, because there were no vacancies that night, but she quietly suggested to Violet that they might find lodgings at the Travellers' Aid Society through inquiries at Flinders Street Station.

They stepped back out into the dark to find that the weather was worsening. After they had found somewhere to shelter from the rain, Violet told the women to wait for her there while she found them a place to stay. She chose Bea Ogilvie to accompany her and set off into the night.[3]

At the station, they located a representative of the Travellers' Aid Society, who took them to the society's building at 235 King Street, just off Lonsdale Street. She introduced Violet and Bea to Nest Malcolm, a genial woman of Violet's age. Malcolm ushered them into her interview room.

The Travellers' Aid Society was a privately run charity that offered crisis accommodation to runaway children, women fleeing violent husbands, migrants who had stepped off ships without any local currency, families visiting Melbourne due to relatives in hospital, and itinerants and drifters of many kinds. Nest Malcolm's helpers frequented the train stations and ports to offer accommodation to new arrivals, particularly young women and children.

Violet explained the situation. There were nine of them in total; they had arrived that day from Sydney, and they had nowhere to stay. Malcolm offered them beds for the night, if they were prepared to sleep two to a room.[4]

The others were relieved when Violet and Bea emerged from the night bearing the news that they had found somewhere to stay. They all trudged through the rain to the Travellers' Aid Society, lugged their suitcases up the stairs, slid under the sheets on the hard little beds and slept.[5]

The next morning, they reported to Flinders Naval Depot, where Jack Newman greeted them. When Violet told him about the accommodation debacle, Newman apologised and offered to pay for the women's lodgings.

Newman was keen to start training, but first things first. The women had not undergone the medical fitness examination in Sydney and would have to be assessed immediately to ensure that they were fit to serve. Newman was cutting corners to enlist them quickly and without fanfare, but he was not prepared to cut that one.

The weight requirement was a problem. The navy had a minimum acceptable weight for recruits, but it had been set with only male recruits in mind. Several of the women barely weighed enough, and Jo Miller—who was almost as tiny as Violet—was under the limit. Violet hurried out of the medical centre and across to Newman to tell him of the situation. Newman ordered a sailor to fetch him a pair of heavy rubber sailor's boots.

With the boots in hand, Newman accompanied Violet across to the medical centre, where he instructed Jo Miller to put on the boots. He told the physician that Miller could only be examined while she was wearing the boots. She looked ridiculous with her thin little legs in those enormous sailor's boots, but when she next stepped onto the scales, she passed the weight test.[6]

Another issue was how long they could stay at the Travellers' Aid Society, which typically provided only short-term accommodation. But Nest Malcolm was happy to oblige. She told Violet that the eight young women were welcome to lodge there for the duration of their eight-week training course in Melbourne.

The Travellers' Aid Society worked out for them in several ways. The building was only a year old, it was conveniently located in the city, it was near the naval base, and there was a cafeteria on the ground floor that served cheap lunches and dinners.[7]

A variety of lodgers stayed at the Travellers' Aid Society while they were there. Refugees came from war-torn places in Europe and Asia. There were wives and children of servicemen, who had come from the country to see their husbands and fathers on shore leave. Unmarried women who had fallen pregnant stayed at the Society until their pregnancy ended one way or another. And there was a steady stream of unaccompanied children from London who had been sent on ships to Australia by their parents so that they would be safe from the Blitz, Germany's bombing campaign.

For the eight young women—none of whom had been to Melbourne before, and all of whom still lived at home—it was an educational experience in the varieties of human experience, and in misery as well as compassion, which they had barely imagined in their suburban childhoods. For a long time afterwards, these women remembered those eight weeks with fondness—including the eye-opening lessons in life, and the care and interest shown towards them by Nest Malcolm and her staff.[8]

Jack Newman paid for the women's lodging out of his own pocket. He said that he would recoup the costs from the women once they were on the navy payroll, but he never did. Newman and his wife hosted the eight telegraphists for afternoon tea on weekends at their home, and his second-in-command, Lieutenant John A.S. Brame, did likewise.

Violet stayed on for a few days at the Travellers' Aid Society, then bid the women good luck and departed from Spencer Street Station on the Sydney-bound train.

•—•

During their eight-week training course, the women learned the Japanese variant of Morse code known as the *kana* code. Their job, once they were on duty, would be to monitor Japanese naval frequencies, on which all messages were encrypted and sent in *kana* code.

Japan had not yet entered the war. Even so, the wind was blowing in that direction. Japan's government had a pact with Germany and was considered a part of the Axis alliance. Tensions were mounting between Japan and the United States, and British and American intelligence agencies concluded that Japan was preparing for war.

For over a year, Jack Newman had been nurturing a code-breaking unit at Melbourne's Victoria Barracks called the Special Intelligence Bureau. His chief code-breaker was Eric Nave, an Australian who had worked for many years at Britain's Government Code and Cipher School and who had recently returned to Australia from his posting in Singapore due to illness.

Nave was attempting to break certain Japanese naval codes, but to do so he needed lots of sample messages to study. That's where the telegraphists would come in. Instead of communicating with Allied ships and friendly stations, they would scan the airwaves for Japanese naval communications, transcribing encrypted Japanese messages and sending them to Melbourne for Nave and his code-breaking team to study.

Newman's task was to provide the infrastructure around Nave so that he could build an Australian code-breaking centre. And so, for the next eight weeks, Newman trained the eight young women in the various arcane skills required in the navy's signals intelligence, including mastery of *kana* code and the conversion of *kana* code into *katakana* (a Japanese syllabary). When their training was completed, he escorted six of them to Harman, while Joan Cowie and Jo Miller—whom he had identified as the most talented of the group—stayed in Melbourne.

The six telegraphists who went to Harman had been trained in secret techniques, but they were never told how their work would be used. They did not know of Eric Nave, or the Special Intelligence Bureau, or the network of Allied code-breaking units around the world, even though they were part of that network. Only Cowie and Miller, who stayed behind, learned of the bigger picture.

Newman planned to increase the size of his code-breaking operation using WRANS, and he needed Cowie and Miller to help him by training and coordinating the many women that he planned to employ. When he returned from Harman, he gave them desks in his offices at Victoria Barracks, alongside a small number of staff, including Joan Duff (later Joan Fairbridge).

Desperate for personnel to support his burgeoning intelligence operations, Newman had recruited Duff before the creation of the WRANS and, as a result, he employed her as a civilian. Cowie and Miller called her the 'also WRAN'. They processed intercepted Japanese messages and liaised with Eric Nave's Special Intelligence Bureau, which was further along the corridor.

In December 1941, after the Japanese attack on Pearl Harbor, the code-breaking operation expanded as Newman had planned, and there were large intakes of telegraphists and coders. American code-breakers, who had escaped from the Philippines, arrived. The code-breaking operation outgrew its rooms at Victoria Barracks, so it relocated to a nearby apartment block called Monterey Flats.

Cowie and Miller played a vital role in training, organising and supervising the WRANS who worked at Monterey Flats, although their ranks did not reflect the level of responsibility that they had been given. Newman, as usual, did things informally and without filling out all the requisite forms. Even when there were large numbers of WRANS living on naval establishments, Cowie and Miller continued to live in private accommodation.

When Violet learned that Cowie and Miller were living on their own in Melbourne and were there permanently, she worried about them. She often wrote to them breezy, lighthearted letters that began, 'Dear Jo 'nd Joan', or sometimes 'Dear Joan 'nd Jo'. At Christmas time, she sent them each a blue vase as a gift.[9]

Miller and Cowie became the subject of gossip among the

WRANS under their supervision. They appeared to have a close and special relationship with Newman, who was aloof and inaccessible to other WRANS. Cowie and Miller were inseparable, and remained so after the war, travelling the world together.

Jo Miller remained in contact with Violet for the rest of Violet's life. After Violet died in 1982, Miller gave a eulogy at the funeral, in which she revealed that she still had the blue vase that Violet had sent her for Christmas in 1941.

21

MUSICAL MORSE

— — ••— ••••• —•—••— •—••   — — — — — •—• ••• •

*The women considered Morse code to be quite musical,
even when they did not feel they were learning music.*

Cassandra Mohapp, 'The Rhythm of Life'[1]

An army major came to the Clarence Street woolshed,
desperate for help from Violet. The officer said to her,
'I've got a problem, a serious one. You might help me.'

She said, 'I'll try.'

The major explained his situation. 'I'm going to Egypt in
three weeks to fight the Germans, and I haven't one man in
my unit who can send and receive Morse code accurately.
Can you advise me what to do?'

Violet told him, 'I can help you if you'll take my advice,
but if you doubt it, and have some ideas that don't agree
with my experience, then I can't help you.'

When the major agreed, she proposed a solution. 'I want your men to come in every day, all day, for about six hours for the three weeks, and only do slow Morse. Only get up to eight words per minute.'

That was well below the army's minimum Morse proficiency of twenty words per minute. The major blustered, 'Eight words per minute? That's nothing!'

Violet replied, 'I know that's nothing compared with fast Morse, but you only want to send little odd messages like "We need 100 reinforcements" or something. Four or five words. You take my advice, and you'll find it will work.'

Her advice was based on her belief that training for accuracy is more important than training for speed, when the ultimate goal is to have both. Speed comes naturally once the skill itself is mastered. Violet put it like this: 'You must get it right. It doesn't matter how slow it is, it must be right.'[2]

The major returned the following day with his signallers. She was appalled by their lack of skills and their poor basic knowledge. None of them knew the Morse alphabet; worse than that, many of them did not know the *English* alphabet. They were illiterate. She did the best she could, and then put them to work at Morse stations, where they trained all day, every day, tapping out Morse messages at slow speeds. Three weeks later, they were gone.

Some time later, Violet received a letter from the major, praising her for the work she had done with his signallers. They had, as it turned out, performed well. The major boasted, 'Our boys left all the 25-word-per-minute boys cold.'[3]

•—•

The woolshed always hummed with activity. Men and women filed up and down the narrow, rickety staircase at all hours of the day and every evening. Some of the women—including all of the instructors—wore WESC uniforms, while other women came in civilian clothes. Men who were waiting for call-up came dressed in civvies, while those already enlisted came in their uniforms. Officers from all services visited from time to time.

At the top of that first flight of stairs, the dim, cavernous interior was dotted with trestle tables that seemed to go on forever, the occasional shaft of sunlight causing a flare off a Morse key or the back of a chair. People sat at the tables with headphones over their ears.

Near the door was the two-words-per-minute table. This was for absolute beginners, who listened intently to a Sigs instructor sending Morse code at a speed that anyone could keep up with. Another table was for Morse code at ten words per minute, another for fifteen words per minute and so on.

Former Sigs student Jean Nysen explained how a newcomer would progress:

> You would start off as a beginner, then you go to two words per minute and then when you could do that comfortably you go to the six words per minute table and work up to the one that went . . . *brrrrt* . . . that would be Marion Stevens from the top table sending something from today's paper.[4]

Breaks for morning tea and afternoon tea were a daily ritual when students and instructors could briefly chat over a cup of tea.[5] Cecil would come in after work or on weekends to maintain the lattice of circuits that weaved throughout the woolshed, from sending keys to receiving stations, from zone to zone and between floors.[6]

WRANS who had been posted to Harman (and later all over Australia) would call in when they were on leave in Sydney. When the navy finally got around to issuing uniforms to WRANS, the women would visit the woolshed in their uniforms, causing a stir with students who hoped to emulate them soon, and invariably causing Violet to make a fuss like a proud relative.[7]

Everyone was welcome. Older people, well past the age limit for joining the forces—some of whom weren't interested in learning Morse code themselves—volunteered and helped in various ways, such as cleaning and tidying, making sandwiches and doing various ad hoc tasks. Some of the older women spent their time knitting balaclavas and scarves for the male trainees to take with them when they departed for war. A young woman who had been born with a deformed arm learned to send with her 'good arm', and was an enthusiastic helper in the kitchen.[8]

With the entry of the first groups of women into the WRANS and the WAAAF, where they were quickly issued with proper service uniforms, there was for a moment a booming market in second-hand WESC uniforms. Women posted to Harman or elsewhere sold their no-longer-needed green, brown and white outfits to newer members, freeing them of the need to expend scarce clothing vouchers when they qualified for the uniform.

There was an order to the place that came from a common purpose and from Violet's unwavering supervision. Former Sigs student Alison Armstrong recalled: 'I wouldn't say there was discipline, and yet it was disciplined.'[9]

In an interview for an ABC Radio National program about Violet, Former Sigs student Margaret Taylor said, 'There was no nonsense in Mrs Mac's classes, I can tell you.'[10]

When the interviewer asked Taylor for an example of

Mrs Mac's 'discipline', she answered, 'Well, she just had to really *look* at you, you know. It was just her bearing, her expression. She was strict, and yet she was soft as butter. She was a lovely lady.'[11]

As enrolment numbers climbed ever higher, Violet continued to innovate with her teaching techniques. She was convinced that musical ability corresponded with Morse ability, and continued to try various techniques that tapped into rhythms and beats. *The Daily Telegraph* reported in August 1941 that Violet had organised a 'Morse orchestra' in order to teach large classes of newcomers.

Girls in Morse Orchestra

New System Speeds up Telegraphists' Training

Morse code instruction has been speeded up by a new 'Morse orchestra', organised by Mrs. F.V. McKenzie at the Women's Emergency Signalling Corps' headquarters in Clarence Street.

The orchestra was established after Mrs. McKenzie had tried it out successfully on a batch of 100 new girl recruits for the corps. When it proved immediately effective, she began to train girls for the WAAAFS in the orchestra.

'It is important that girls be taught Morse quickly,' said Mrs. McKenzie, who was recently appointed hon. Flight Officer in the WAAAF.

She based her orchestra on the rhythm of Morse code. It works thus: The instructor of a class sends a letter or word repeatedly over the transmitter, and the pupils listen in to it with their earphones.

When each pupil feels she has the rhythm of the letter she works her own key, joining in with the instructor and other pupils.

In this way dozens of girls are sending the same signal

with the same rhythm at the same time like musicians playing together in a symphony orchestra.

Girls at the corps headquarters are now taught, when receiving, to whistle the Morse symbols softly instead of the old-fashioned method of 'singing' them. This is because a whistle is very similar to the sound made by a wireless signal. The 'singing' of symbols introduces an intermediate stage of thinking which has to be discarded before speed can be obtained.[12]

Violet worked at Sigs for about 70 hours each week. She was there to open the doors in the morning, and she was the last to leave in the evening. Two of her volunteer assistants, Beryl White and Ruby Hughes, were also a fixture throughout the war, and worked around 60 hours a week. Several other instructors were also putting in long hours.[13]

In spring 1941, Violet organised a weekend camp—only for instructors—at a holiday house by the water in Broken Bay, about 30 miles (50 kilometres) north of Sydney. This was unlike the large camps that she had previously held at Easter and other times, where the women trained all day and lived in military-like conditions. Instead, this was actually just a treat as a way of thanking them, and a chance to get away for a couple of days and recharge. They did a bit of signals practice, but mostly swam, lazed about and had fun.[14]

Gwenda Moulton was one of the women at the camp. She hoped to join the navy, but she didn't expect to get in any time soon, as there were plenty of highly skilled women who would probably be chosen before her. In the meantime, she was happy to contribute in her role as an instructor.

Her opportunity to enlist came sooner than she expected—and without warning. When the navy was next running telegraphy entrance tests, Violet encouraged her to come along. 'We're going for a test tonight, Gwenda. You might as well come for the practice.'

Gwenda attended, passed the test and, on 21 December 1941, found herself leaving Sydney as one of the 24 women in the next contingent to Harman.[15]

The navy had still not adjusted its physical entrance requirements since the first fourteen women had left for Harman in April, but the practice of boosting women's weight and height had become more or less standard practice at the examination centre. Gwenda was too short according to the height limit, but the doctor had a pair of women's high heels at hand, and invited her to wear them before being retested. She passed the medical test, and was dispatched to duties at Harman.[16]

The navy assigned an officer to administer naval proficiency tests at Sigs on prospective candidates. He would always turn up after lunch with a faint smell of beer, due to his habit of stopping at a nearby pub for a couple of drinks before arriving. His Morse code was flawless, but the women of Sigs were unimpressed because his sending speed was only fifteen words a minute. For candidates who were attempting to pass the navy's 22-words-per-minute benchmark, the drunken sailor made it easy.[17]

22

THE GENERAL AND MRS MCKENZIE

— •••• • — —• • —• • •—• • •—•• •— —• —••
— — •—• • ••• — — —•—• —•— • —• — —•• •• •

Mrs McKenzie has achieved more than any other woman, in this work of training women to under-take special wartime duties, work in which she is a pioneer.

Lady Margaret Wakehurst, 1941[1]

In November 1941, General Thomas Blamey gave a speech to the Australian Imperial Force Women's Association (AIFWA) in Melbourne. He said: 'It is not a bit of use women training to be dispatch riders and signallers or doing any military things. Your work will inevitably be to train yourselves to take the place of men in industry.'[2]

His audience was far more receptive to his theme than a gathering at Violet's corps would have been. There may have been some among them who harboured a secret desire to drive dispatch motorcycles and learn Morse code, but by and large the women gathered before him had no intention of joining the military. Their association was a club for officers' wives, whose main activity was hosting social events and providing a forum for emotional support. This is not to say that it had no merit: their husbands were on active service, and many would soon be dead.

It was a bizarre speech for Blamey to make. The Women's Auxiliary Australian Air Force (WAAAF) and the Women's Royal Australian Navy Service (WRANS) were both up and running, with uniformed women working alongside men at several military establishments. And, at that moment, the Australian Women's Army Service (AWAS)—having been gazetted in August—was holding a training school for its first officers at a Girl Guides campground in the hills east of Melbourne. Across all three military services, women were already 'doing military things'.

He had whistled a different tune two years earlier when, as head of the Manpower Committee, he had written to the state directors of the Women's Australian National Service (WANS), thanking them for their efforts. He had also written to Violet directly, telling her: 'It is with great pleasure that I have learnt of the excellent training being put into force by the signalling corps.'[3]

But back then, Violet had not been advocating for women in the military. She was still telling people that all she wanted to do was help women fill men's jobs on a temporary basis while the men were at war.[4]

Perhaps Blamey—having been in the Middle East for the past year and a half as Australia's army chief—was annoyed that women's military services had been formed in his absence. On this brief visit home, before he returned to his command in Egypt, he made his views known about women serving in the military.

Violet retorted in an article printed in the *Sunday Sun and Guardian*: 'I am writing General Blamey a letter to explain the work our organisation is doing. By his statement on the uselessness of women training to be signallers, I am convinced he has no knowledge whatsoever of the work which the Women's Emergency Signalling Corps are doing.'

She noted that there were already 100 of her women currently serving in the navy and air force: 'There is a great demand for them. The air force asked us to supply 250, a demand we were unable to fill because we didn't have them . . . Liaison officers from the army, navy and air force are attached to our service, and the course we follow is based on their advice.' Yes indeed, the army under Blamey's command had a liaison officer posted at the Women's Emergency Signalling Corps. Perhaps nobody had bothered to tell him that before he castigated the women's corps in public.[5]

But while he was at it, he took a swipe at the practice of sending gift parcels to overseas units. The Women's Emergency Signalling Corps sent comfort parcels to various signals units and, similarly, other women's groups provided comfort parcels or cash donations to units that they wished to support for whatever reason. It was true that this practice resulted in somewhat patchy support across the various units among the fighting forces, and probably looked unfair to the ones that didn't get presents. But from the point of view of the women's groups, it was far more motivating to send gifts to specific units than to drop donations into the bucket of an impersonal general fund. But Blamey didn't like it, and he railed against it:

The sending of money to individual units is not needed, nor desirable, and weakens Australia's economic position. I would like to see you drop unit funds and give to the Comforts Fund, which is responsible for many of the clubs for the men abroad. I do not want to interfere with the sending of private parcels, most of which reach the men. If there are any delays, they are due principally to the necessary movements of troops.[6]

There were plenty of other things occupying Blamey's mind during his month-long visit to Australia. He briefed the government on the general strategic position in the Middle East, the Western Desert campaign in North Africa, the disastrous Greece campaign and plans for future operations, including in Sicily and Turkey. He was intensely involved in decisions relating to Australian Army organisation and recruitment, and discussions about the working relationship between Australian and British forces.[7]

The women's organisations were not alone in drawing flak from the hot-headed general. He fired volleys left and right during his visit to Australia, deriding the extraordinarily large sums of money the government was lavishing on air-raid drills (he might have had a point on that one); the paltry output of military production (he had a point there, too); enlistment rates; and obsolete training methods.[8]

He was particularly appalled by what he saw as widespread apathy. In Sydney, he said, 'I am astounded at the complacency with which people in Australia view the war situation. You are living a carnival life and you are enjoying it. But if you do not take your part you will find your homes overwhelmed, as were the homes of people in France and Belgium. We are in a position where we must fight or perish.'[9]

In Melbourne, he bemoaned what a 'fool's paradise' the

country had become, saying, 'Candidly, it sickens me. I want to get away from it as soon as I can. Don't people realise we are up against it? If we don't win this war it means the end of us and the whole of the rest of the British Empire.'[10]

When, only days later, he attended the Williamstown Cup horse races and presented the winner's trophy, he copped some deserved criticism from diggers and journalists. They noted that, after denouncing the Australian public's 'carnival life', he had attended an actual carnival.[11]

•—•

Coinciding with Blamey's visit, the government introduced a new regulation banning women's organisations from adopting uniforms that resembled military uniforms: 'It is illegal for any unofficial women's organisation to adopt a uniform resembling that of enlisted men.'[12]

Naturally, the media gaze fell on Violet and the Women's Emergency Signalling Corps, the most prominent women's organisation whose members donned their own military-style uniform. With a shrug of disinterest, Violet dismissed the regulation as not applicable to her. In fact, she said, 'I was pleased to see the statement, as I know that great confusion is caused.' (She did not suggest where this 'confusion' was occurring, other than to say it was not coming from her.) 'The green uniform of the WESC is sufficiently distinctive to be exempt from the new regulation.'[13]

Leaders of other women's organisations responded in the same vein. Jean Allen of the Australian Women's Flying Club (whose uniform was blue) said, 'Our uniform is distinctive enough not to cause any confusion.'[14]

The head of the Sydney WANS said, 'As no service uniform resembles the W.A.N.S. uniform in colour, I do not think we would come under the new ruling.'[15]

The honorary secretary of the National Emergency Ambulance Drivers, H.B. Jamieson, complained that her group's uniform had been approved by the National Emergency Services (a government agency that was coordinating civilian defence activities); likewise, the head of the National Defence League Women's Auxiliary complained that the army had given her group permission to adopt khaki uniforms.

Violet and the other leaders of women's groups were making a stand. They were, in effect, saying to the government: *We're not breaking the law, and if you think otherwise, come and get us.* The government went into reverse.

Prime Minister John Curtin, who had only held the top job for a month, did not relish the prospect of starting his prime ministership by antagonising grassroots women's organisations. He issued a hasty clarification at the end of the week, explaining: 'A recently gazetted amendment to the national security regulations was not designed to prohibit members of women's unofficial war organisations wearing uniforms if they wished to do so.'[16] The only condition, he added, was that, if they wore uniforms, they should not resemble the uniform of any Australian services or, for that matter, the services of any other Commonwealth country.[17]

That sounded reasonable, except that the buying, selling and wearing of military uniforms by those not entitled to do so was *already* illegal. What was the point of regulations that restated existing regulations? Following Curtin's curious statement, the issue was quietly dropped.[18]

At any rate, the WESC uniform's heyday had passed. With the huge volume of students coming through Sigs every day, the opportunities for marches and parades through city streets were rare, and field days to parklands such as the Domain and Centennial Park were a luxury they could no longer afford.

•—•

Meanwhile, Violet's vision of sending her women into civilian roles was shattered when the Postmaster General turned his back on her.

The Postmaster General's department was the largest employer of civilians, and it was there that Violet had for a long time envisaged that her girls would be most needed. Originally established to handle physical mail, the Postmaster General's department had by degrees become involved in modern telecommunications, starting with the invention of the telegram. Transmitted by national and international cable networks, telegrams were an early analogue version of modern-day email. Telegrams were relayed by Morse code, necessitating post offices all over the country to have a Morse code expert for sending and receiving them.

With military signals bases perilously short of telegraphists, the Postmaster General, Thomas Joseph Collins, came under enormous pressure to relinquish staff for military service. The case was made to him that he could bring in women telegraphists from the Women's Emergency Signalling Corps. But when the unions got wind of this proposal, there were mass strikes by male civilian telegraphists in protest against the possible use of women.

On top of this, a man based in Sydney had been assigned the task of reporting on the viability of employing Mrs McKenzie's women in this way. He eventually informed Collins that they lacked the skills to do the job.

Collins dug in his heels, using as his cover the exemption from military duty of 'protected professions'. He made the case that there was no point stripping his department of telegraphists to rescue the military's shortages, only to cause the civilian communication network to fail instead. Given the negative report he had received on the women's capability, Collins may have seen the controversial proposal as nothing more than a ruse to lure him into surrendering to the military his most valuable workers. In the end, Collins won both of these political battles: he shielded all his workers from military service, and he blocked the entry of women into their jobs.

With civilian jobs out of the question, the only option left for Violet's girls was enlistment.

•—•

Recruitment at Sigs was soaring, and training demands soared with it. Most of the earliest members of Sigs—those who had been there at the start, almost three years earlier—had either now gone into military service or were senior instructors. The newcomers, men and women, were passing through Sigs and into the forces at a rapid rate. By the time they qualified for a uniform, many women were already on their way into the armed forces. Violet was in more demand than ever, but she was being supported by a declining number of volunteer helpers.

In June 1941, during a widely publicised visit to the Women's Emergency Signalling Corps headquarters in Clarence Street, the NSW governor's wife, Lady Wakehurst, had claimed that Violet had done 'more than any other woman' in her contribution to Australia's war effort. It was a bold claim but a defensible one, given that she had been responsible for the training of thousands of Allied troops.

23

HARBOUR INTRUDERS

•••• •— •—• —••• — — — ••— •—•

•• —• — •—• ••— —•• • •—• •••

The audacious attack by the Japanese midget sub-marine crews proved to be a sharp wake-up call to Sydneysiders for whom the war had hitherto seemed somewhat distant.

John Perryman, RAN Seapower Centre[1]

World War II escalated abruptly when the Imperial Japanese Navy attacked the American naval base at Pearl Harbor on the morning of 7 December 1941, destroying or damaging several ships including four battleships, and killing 2335 military personnel. The Imperial Japanese Army then quickly spread through East Asia and the Pacific with the precision of a Swiss clock, capturing Hong Kong on Christmas Day, the Philippine capital Manila on 2 January

1942, and Singapore on 15 February. Four days later, 235 Japanese planes—launched from nearby aircraft carriers—attacked Darwin, causing devastation and killing over 200 people; it was the first of 64 air raids on the Australian city over the next two years.

The telegraphists at Harman tracked the course of the Japanese advance as the Allied stations progressively went off the air. First went Hong Kong, then Singapore, then Java, until Harman was the only major Commonwealth signals station in the Pacific area.

The first American servicemen arrived in Australia less than two weeks after the outbreak of the Pacific theatre of war, when a convoy on its way to the Philippines was diverted to Brisbane, arriving at Hamilton wharf on 22 December.[2]

Within weeks, American warships were anchored in Sydney Harbour; some of them had been diverted from their voyages to Manila. Fresh-faced young men wearing American uniforms were a common sight on the streets, and in bars and clubs. They were flush with money (being paid twice as much as Australian servicemen) and bravado, and brought with them novel tastes in music, such as jazz. The nightclub area of Kings Cross boomed with American customers and was permanently transformed.[3]

Australian servicemen were more frequent, too. Diggers fighting in Africa and the Middle East were recalled to boost the forces needed to fight the Pacific War. Hardened veterans of bitter desert campaigns resented the way that the cashed-up 'Yanks' managed to attract female attention more easily than the battle-weary but impoverished Australian men. In the port cities of the east coast, the tension between Australians and Americans sometimes sparked fights and brawls, the most notorious being two days of widespread rioting in Brisbane in November 1942, ironically dubbed the 'Battle of Brisbane'.

In Sydney, Violet was to play a role in bringing Australians and Americans together in the friendly, harmonious environment of Sigs. US army signallers learned about 'Mrs Mac's signalling school' and inquired about whether they could attend. Violet welcomed them. Americans were soon attending in large numbers, filing up those rickety steps and learning Morse code alongside the Australians.

Men of other nationalities also came to the woolshed for training, including Dutch, Indians, Norwegians, Chinese and French. Some were enlisted men, while others were merchant mariners.[4]

●—●

A reporter visiting the Clarence Street woolshed inquired whether Violet had trouble adjusting to these new students. She replied that the Americans were no trouble at all, and she was glad to have them: 'The only change we've made for the US lads is to alter our morning and afternoon tea, to morning and afternoon coffee.' She also told the reporter: 'The Americans were greatly surprised to find our girl signallers capable of their fastest speed.'[5]

The United States Army officers were appalled when they learned that Violet was running her signalling school voluntarily, without any kind of payment or subsidy from the Australian government. A sergeant passed a hat around among his men to collect cash as a donation to the Women's Emergency Signalling Corps, but when he presented the cash to Violet, she refused to accept it.

Taken aback, the sergeant asked, 'But Ma'am, what will I do with this money?'

She answered, 'Donate it to your own canteen.'[6]

●—●

Given the parlous state of the navy, a volunteer coastguard had been formed in 1941, called the Naval Auxiliary Patrol. Men who were either medically unfit to serve or who had been barred due to being in a reserved occupation were invited to apply. Likewise, anyone with a seagoing vessel was encouraged to apply.

There were already two civilian volunteer coastguards, the Volunteer Coastal Patrol and the National Emergency Service Yachting Auxiliary. Many of these members took umbrage at their role being usurped, and they refused to join the newly formed service.[7]

Cecil was one of the first in Sydney to join the Naval Auxiliary Patrol, offering the services of his yacht, *Pilgrim*. He had purchased the 30-foot cruiser, which had previously belonged to aviator Charles Kingsford-Smith, in 1936. Since purchasing *Pilgrim*, Cecil had become a keen yachtsman, competing in weekend races on Sydney Harbour. He and Violet had also made at least one lengthy voyage north along the New South Wales coast before the war.[8]

As the commander of his own vessel, he was given the rank of 'skipper' in the NSW Division and was soon appointed as the Chief Instructor.[9] He and the other skippers patrolled Sydney Harbour and nearby waterways at night, according to a roster they had arranged between them. *Pilgrim* was on patrol about once a week.

Cecil was not rostered on patrol on the night of 31 May 1942. Instead, his colleagues Leslie Winkworth and Hayden Arnott were on the water in the timber ketch *Lauriana* when three Japanese midget submarines slid through Sydney Heads and into the harbour. The first midget sub hit anti-submarine netting and blew up. The second fired two torpedoes at the American cruiser USS *Chicago*, but missed. One of the torpedoes skidded ashore at Garden Island without detonating, while the other hit the seawall and exploded near HMAS *Kuttabul*, a Sydney ferry that had been requisitioned as a navy depot ship. The explosion destroyed *Kuttabul*, throwing debris into the air and causing the stern to sink instantly. A crew of between 35 and 40 were asleep on board at the time of the explosion. Twenty-one of them died.

A naval review of the attack incorrectly claimed that a coordinated response had been impaired because the Naval Auxiliary Patrol boats were unarmed. The perceived problem was quickly remedied: like the other skippers in the Naval Auxiliary Patrol, Cecil McKenzie was supplied with depth charges, a pistol and a machine gun to take with him on all future patrols.[10]

24

CORVETTES

—•—• ———— •—• •••— • — — • •••

Wherever she saw a need, she filled it.

Jean Nysen[1]

The shipyards in Sydney Harbour built corvettes—small, fast, manoeuvrable ships. Known as the *Bathurst*-class corvettes, four of them were commissioned by the Royal Indian Navy. The first of those ordered by the Indians was HMIS *Punjab*, launched in October 1941, with HMIS *Madras*, HMIS *Bengal* and HMIS *Bombay* completed in 1942. While they waited to take possession of their ships, Indian sailors attended training courses in Sydney, including signals training at the Women's Emergency Signalling Corps in Clarence Street.[2]

Lieutenant Chitravati of the Royal Indian Navy was assigned to *Bengal*, which was launched from the Cockatoo Island dockyard in May 1942. While in Sydney he met

Jean McKenzie (no relation to Violet), the daughter of an Australian naval officer, and he courted her for a while. During that time, he learned that Jean was a student of Mrs Mac's at Sigs.[3]

One afternoon, Jean was chatting with her friends over a cup of tea at Sigs when she noticed her former suitor enter the building. Hoping to avoid an awkward interaction, she suggested to her friends, 'Let's go upstairs.' They hurried away to the floor above, but it was to no avail. One of Mrs Mac's green-uniformed instructors came up with a message for them: 'Mrs Mac wants you downstairs.'

Returning to the lower level, they were met by Mrs Mac; Lieutenant Chitravati was standing next to her. Violet smiled at Jean and said, 'Lieutenant Chitravati has something wonderful to ask you!'

All Jean could manage in response was a hesitant, 'Oh, yes?'

Mrs Mac turned to the lieutenant, who said: 'We had Mrs Curtin on board our ship this morning for lunch. Well, the ship's looking so smart we thought that, in the afternoon, we would have some of our friends [visit]. So if you, Mrs Mac and your friend Peg would like to visit, we would love to have your company.'[4]

This introduced an intriguing, and welcome, possibility for Jean: perhaps the lieutenant was not hoping to rekindle their relationship, as she had thought, but was instead interested in her friend, Peg. Maybe there was no need to avoid contact with him after all. She graciously accepted, and Peg did, too. So did Mrs Mac.

The three women were soon at Garden Island, walking the gangplank onto *Bengal*, where they met the lieutenant and the other officers, including the commander. The ship's crew was a mixture of Australians and Indians. Despite

Jean's initial misgivings, the three women had a delightful afternoon on board. The officers treated them to afternoon tea and gave them a tour of the ship. Jean later recalled that Mrs Mac took great interest in the corvette's communication systems.

Lieutenant Chitravati showed them the ship's guns and allowed the women to hold the handles and move them around. One of Jean's most vivid memories of the day was of Mrs Mac behind the sights of a large naval gun, swinging it around as if aiming at distant targets, shooting at imaginary enemies.

Before long, *Bengal* and its crew had slipped out past Sydney Heads and were gone. The next time the Sigs women heard anything about Lieutenant Chitravati's ship was in the news, after it had been in a naval battle with the Japanese raider *Hōkoku Maru* about 1000 miles (1600 kilometres) south-west of Java. *Bengal* was escorting the Dutch tanker *Ondina* when the raider attacked. Rather than flee and leave the fighting to *Bengal*, the captain of *Ondina* decided to sail towards the raider and use the tanker's own guns to join the battle.[5]

Hōkoku Maru scored direct hits on the tanker, strafing its deck with machine-gun fire and killing the captain; however, it failed to sink the tanker. *Bengal* and *Ondina* both scored hits on *Hōkoku Maru*, which then sank. The question about which of the two ships—*Ondina* or *Bengal*—actually deserved credit for sinking the Japanese raider was a source of controversy for many years.

Many men died on the other two ships involved that day, but Lieutenant Chitravati and the rest of the crew of *Bengal* survived the battle.

●—●

Jean's father was Lieutenant Commander Donald McKenzie. In 1915, he had been the navy's first signalman, and in 1916 he had served in the Battle of Jutland. He was now the head of the Flinders Naval Depot signals school. Another member of Sigs with a prominent father was Valerie Ashley, the daughter of Senator Bill Ashley, the Minister for Information in Prime Minister John Curtin's cabinet. Being the daughter of a senior naval officer and important politician, respectively, Jean and Valerie were called upon from time to time by Violet for photo opportunities with the press.

One such publicity event resulted in a news item in *The Sun*, featuring an article about Jean and Val sending Morse code to each other. Under the heading *SENATOR'S DAUGHTER AS INSTRUCTOR*, the story recounted: 'Side by side at No. 10 Clarence Street, WESC headquarters, Miss Jean McKenzie and Miss Val Ashley work together decoding Morse signals. They share a common interest, to be of use in Australia's war effort.'[6]

Jean was enlisted into the WRANS in September 1942 and reported to Harman for duty on 1 October. Val reported for duty two months later, commencing on New Year's Eve.[7]

A couple of days before Jean's group left for Harman, Violet organised a small send-off party for them at the woolshed, including a cake that she had baked for the occasion. She invited a press photographer to the event to take some snaps for the daily paper. Although Sigs was well known, Violet needed to keep up the publicity to combat a drop in new enrolments of women.

25

THE LADY AT THE TOP

— ••••• • •—•• •— —•• —•— —

•— — — ••••• • — ——— •—•

Florence Violet McKenzie, a remarkable woman, as
charming and as admirable as she is clever.

Smith's Weekly, 1943[1]

Gwenda Cornwallis and Shirley Kingsford-Smith were
both eighteen, and both hoped to join the navy as telegraphists. In fact, Gwenda was so keen that she had joined
Sigs while she was still at school, so that when the time came,
her Morse code would be up to speed. But the navy—and
Mrs Mac—had other plans for them.[2]

One winter's day at Sigs in 1943, Mrs Mac pulled Gwenda
and Shirley aside. She informed them that Sydney naval base
HMAS *Penguin* had sent an urgent request for two visual
signallers, requiring them to commence in a week's time.

They were the two best suited to the job. They were both proficient with a Morse key, but had not mastered the other skills that were taught at Sigs: neither of them knew anything at all about flag signalling—either semaphore or the international code—and they had never practised Morse code with an Aldis lamp. It didn't matter, Mrs Mac told them, because they had a whole week to get trained up to standard.

They were enlisted in August. However, after their frantic rush to cram in everything there was to know about visual signal systems, they were then told by the navy that they had to wait to be trained at the signals school at HMAS *Kuttabul* (a new naval base named after the ship sunk by a Japanese submarine the year before). While they waited, the two young women continued practising their signals, spending their afternoons sending semaphore to each other beside the swimming pool at the HMAS *Penguin* naval base.

Ultimately, the two women were posted to the degaussing range at Bradleys Head, on the harbour's north shore. Magnetic mines were an ever-present threat to ships. The best preventative measure available was to 'degauss' a ship's hull: to demagnetise it in such a way that it did not attract the mines. To undergo degaussing, ships would sail across the range, passing over finely calibrated underwater coils. The United States Navy had built the Bradleys Head degaussing range, and had then trained Australian naval personnel in its operation.

The role of the two WRANS there was to assist communication between the shore station and the ships. The women taught the range's instrument panel operators how to do the signalling, and they themselves were taught how to run the degaussing equipment, so that everyone on the base had a broad, versatile skill set.

Some of the ships being degaussed were fresh out of the dockyards, while others had been battered by previous exchanges with the enemy. The benefits of the program were real, but invisible to those at the degaussing range. After treatment, the ships disappeared through the Sydney Heads, leaving the workers at the range to trust and hope that their work would help the ships' crews survive the war.

•—•

The newspaper *Smith's Weekly* ran a half-page feature about Violet in June 1943 titled 'The Lady at the Top'. In part, it said:

Florence Violet McKenzie, for all her managerial, adminstra-tive, and technical ability, is dainty and essentially feminine. Unobtrusively, she has done this remarkable work for the forces, for the nation. She remains kindly, human, with a genial sense of humor, with fine understanding of her students, and radiating an atmosphere of friendliness which must remain a sweet memory for the thousands of students who have become indebted to her.[3]

In mid-1943, the woolshed on Clarence Street hummed to the sound of Morse buzzers and key clicks, some at a rapid staccato, overlaid by the slow tap-tap of beginners near the entryway. The trestle tables were crowded with women along-side men in the Australian Army uniforms, who were also shoulder-to-shoulder with air force and navy servicemen, Americans, Britons and New Zealanders. Their collective attention was on the women in green uniforms instructing them.

However, unless something changed, the whole operation would soon become unsustainable because, by the middle of 1943, the number of enrolments into Sigs had dropped to zero. The instructors were working long days with no respite; without new additions to their ranks, they were facing burnout.

Certainly, there were lots of fresh faces at Sigs, but these new students were there to learn signalling and move on; they were not interested in qualifying for admission as a member of Sigs itself, much less becoming an instructor. By the time they qualified for membership they had also qualified for the navy, which had by then reduced its Morse proficiency criterion to fifteen words per minute.

Initially, the intakes of telegraphists from Sigs into the air force had been treated with scorn. One memo noted that Violet McKenzie had promised them that the women in a batch she was sending through could receive Morse code at twenty words per minute, but that, with one exception, they could barely do eighteen words per minute. Women who had been trained at Sigs were classified by the air force command as 'self-taught', with complaints from signals officers that the women had 'incorrect technique', particularly wrist technique, and that it was impossible to retrain them with 'correct technique'.

By 1943, all this grumbling from the air force's officers about the women's abilities had disappeared, and was replaced by a panic that they were not meeting recruitment targets. Word had got around at Sigs not to bother applying for the air force, because the likelihood of rejection there was high compared to the army and navy. So, to compete with the other forces for the supply of women, the air force relaxed its standards.

As it got easier and easier to enlist, each wave of young women passing through Sigs spent less time there, and the goal of actually joining WESC as a member—and qualifying for a WESC uniform—became a thing of the past. The newcomers arrived at Sigs, took lessons, attained a Morse speed that was good enough to enlist in the armed forces, and then they were gone. So Violet turned her attention to outreach. As part of her recruitment drive, she contacted a reporter at *The Daily Telegraph* for help. The newspaper soon ran an appeal for volunteers for her:

Signallers Still Needed

Recruiting for the Women's Emergency Signalling Corps has almost ceased in the last year.

The director, Mrs. F.V. McKenzie, said this yesterday.

'I think it is mainly due to manpower call-ups and to the inducement of good salaries offered to girls nowadays,' she said.

Mrs. McKenzie is appealing to girls of 17, who would be willing to join one of the women's Services at 18, to begin their training with the corps.

'After completing this training, they can be accepted by any women's Service as telegraphists,' she said.

Since the outbreak of war almost 500 trainees of the corps have enlisted in the Services.

Thirty of these have become officers in the W.A.A.F., six in the W.R.A.N.S., and four in the A.W.A.S.[4]

An article in *The Sun* four months later also appealed for new members. In it, Violet was quoted as saying, 'If we are to carry on with the work, which is increasing in its demands, I must have more girls to train as instructresses.'[5]

The United States Navy proposed to Violet (or perhaps she proposed to them) that she run a comprehensive signals course for some of their new recruits, who had not had the benefit of training before they had departed the United States.

In other words, this was not a request for supplemental or auxiliary training, or assistance in 'brushing up'—it was for a complete course in naval signalling.

In September 1944, nine sailors from the United States Navy became the first American servicemen to complete a comprehensive signals training course under Violet McKenzie's instruction. Violet awarded 'high marks' to four of them: Joe Smerdel (from Indiana), William Hunter and Eugene Schmahler (Wisconsin), and John Statham (Louisiana). Her signalling school had by then trained over 10,000 servicemen for all three Australian services as well as numerous men from the services of Allied nations, including the United States, India, Britain, New Zealand and China.

The officer in charge of the nine American sailors, Robert J. Wingo, said:

> I have never found any signals school run by women in any other country. Mrs F.V. McKenzie and her instructors are unique as far as I know. The standard is very high. The boys enjoy coming here and do very well indeed. They soon get used to the idea of women instructors.[6]

The success of that class resulted in an official request from the United States Navy for more training. It was the first time that her relationship with any of the American services had been formalised.

•—•

One evening in March 1945, after Violet had gone to bed, one of her neighbours rang the doorbell. When she answered, the neighbour told her to come down to the water's edge quickly. There was a ship nearby in the harbour, flashing Morse code messages at the shore. None of the locals who had come out of their homes could read the message but, as they were concerned that the ship was in distress, a delegation was sent up the headland to fetch Violet McKenzie.

She grabbed a flashlight (so that she could signal back to the ship if necessary) and hurried down to the water's edge. Sure enough, a warship loomed in the darkness close by, and was signalling with an Aldis lamp.

The message (in Morse code) said something like this:

Attention Violet McKenzie.
We are United States naval personnel.
We request training at your signals school.

The ship had arrived that day from the United States, and the naval officer in charge of Sydney, Admiral George D. Moore, had given the ship's commander the location of Violet's home (apparently, Moore had a mischievous sense of humour). The following morning, Moore visited Sigs with a delegation of United States Navy officers, as well as the ratings from the visiting ship who were in need of training.[7]

Another group of American sailors in May were sceptical when they learned that a woman would be instructing them in a refresher course in signals. They were even more sceptical, as they stood in front of her holding their semaphore flags, when she told them that they would be practising semaphore to music. She then turned on her jukebox, selected the song 'The Teddy Bears' Picnic' and commenced the semaphore drill, calling out letters in time with the music.

A week later, the sailors had come to love their teacher and her unusual methods, declaring that she was 'the tops'. They vowed to encourage signals instructors back home to adopt her musical teaching methods.[8]

•—•

New students continued to flood in, but the supply of new instructors remained at a trickle. Violet and her loyal coterie continued to shoulder the burden, because—as they saw it— they had no choice. There was nobody else who was willing and able to do what they were doing.

26

PEACETIME

•— —•••— —•—•• — •• — — •

*Fellow citizens, the war is over. The Japanese govern-
ment has accepted the terms imposed by the Allied
Nations and hostilities will now cease.*

Ben Chifley, 15 August 1945[1]

The last group of women sent by Violet to the navy enlisted
on 15 August 1945, the day the war ended. Marie Davis,
nee Munns (who was one of the people interviewed for this
book) was in that contingent.

When she had joined the Women's Emergency Signalling
Corps six years earlier, at the age of fourteen, she was its
youngest member. She worked in the city during the day,
attended Sigs after work, and caught the train home in the
evening with her friend Pam, who was also in Sigs. Before
long, she qualified to become one of Mrs Mac's instructors.

For years she watched older girls depart for different signals bases; she had hoped that, when she turned eighteen, she could join them.

It wasn't that easy. When she applied for the navy (soon after turning eighteen), she discovered that as a clerk with the Department of Trade and Customs, her job was deemed a 'protected occupation'. This prevented her from enlisting until her boss signed a release form.

When Marie and Pam were called up to commence duty it was already clear that the war's end was imminent. Most of the territory conquered by Japan in the early part of the war had been recaptured by the Allies, and the Japanese homeland islands were under constant bombardment. The United States had dropped an atomic bomb over the Japanese city of Hiroshima on 6 August, and a second over Nagasaki on 9 August.

When Marie and Pam reported for duty at the Sydney naval centre near Rushcutters Bay, the news had already come through that the Japanese emperor had announced that Japan would surrender. So their first duty was to participate in the navy's official victory march through Sydney a few days later, a role for which they were urgently needed because most of the navy's personnel were overseas. People cheered, applauded and threw streamers at them.

Following the march, they were sent to HMAS *Harman* (which had been officially commissioned on 1 July 1943). There they were embarrassed to learn that they were also required to participate in a victory march in Canberra.[2]

Despite the war being over, their services were still needed. HMAS *Harman* remained operational (as it does to this day), and the navy still had a lot of work to do. Australian naval forces were deployed across the globe, and the demobilisation process for most of these forces would take another year.

In 2018, Marie said that she still sometimes practised Morse code in the evening, with her finger on a table. 'Once you've been to Morse school, you never forget it.'[3]

One of Violet's mnemonic tricks for learning the Morse alphabet stuck with her, a method for remembering the letter U. Mrs Mac had told her, 'The letter U is "make it square." *Dit-dit-dah*. Make it square. Ever since then, all my life, whenever I write the letter U, I make it square.'[4]

•—•

During the war years, a miscellaneous collection of items had accrued at the woolshed—gifts from men in far parts of the world who had been trained there. The first had been an Italian flag from Tobruk. Signaller Michael O'Ryan had written to Violet in January 1941, giving his sender's address only as 'somewhere in the Middle East':

> Best wishes to you and your Corps from the boys in the unit here . . .
> Would you like some souvenirs of Tobruk for the walls of your club? Especially I should like to send you the national flag which I myself had the honour of hauling down the left wing of Tobruk.[5]

Several weeks later, a large, weather-beaten Italian flag arrived at 10 Clarence Street. They hung it on the wall.[6]

After reading in the news about O'Ryan's generous gift, another digger wrote to Mrs Mac, promising to also obtain a flag for her. Gunner William Stewart's letter said:

> Dear Mrs. Mac.
> Thanks for the Christmas parcels. I am not going to be outdone by Michael O'Ryan, who sent you a flag captured

from the Italians in Syria, and have made up my mind to secure one with the red sun on it from the Japs.

Like a lot of other chaps, I'm eternally grateful to you and your girls for the great job you are all doing.[7]

On Armistice Day (now known as Remembrance Day) in 1941, another flag was delivered, this one from a signals unit in Syria. It was a plain white flag with a big red X in the middle, the words 'Lest we forget' underneath in gold and the name of a single soldier who had been killed in action. In his memory, the members of the unit had made the flag, and then each of them had signed it before sending it home to be delivered to Mrs Mac.[8]

More items came from afar, souvenirs of travel and war sent from exotic places: an Italian army helmet; a fragment of a Japanese Zero fighter; a large wall map of the United States; a Japanese military map of the Celebes.[9]

A particularly unusual item was a revolver-like unidirectional Chinese signalling lamp that had been salvaged after the Battle of Milne Bay. When she received it, Violet commented with delight: 'Our latest gift will be useful, as well as a relic, for we can teach trainees slow light-touch signals on it.'[10]

The collection of gifts and souvenirs became known as 'Museum Corner'.[11] As Museum Corner grew, so did the collection of portrait photographs. The only thing Violet requested in payment from her students, the photos spread across the hessian-lined walls like shiny grey ivy.

•—•

By the end of World War II, Violet's signals school had trained more than 3000 women, over 1000 of whom had entered the WRANS; many others had entered the army and air force.

She and her instructors had also trained more than 12,000 men.[12]

The question of what to do with Sigs when the war ended had occupied Violet's mind for some time, long before the end was in sight. As far back as 1941, she was making plans for an employment bureau that would assist members of the Women's Emergency Signalling Corps to re-enter civilian life. She was also promoting a provident fund that she had established to assist members in need, once they had returned from service.[13]

In 1943, she had speculated that when peace finally came—whenever that would be—she would resume the activities of the Electrical Association for Women, which had been completely subsumed by the activities of Sigs.[14]

From 1944 onwards, an increasing number of students had been merchant seamen, who needed to pass the signals requirements for mate's and master's certifications. Violet anticipated that, even in peacetime, they would keep coming. She also believed that she might install a short-wave radio station at the woolshed, to encourage young women to take up radio.[15]

•—•

In late 1945, with the various branches of the Women's Emergency Signalling Corps outside Sydney long since closed, only the Clarence Street woolshed remained, but there were fewer newcomers now. The woolshed no longer thrummed with activity across two vast floors. The trestle tables that stretched off into the distance were no longer crowded with men and women side by side, headphones over their ears, their faces frowning with concentration. The instructors, who had given so much over the past five years, stopped coming. Only one, Esme Murrell, remained.

But the young men from the merchant marine continued to come, just as Violet had expected. Ships sailed the oceans in peacetime as in war, but now there were fewer cargoes of weapons, ammunition and military supplies. They were replaced by shipments of food, clothing and other goods, many of which had been restricted by rationing. During the war, shipment of the most harmless stuff across the ocean had carried the risk of a submarine attack. Now that submarines and raiders no longer prowled the seas, trade boomed.

Yet it wasn't just merchant mariners who kept her busy. Violet also had a steady intake of young men who had been discharged from the air force; they lacked a job, but they had experience with aircraft and hoped to transfer their wartime skills into the civilian air industry.

Installed at the Clarence Street woolshed was a complete fit-out of an aircraft communication system manufactured by US aeronautical firm Bendix, including a transmitter, receiver and radio compass. The Department of Air had donated it during the war specifically so that Violet could train commercial pilots.[16] Believing that if she was going to teach it she had to understand it, in February 1943 Violet had made a trip to Adelaide, where she had been trained in the use of the Bendix equipment.[17]

After the war, the Department of Air posted an employee to Sigs, an Englishman named Arthur Copeland, who worked at the woolshed as an assessor and instructor for pilots. Copeland issued students who mastered the equipment and whose Morse code speed was at least twenty words per minute with an Operator's Certificate.

In the post-war years, Sigs became the go-to place in Australia for training in aviation communication systems. Between 1946 and 1953, virtually everyone who qualified as a pilot in Australia—including the pilots for the four major airlines (Qantas, TAA, Ansett and Butler Air Transport)—was trained in signals by Mrs Mac at the Clarence Street woolshed.[18]

The nation was awash with veterans—men who had left Australian shores as boys, and who had returned having spent years (in many cases) learning the art and craft of warfare, skills that were no longer useful. They were intimate with death and destruction, but the humdrum world of civilian life—and how to make a living in it—was a mystery to them.

With no job, no skills and no other promising avenue open to them, many unemployed veterans became devoted students, spending their days at the woolshed, learning whatever there was to learn. A visitor arriving at the top of the stairs would see fifteen to twenty men at the nearest Morse table. Another three or four could be seen at the Bendix equipment. Seeing that the school was still open and in need of volunteers, several of Mrs Mac's former students and instructors returned to help.

Former students would also just drop in for a visit, sometimes in such numbers that the woolshed became a sort of informal clubhouse for 'alumni' of Mrs Mac's signals school. In dark nooks of the myriad partitions or under obscure brick archways, a visitor might see a pile of gear left with Mrs Mac by a mariner for safekeeping while sailing distant shores, or by a pilot on contract to remote parts of the country.[19]

In years to come, some of her students would go on to prominent positions, including the heads of the navigation schools in Melbourne and Sydney, and the NSW commissioner for police.[20]

His health failing, Arthur Copeland was finally forced to resign his position with the Department of Air. He wished everyone at the woolshed farewell and went home to England, never to return. During his stint at Sigs, he and Violet had become friends. After he moved back to England, he corresponded with her as well as with several of the students who had studied under him.[21]

•—•

Journalist Norman Ellison visited Sigs in 1948, as he was writing a feature article about Violet for Butler Air Transport's in-flight magazine, *Sky Script*. Interviewing Violet proved to be a struggle, as he subsequently described in his article:

> While you're doing the interview there are frequent interruptions. One pupil, a mercantile-marine type, wants to know what the letters are for *'At one time indicated'*. 'BMS', answers Mrs Mac.
>
> Another chap, also of the sea, asks: 'What does NNS represent?'
>
> 'Hope you never have to send this signal', replies Mrs Mac. 'NNS is, *in imminent danger of sinking.*'
>
> Then there's a chap, airline type, who has a spot of bother. Mrs Mac goes with him (you also tag along), to the aircraft wireless set. This is the senior 'doover' in the establishment. It's a complete unit—transmitter, receiver, and compass—as set up in an airliner. This is where the pupils finally train for their air-wireless tickets.[22]

Ellison asked her why she did it. She answered, 'The boys deserve it.'

Ellison finished by asking rhetorically: 'But what does Mrs Mac deserve? That's a question officialdom should ponder.'[23]

•—•

A revised certification system came into effect in 1948, requiring pilots and aircrew to hold a Flight Radio Telephony

Operator's Licence. Violet was awarded a first-class category aircrew licence in Melbourne in June of that year. This was an internationally recognised qualification that required her, among other things, to have logged 50 hours of flying.

Despite her penchant for publicity, there were no news reports for this, no mentions in magazines, no cakes and no photographs. How and where she put in 50 hours of flying as trainee aircrew is a mystery.[24] The only reason we know she did this is that her first-class aircrew certificate was discovered by a journalist in a box of old documents at the Spectacle Island naval archives more than 50 years later.[25]

At any rate, Violet was not the first Australian woman to obtain the qualification. That distinction was achieved by Patricia Whyte, one of her wartime students who had served in the WRANS and who was employed at Sydney Airport. Whyte's success was widely reported in the papers, while Violet's achievement escaped notice.[26]

•—•

In the 1940s, there were two nautical schools in Sydney, both near Circular Quay. Both were privately owned colleges that had been operating for several decades. They were the Sydney Nautical School at 54 Pitt Street, and the Richmond Nautical School at 30 Pitt Street. Francis Bayldon, a master mariner who had founded the Sydney Nautical School in 1898, decided to retire at the age of 75; one of Mrs Mac's former students, Captain William D. Heighwey, purchased the school from Bayldon.[27]

Heighwey and Violet formed a working relationship, whereby Heighwey would send his students to her for training in signals. The skills that the nautical students most needed for their certification were those involved in visual signalling: semaphore (signalling with handheld flags) and visual Morse code (sending and receiving Morse code as flashes of a light).

A former trainee at the Sydney Nautical School, Mark Sunter, recalled that Heighwey would send students over to Mrs Mac for signals training, instructing them to take packets of tea or some other small gift for her. That was because she refused monetary payments, but always accepted gifts. Sunter remembered her as 'a lovely little lady with dark hair'.[28]

Heighwey's competition down at Circular Quay, the Richmond Nautical School, was run by Captain W.A. Pearson, who also got on well with Violet and outsourced his signals training to her.[29] In 1948, Pearson had a letter to the editor published in *The Sun*:

> The high praise accorded to Mrs. F. V. McKenzie (Women's Emergency Signalling Corps) by a recent correspondent could well be amplified by thousands of officers and men of the Merchant Navy and the Services.
>
> For over 10 years, Mrs. 'Mac' has devoted her whole time to training men and women in every specialised branch of signalling, at no cost whatever to the student, the success of students at examinations being her only reward.
>
> The magnificent service to the community of this generous little lady must not be overlooked or forgotten. Mrs. McKenzie is worthy of the highest honour Australia can bestow. All who can help to advance this recognition are invited to contact us. This is not an appeal for funds, but for support in placing the facts in the right place for appropriate recognition.
>
> Captain W. A. Pearson,
> principal, Richmond Nautical School,
> Sirius House, Macquarie Place, Sydney.[30]

Pearson's letter prompted a reply from Violet:

Many thanks to your readers for proposing that 'honors' should be bestowed on me; but they can rest assured that Australia has already bestowed its greatest gift—the quiet serenity of mind and complete happiness which follow the giving of our little all in 'brotherly love.'

We look forward to the time when this spirit will prevail in our international relationships, and it may be sooner than we think.

'Mrs. Mac'[31]

She could protest all she liked, but the push was on. She'd had a direct impact on thousands of people's lives, and many Australians believed that Violet McKenzie's services should be formally acknowledged.

27

EINSTEIN'S CORRESPONDENT

• •• —• ••• — • •• —• •••

—•—• — — — •—• •—• • ••• •—— •• — — — —• —•• • —• • —

If I were not a physicist, I would probably be a musician.
I often think in music. I live my daydreams in music.
I see my life in terms of music.

Albert Einstein[1]

Anews article caught Violet's attention in early 1949, reporting that Albert Einstein had undergone gall-bladder surgery in New York. She sent him a cheery letter accompanied by a boomerang as a gift. It was the first in a series of letters between them:

Dear Dr Einstein,
    Will you please forgive an elderly woman for writing
to you to express my joy and thankfulness at your recovery
from recent illness?

219

I conduct a Signal School (free) to help returned servicemen, and take most of the passages for Morse code and semaphore practice from books such as your 'Life and Times'.

This means that we feel deeply indebted to you—who can see so much more clearly than the rest of us—can yet live cheerfully and serenely.

Our perspective has been greatly improved and our minds enlightened and stimulated by the study of your discoveries. It may seem strange to you that away 'down under', there is a newspaper photograph of yourself leaving hospital, pinned on our notice board, and a very genuine feeling of affection and gratitude to you.

Please accept our most sincere wishes for your complete recovery.

Yours respectfully,

F. Violet McKenzie

('Mrs Mac')

P.S. I am taking the liberty of sending you an Australian blackfellow's boomerang. Its queer habit of returning to the person who throws it, after traversing a curve, will no doubt seem simple to you, but you might like to explain it to some lucky small boy of your acquaintance, if no one has thought of sending you a boomerang before![2]

She received a reply from him three weeks later, thanking her for the letter and the boomerang. That inspired her to write again.

In your letter you refer to the connection between your work and my own being very slight. Actually the only connection is that you have helped us immeasurably, and my letter to you was only written because I wanted to express deep gratitude to you, and to let you know how much you are appreciated down here.

My work could be horrible routine—like soldiers drilling, and just as regimentation brought grief to you as a child, so it grieves me to see so many airline pilots etc., having to spend hundreds of hours gaining Morse speed.

I have often thought that if soldiers could march only through beautiful and interesting country it would not be so bad, so I take my pupils through interesting Morse passages, mostly about your life and work. They are now so interested in their Morse practice passages that frequently they will beg to carry on through meal hours, being anxious to learn more of the new outlook opened up by your discoveries, and not realising that they are gaining proficiency without drudgery, even enjoying it, and benefiting in so many other ways.[3]

Her flattery was a bit of an exaggeration, and downplayed her own teaching skill. Certainly of late she had been sending her students extracts in Morse code from the recently released biography *Einstein: His life and times* by Philipp Frank, which a former student had sent her as a present the previous Christmas, but she had been successfully engaging students and exciting them about Morse code, radio and electricity for many years prior. Before Einstein, it had been *Popeye* and 'The Teddy Bears' Picnic', among other things, that had given many pupils a 'new outlook' on their learning.

Violet also made the following offer: 'If there is ANYTHING you want from Australia, we should be proud and honoured to send it to you.' Presumably he asked for a didgeridoo, because that's what she sent to him in November.

A pilot had acquired one for her from the Kopapinga tribe in Arnhem Land.[4]

While the didgeridoo was in transit, Einstein sent Violet an autographed photo of himself as a gift.[5] He wrote again in February 1950, after the didgeridoo arrived:

> After having received the instrument and being aware that it is simply a tube of nearly cylindrical shape, I wondered how the natives of Australia are producing sounds with it.
>
> First I tried it, without success, using it like a flute, then like a trumpet—but with no satisfactory results.
>
> Then I tried it with singing while tightly pressing the openings of the tube against the surroundings of my mouth.
>
> I discovered indeed startling resonance effects in certain regions of pitch, and I concluded tentatively that this might be the way the instrument is used. But I should be grateful if you could tell me better![6]

Violet replied, telling him that his didgeridoo technique was wrong. The sound, she explained, was meant to be a sort of 'boom-ho-ho'. She posted a recording of the sound of a didgeridoo, so that he would have some idea of what he should be aiming for.[7]

Violet also corresponded with Einstein's stepdaughter, Margot, sending her a book about seashells. Margot replied, thanking her for the book and inviting her to stay with Professor Einstein if she ever happened to be in the United States.[8]

Violet never had the chance to take up the offer, because Einstein died in 1955. But the signed photograph of Albert Einstein had pride of place in Violet's living room, and each year on his birthday she would decorate it with flowers.[9]

28

HONOURS

•••• — — — —• — — — ••— •—• •••

My satisfaction comes from getting boys through their examinations.

Florence Violet McKenzie, 1952[1]

I was awakened at dawn by a Qantas pilot, who said he jumped out of bed and hit his head on the electric light globe when he saw my name in the paper. The phone has not stopped ringing since.'[2] The list of OBE recipients for 1950 had been released, and Violet McKenzie's name was on it 'for voluntary services to the Women's Emergency Signalling Corps'.[3] The Order of the British Empire (OBE) awards, a legacy of Australia's history as a colonial outpost of Britain, were discontinued by the Whitlam government in 1975 and replaced by the Order of Australia (which amounted to the same thing but with a more appropriate name).

In 1948, Captain Pearson had called for Violet to be given 'the highest honour Australia can bestow'. She was not getting that (this would have been a damehood), but in 1950 an OBE was the next best thing.

The governor-general had informed her in writing of her award three weeks earlier, but that didn't make the accolades and support any less overwhelming.[4]

A group of air force Douglas pilots who were former students of hers sent a message from all of them: 'Congratulations! OBOE BAKER EASY.' ('Oboe baker easy' spelled OBE in the phonetic radio code.)[5]

The federal Minister for Supply, Howard Beale, revealed that he had been a student of Mrs Mac's during the war.[6]

The publishers of the *All Electric Cookery Book* got on board the publicity train, announcing the release of a new edition of Violet's book later that year.[7]

•—•

Violet wrote to two of her former students to tell them her good news. Joan Cowie and Jo Miller, who had worked in the naval code-breaking centre at Monterey Flats in Melbourne and who had each received a blue vase from Violet on their first Christmas away from home, were living in Rhodesia (today's Zimbabwe).

She addressed the letter, 'Dear Joan 'nd Jo / Dear Jo 'nd Joan'. In her letter, she told them that she didn't regard the OBE as for her personally, but for everyone associated with the Women's Emergency Signalling Corps, including them. The award, she explained, was for 'all my boys and girls'.[8]

Joan Cowie's father, Robert, had been lobbying the government to recognise Violet's efforts since 1945, when at the conclusion of the war he had written to the prime minister about her:

Dear Sir,

I am taking the liberty of addressing a matter which I feel, now that peace has once more come to our land, should be brought under your notice so that it may receive the consideration of the appropriate authorities.

I refer to the magnificent work carried out by Mrs F. McKenzie, commandant of the Women's Emergency Signalling Corps, 10 Clarence Street Sydney . . .

Not only has Mrs McKenzie done this tremendous work but, I can safely say, acted as 'Mother' to thousands of lads of the various services who having passed through her hands, have constantly kept in touch with her and who have received parcels and many comforts. A great portion of the cost of providing these parcels and comforts has been provided by Mrs McKenzie.

Should you desire any further information I would be very pleased to obtain and furnish same to you.

In addressing you on this matter I feel I am voicing the sentiments of many thousands of people who are cognisant of the work that Mrs McKenzie has performed during the past five years and who consider her great work should receive some official recognition.[9]

Robert Cowie had particular reason to be proud of his daughter—and grateful for the opportunity created by Violet McKenzie—because Joan Cowie was the only enlisted WRAN to serve outside Australia in an operational zone.[10]

In November 1950, Violet was made a Fellow of the Australian Institute of Navigation.[11]

●—●

Accolades were a pleasant distraction but, after the fuss had subsided, the woolshed door still had to be unlocked each morning, and bills still had to be paid. Violet had been bank-rolling Sigs for more than a decade, using the money she had made from her string of successful businesses in the 1920s and 1930s, and with support from Cecil as well.

But, after financing Sigs for more than ten years, she had run down her business fortune and her finances were tight. She and Cecil lived frugally; she told a reporter in 1952: 'I never spend anything on myself, and by absolute economy, I get by.'[12]

29

OUT OF THE WOOLSHED

— — — •• — —   — — — ••—•   — •••• •

•— —   — — —   — — —   •—•• ••• •••• • —••

Apart from Mrs McKenzie's school, these men have nowhere for practical signal training.

Captain McLean, Senior Examiner, Commonwealth
Board of Trade, 1953[1]

An envelope arrived in October 1952, addressed as follows:

F.V. McKenzie (a female)
10 Clarence St, Sydney[2]

Violet opened it to find a letter from Australian National Airways, the airline company that owned the Clarence Street woolshed. The letter informed her that her lease was being terminated and that she had to vacate the premises. The letter

227

was subsequently pinned to the wall among the photographs, many of which were faded and yellow, others smudged from a water leak during a winter storm.[3]

Although she made half-hearted, dismissive jokes about the eviction notice to 'the boys', she was deeply offended. This was in no small part because of the rather rude way it was addressed: 'F.V. McKenzie (a female)'.

The airline had been a bad landlord before the eviction. As activity at Sigs declined, Violet had relinquished the upper floor; the airline had leased it to a tyre-retreading factory, with no consideration of the impact that the noise from such a business might have on her signals school. The airline had neglected maintenance and repairs, resulting in a roof leak earlier that year, which—quite apart from the damage to her memorabilia—created a safety risk because of the electrical equipment used at the Morse stations.

If the eviction letter sounded cold and impersonal, that's because it really wasn't personal. It had nothing to do with Violet and everything to do with the airline's financial situation.

For years, Australian National Airways (ANA) had been the country's biggest airline, with the most routes and destinations. It continued to operate throughout World War II, despite having several of its aircraft commandeered for defence purposes and losing many of its pilots to the air force. When the war finished, it controlled 80 per cent of the domestic market.

But in 1946, the Curtin government created a state-owned competitor, Trans-Australia Airlines (TAA), which was given exclusive access to government business, mail routes and some passenger routes. Two other upstarts—Butler Air Transport and Ansett—were snapping at its heels. By 1952, ANA's financial situation was so parlous that it was in need of a large loan—effectively a bailout—from the Menzies government.

Hence the airline had a desperate need to sell any unwanted assets, such as the woolshed at 10 Clarence Street. The irony was that most of ANA's pilots and aircrew had been trained at that same woolshed. Between the war's end in 1945 and the day she received the eviction notice in 1952, Violet's signals school had trained 2450 civil airline crew as well as 1050 merchant navy seamen.[4]

•—•

True to form, Violet leveraged the media to fight back. She contacted a senior journalist at *The Sydney Morning Herald*, who ran a long piece for her in 'Column 8'. Famous for its usual collection of brief, quirky items, the next day's 'Column 8' made an exception by devoting most of its space to Violet's cause:

> IN 1950 Mrs Florence McKenzie—one of the few women electrical engineers in this city—was given the Order of the British Empire. The award was made for honorary services to the Women's Emergency Signalling Corps, which she founded during the war . . .
>
> These premises are now required for other purposes, and Mrs McKenzie has been given notice to quit.
>
> She doesn't object to that—although she hasn't yet been able to find other accommodation—but she strenuously objects to the form it has taken. The only official notification she has received begins:—
>
> 'F.V. McKenzie (a female), 10 Clarence Street.'
>
> It may be a strictly business form of address—but in the circumstances, you can't say it's nice, can you?[5]

The article had the desired effect, in that it caused a stir in Canberra. The member for Gwydir, Thomas Treloar, sent a copy to the Minister for Air, along with his opinion that the department should provide her with alternative premises. Memos flew back and forth, but it turned out that the department's bureaucrats had not heard of her and could not find any paperwork to explain what she had been up to.[6]

One handwritten note asked: 'Is there any record of Mrs McKenzie carrying out training of RAAF members?'[7]

Another public servant reported fruitless lines of inquiry: '[I] rang Wing Commander Duval, EAHQ, who advised he had no knowledge of Mrs McKenzie. Promised to make enquiries at EAHQ and ring back.'[8]

Sadly, in the end nobody could find any evidence that Mrs McKenzie had done anything at all, but maybe (they speculated) that was because she changed her name in the meantime: 'There is no record of Mrs McKenzie acting for RAAF or WRAAF during or after the war. She may have been "Miss" somebody at that time.'[9]

News of Violet's predicament reached air force headquarters, where there were still memories of Mrs Mac's signals school among serving members. Air Vice-Marshal Frank Bladin wrote a rather tentative confidential memo to the minister in favour of Violet's cause:

Despite the lack of any official records I am aware that Mrs McKenzie provided facilities at night and at weekends during the war years whereby a great number of aircrew trainees were enabled to practice and improve their Morse free of charge. Probably it is quite out of the question to provide accommodation but I feel the case merits consideration.[10]

The minister was unmoved. His secretary, Joe Hewitt, responded to the air vice-marshal, spelling out why the government would not step in. But first (since the air force had helpfully informed the department of Mrs McKenzie's contribution), he patronisingly outlined the history of the Clarence Street signals school:

During the war, Mrs McKenzie operated a Morse Code signalling training school on a purely voluntary basis. Young men and women who desired to enter the Services in signalling trades went to Mrs McKenzie for preparatory training in order to better their chances of enlistment. There is no record of Mrs McKenzie's school having been recognised as an official one.

Today, Mrs McKenzie continues to operate her training school in Sydney in a building owned by A.N.A. from whom she rents the space. She has about 12 pupils daily comprising:

- Prospective air line pilots
- Merchant Navy personnel
- Air line pilots endeavouring to pass higher examinations.[11]

As for financial support, as Hewitt made clear, it wasn't as if she had done it all on her own. Hewitt went on to explain that Mrs McKenzie had been the recipient of free equipment:

Department of Civil Aviation use Mrs McKenzie as an official examiner and has supplied her with radio equipment, approximate value £1000 and maintains this equipment on a monthly overhaul basis. Space occupied by Mrs McKenzie consists of three rooms for flag signalling, Morse signalling, and technical equipment demonstration.

Indeed, the generosity of the government knew no bounds.

Hewitt had learned that Civil Aviation was desperately keen for this woman to find alternative accommodation. His attitude to that was: *Perfect. Let them pay for it then.* His response to the air-vice marshal continued:

> Mr Hodder (DCA Radio Examiner) is very interested in Mrs McKenzie's activities, and he is endeavouring to arrange through the Civil Aviation Regional Director in Sydney other accommodation for Mrs McKenzie.
>
> I recommend I might add that the Department of Air has no contact with Mrs McKenzie now and it would be extremely difficult to find her accommodation out of this department's current resources in Sydney.[12]

So that was it: *There's no money, and the school isn't that important anyway. If someone else thinks it is, then they can pay to keep it going.*

•—•

By the end of January 1953, there was no deal and Violet had to go. Bailouts are for things that politicians care about, such as airline companies. Not volunteer-run signalling schools operating out of repurposed woolsheds.

She found a space for rent at Wharf 6, Circular Quay. At this time, there were large, multistorey buildings at the Circular Quay wharves, where maritime-related businesses rented space. The new location was much smaller than the woolshed; however, that no longer mattered, given that the number of students was just a fraction of the number who had passed through the school during the war.[13]

There were some advantages. For one thing, it was much closer to the Sydney Nautical School, from which most of her students were now coming. It was easier to clean and maintain. And it was more convenient, since Violet travelled into the city every day on the ferry from Greenwich Point to Circular Quay.

So the hundreds (or maybe thousands) of student photographs were unpinned from the woolshed's walls and lovingly transported to her home at Greenwich Point. The Morse stations were uninstalled, and a few of them were set up at the Circular Quay premises. The Bendix equipment was removed (its fate is unknown).

Without the Bendix set-up, Violet could no longer train pilots, so she dealt exclusively with merchant seamen, mostly from the Sydney Nautical School. According to the senior Board of Trade examiner, Captain McLean, her lessons were so effective that men who studied there usually 'sailed' through their tests.

There were no women students anymore. But if that disappointed her, she did not show it; she embraced her role as teacher and mother figure for the young men in her classroom. She told a journalist from *Woman's Day*: 'It seems that losing my only child left me free to have many thousands of sons.'[14]

But then, after two more years, she had had enough. After informing the navigation schools that she would cease taking students, she closed the school entirely. By then, the only volunteer there (apart from herself) was Esme Murrell, her longest-serving and most devoted volunteer helper.[15]

After winding up Sigs, Violet spent some time at the Sydney Nautical School, transferring her teaching systems to Captain Heighwey so that someone else could continue her work and so that all that she had learned about the teaching of signals would not be lost.

In 1955, she was asked to teach at a new government-funded maritime signals school. She recalled, 'They offered to pay me a generous 15 shillings a day, which I refused.'[16] She turned down the offer of employment.

Some years later, the Sydney Institute of Technology created a School of Navigation. The Sydney Nautical School was incorporated into it, creating a line of descent between modern-day navigation studies and Violet's signals school. However, most of Violet's innovative teaching methods were lost in the transition. No aspiring sailors at the School of Navigation were made to practise semaphore to the accompaniment of 'The Teddy Bears' Picnic'.

•—•

The aero clubs continued to offer pilot training at a cost, but had limited capacity and no facilities for signals training. For several years after the closure of Sigs, the only realistic route for many aspiring pilots—including those with qualifications gained during the war—was to move to the outback and work as a crop duster to gain flying hours.

The airlines did not care about the closure of Violet's school, in part because World War II had left Australia with a surplus of trained pilots. Airline executives believed that the surplus would get even bigger with the advent of jet airliners such as the Boeing 707. Compared to anything that had come before, these aircraft were huge, with the capacity to carry more than 100 passengers at a time. Based on advice from the best accountants, the executives figured that the volume of passengers would remain the same; they would need fewer planes, and therefore fewer pilots, to move them.

They were absolutely wrong. The jet airliners carried more passengers, but they also made flying much cheaper, ushering in a new era that was being dubbed the 'jet age' of international travel. Flying was no longer a luxury that only the ultra-rich could afford. Demand boomed, and by the early 1960s there was an acute global shortage of pilots. In Australia, where pilot training had remained the responsibility of the aero clubs, the shortage was severe.

The blame game ratcheted up, with executives, pilots' associations, politicians and bureaucrats all pointing fingers in a variety of directions to identify the cause of the dire pilot shortage. An editorial in *The Canberra Times* advised everyone to calm down: 'Recriminations being indulged by the pilots, the operators, and the Department of Civil Aviation [DCA] will not solve the problem. DCA could help by inaugurating a training system . . .'[17]

The Minister for Air was soon busily announcing new training programs and scholarships to train pilots. But the government had to pay dearly to establish and run all these new programs, including signals training. The school in Clarence Street—which Violet had run for free—was long gone.[18]

•—•

Much later again, on the occasion of Violet's funeral, one of her former pilot students wrote to Jess Prain (one of the first fourteen at Harman), who was helping to coordinate the service:

> It would be true to say that a great number of the pilots whose futures were finally fulfilled in airlines in Australia owe a deal to Mrs Mac. This includes those in all the major airlines, Qantas, TAA, ANA, Airlines of NSW, Butler's and so on. Unfortunately, she was not personally thanked in the way she deserved, and I am ashamed to say that I myself must be placed into that same category of neglect.[19]

30

THE SAILOR'S LESSONS

– •••• • ••• •– •• •–•• ––– •–• •••
•–•• • ••• ••• ––– –• •••

In the seafaring fraternity today, and indeed over
British Commonwealth merchant navies, the name of
Mrs McKenzie is legendary.

John Dodwell, former Commissioner of Maritime
Services, 1987[1]

O ne of Violet's most poignant and significant achievements as a teacher occurred in 1957, two years after she
had permanently shut the doors of her signals school.

A young sailor named Edgar Gold was living in Sydney,
trying to pass the requirements for the Second Mate's
Certificate at the Transport Department's examination office
at Circular Quay.[2] He had dropped out of school against
his father's wishes and taken a sailor's apprenticeship with

coalmining company BHP, sailing as a crew member on coal ships around the Australian coast as well as in south-east and east Asia. At the conclusion of the apprenticeship, the apprentices sat for their Second Mate's exams, which they needed to pass in order to progress in the maritime industry with BHP—or, for that matter, with any other shipping company.

There were three components to the Second Mate's examination, all of which were tough. This was no exercise in rubber-stamping. The first was a written examination. The second was an oral examination, which was essentially a practical examination administered by a captain. The third was the signals exam. The signals component in turn comprised three parts: semaphore, international code (flags) and visual Morse code.[3]

Edgar passed the written and oral components, but could not pass the signals exam. Specifically, he could not pass the visual (Aldis lamp) Morse component. He enrolled at the Sydney Nautical School, where the instructor, Captain Heighwey, even gave him private lessons to help him get over the line after he failed the signals test, but it was to no avail.

Even after Captain Heighwey retired, Edgar kept practising Morse and kept failing. His apprenticeship ran out and so, to make ends meet, he took odd jobs around the city, selling tickets at a cinema for a while, and labouring on construction sites. He was out of options: having dropped out of school at a young age, he had no academic qualifications, and he was alienated from his father. The only way forward that he could see was to pass the certificate, yet it eluded him.

Over a period of a year and a half, Edgar failed the signals test fourteen times. This created problems with the other examination components because, although he had passed them, the results had an expiry date of six months, forcing him to resit those as well.

His continued failure baffled him. He practised Morse so hard for so long. Nobody else seemed to have the problems with it that he was having; he was, in his own words, 'almost suicidal'.

One evening, he was drinking at the Exchange Hotel, a pub on the corner of Pitt and Bridge Streets that was popular with sailors, when he ran into Captain Heighwey, his former signals instructor. When Edgar told him about his troubles, Heighwey was aghast that he had not yet passed the signals test.

The captain said to him, 'I know an old lady I worked with during the war, who might be able to help you. She's very elderly and long retired but it can't hurt to try. I'll ring her and see if she can help.' He explained that her name was Mrs McKenzie, but she was known to all as Mrs Mac.

Edgar was sceptical. As a youth who had worked the seas, he respected tough sailors; the notion that some old woman could help him—when nobody else could—sounded absurd. But he liked the captain, so he accepted his offer, and they arranged to meet there again on the morrow.

The next day at the Exchange Hotel, the captain told Edgar that he had great news. He had phoned Mrs Mac, and she had agreed to meet with Edgar! He slid a piece of paper across the table with a phone number written on it.

His misgivings were amplified when, following their conversation, Edgar called the number on the piece of paper. A woman with a weak and tremulous voice answered the phone. She gave him an address in Greenwich Point, and told him to catch a ferry there the next day.

Doing as he was instructed, Edgar stepped off the ferry, climbed the stairs up the ridge and made his way to Violet's house—a lovely old house with a beautiful garden, over-looking the harbour. A tiny, grey-haired lady answered the door and invited him inside. The ramshackle interior was cluttered with antique furniture and what seemed like enough books to fill a library.

Edgar later vividly recalled the first time he met Mrs Mac: 'What was most impressive were her eyes. They seemed to look right into my heart.'

Mrs Mac said that the captain had told her of Edgar's difficulties, and assured Edgar that she knew all about the requirements for nautical exams, having trained many young men like himself. Then she said, 'Why don't we do a test?'

When Edgar agreed, she turned and disappeared into the depths of the house, announcing that she needed to find her signalling gear. The old lady was gone for some time; finally she reappeared, triumphantly holding a signalling lamp. It was a small, portable variant of an Aldis lamp—the large, powerful signalling light mounted on a ship's deck.

With her trusty lamp in hand, she led him to a dark room— in fact, a room that had been blacked out for the purposes of visual signalling. There she administered a Morse test with the lamp, flicking the light on and off while in response he called out the message—or what he thought her message was—back to her.

At the end of the test, she gave no feedback about how he had gone. She only said, 'Let's do the test a second time.'

When they completed that test, she tested him a third time. After that test, she said, 'I'm not at all sure I can help you, but I want to think about it. Why don't you come back in a couple of days for some tea, and some more testing?' That afternoon, as he sat on the ferry returning to the city across the harbour, Edgar felt that he had failed yet again.

Over the next couple of evenings, at the Exchange Hotel and other sailors' haunts, Edgar asked other sailors whether they had ever heard of someone called Mrs Mac, and was astounded at what he learned. Apparently, that tiny silver-haired woman was a living legend in the maritime world. She was Florence Violet McKenzie, OBE: Australia's first woman engineer, a pioneer of Australian radio and, most importantly, the woman who had run the famous signals school in Clarence Street during the war. He also learned that her husband, Cecil McKenzie, had a distinguished military record as well, having served in both world wars.

This gave him more confidence in Mrs Mac, although he remained pessimistic that anyone—including her—could help him pass the signals test. Nonetheless, two days later he caught the ferry back across the water to her house at Greenwich Point, as he had promised to do.

Mrs Mac and her husband, Cecil (whom she introduced as 'Mack'), were waiting for him, with tea and cake. Being young, physically fit and broke, Edgar was in those days in a perpetual state of hunger, and ate ravenously. As he devoured the cake and tea, Mrs Mac quietly told him that they had a long day ahead of them, and that he should expect to be there for several hours. She told him, 'We'll be doing tests until you literally drop.'

The three of them finished their tea and returned to the blackout room. Mrs Mac performed test after test, her lamp flashing in the dark, while Edgar called out the answers (or what he thought were the answers). Cecil, sitting in the doorway, wrote down Edgar's answers. He could see Violet's implacable face in the gloom, dimly lit from the hallway light behind Cecil. Then, when she clicked the lamp, she disappeared behind flashes of light. When they finally stopped at 11 p.m., all three of them were exhausted.

Mrs Mac said, 'I need to think about what we have done, and examine the information.' Then she told him to go home, and to return in a couple of days.

The next visit was much the same. Mrs Mac flashed her lamp in the dark, Edgar called out the letters that he thought she was sending, and Cecil recorded his responses. During the afternoon tests, Edgar was sure that he saw her smile. Eventually, they stopped for dinner.

Over dinner, Mrs Mac said in a matter-of-fact way, 'I think I can help you.' She then elaborated on a theory that she had about why he could not learn Morse: 'You know, I've been reading all sorts of weird and wonderful technical and scientific journals for some time, and I remember reading something recently about a newly discovered disability called dyslexia, that causes people to mix up letters when they read. I've been wondering if it could also cause people to mix up Morse letters.

'Dyslexia research is still very new,' she told Edgar, and added that its causes were not fully understood. 'But you seem to be exhibiting the traits of dyslexia.' She had identified in Edgar a condition of her own discovery, one that was not in any medical journal: Morse dyslexia.

Edgar's Morse code was perfect, except when it came to four pairs of letters that he would mix up: A and N, B and V, G and W, and K and R. The first three pairs are mirror images of each other:

A is *dit-dah*, while N is its reverse, *dah-dit*.

B is *dah-dit-dit-dit*, while V is *dit-dit-dit-dah*.

G is *dah-dah-dit*, while W is *dit-dah-dah*.

The letters of the fourth pair, rather than being mirror images, transposed into each other by swapping the dots and dashes:

K is *dah-dit-dah*, while R is *dit-dah-dit*.

In all four cases, Edgar would routinely mistake one letter for the other. As he watched the flickers of the lamp, he would perceive an A as an N; likewise, if Mrs Mac sent him the letter

N, he would think it was an A. He'd make the same error for the other three letter pairs.

Edgar felt a surge of optimism that maybe he could pass the signals test after all, although Mrs Mac warned him that there was a lot of work to do yet. Her basic strategy was that he would have to relearn those eight letters, until he could do them correctly and automatically under exam conditions.

When he admitted his embarrassment about the amount of time they were spending on helping him, Mrs Mac dismissed his concerns: 'Mack and I are retired and have lots of time on our hands.' Besides, she added, she and Cecil were learning as much from this process as he was. After dinner, she instructed him to return the following week, and to bring an overnight bag.

The next time he came, he stayed for the whole week. After an early breakfast, Mrs Mac would escort him straight to the signals room, where she would flash her lamp, he would call out letters, and Cecil would write down his answers.

They did drills that focused on those four pairs of letters. Mrs Mac would sometimes use only one of the pair—(such as A)—and not include its opposite (N) in the drill, warning Edgar that if he saw an N, he was mistaken and to instead call out 'A'. Then it would be the other way around. Over and over again, he would call out the letter that he knew she had sent (because she had told him so beforehand), instead of the letter that his lying eyes had seen.

They fed him three meals each day, plus morning and afternoon tea. At night he slept in a spare room, where he dreamed about the eight letters.

During meals and break times, Mrs Mac and Cecil took an interest in Edgar's life story and his family. They regaled him with stories of their own, about the world wars, things they had done and people they had known.

They chatted about current issues, such as the plans to construct the Sydney Opera House on the other side of the harbour, near Circular Quay. The controversial design by Danish architect Jørn Utzon was the topic of much discussion around Sydney, with opinions ranging from it being 'magnificent' to 'a gargantuan monster'. Being from Melbourne, Edgar had no strong feelings either way, but the McKenzies were enthusiastic about it.[4]

At the end of the week, Mrs Mac told Edgar, 'You're ready. We should register you for the exam. But let's do two more practice sessions in the meantime.'

He visited the house at Greenwich Point twice more, then sat the signals test at Circular Quay. He was nervous but confident, and at the end thought he had done well.

Normally the results were available two days after completion of the test, but the next day Edgar received a telegram asking him to come in to the Examination Centre immediately. There he was greeted by Captain Pearson, the chief examiner, who pushed a blue certificate across the desk. Edgar knew what that meant. The blue certificate was a pass, while the white certificate was a fail. Over the past year and a half, Edgar had collected fourteen white certificates.[5]

Captain Pearson said that he, too, had been a student of Mrs Mac's many years ago, and that she had recently spoken to him about Edgar. 'Mrs Mac tried to explain what your problem was, but I didn't understand it. But anyway, you passed. With a score of 99 per cent!'

The captain then asked Edgar to accompany him downstairs to the examiners' luncheon and meeting room. Until that day, Edgar had believed that his misery had been his alone to bear. He'd had no sense that anyone else in the world had noticed or cared about his failures, least of all the captains and staff at the examination centre.

As he walked down the stairs, he saw before him a room full of people. He could see in the crowd the nine nautical examiners. These nine men were respected, accomplished sea captains at the top of their field, men who inspired in Edgar feelings of admiration and awe. The entire staff of the examinations centre was also in the room with them. Everyone rose to their feet and clapped.

When he reached the lower floor, someone handed him a glass of sherry. People crowded to shake his hand. The sea captains shook his hand. Everyone seemed to know of his long and lonely struggle to get the Second Mate's Certificate.

The next day, Edgar found a local florist, bought the largest bunch of flowers he could afford, and requested that it be delivered to Mrs Mac.

She invited him to come over for dinner one more time a week later to celebrate. At dinner, she told Edgar, 'If I was younger, I might have written an article about what we have done, and about the possibility of dyslexia in Morse code. I probably should do it, but I'm too old.'

After eighteen months stuck in Sydney, trying to get his Second Mate's Certificate, Edgar was itching to go to sea again. He never returned to BHP, instead travelling the world crewing ships, eventually settling in England. He got his First Mate's Certificate, then his Master's Certificate, then got one of the most plum jobs you can get at sea: captaining cruise ships. 'I always breezed through the signals component of the tests,' he recalled.

He fell in love with a Canadian woman, who encouraged him to study law. He did so, eventually becoming one of the world's foremost experts in maritime law.

When describing his significant life accomplishments, Edgar said: 'All this, because of Mrs Mac.'

31

THE WAR'S LONG REACH

– •••• • •– – •– •–• ••• •–•• ––– –• ––•
•–•••– –•–• ••••

He was just right for Mrs Mac. They were a very happy couple.

Jean Nysen[1]

The mustard gas attack in France in 1917 affected Cecil's health for the rest of his life. Upon discharge from the army, he seemed to have regained his health thanks to a period of convalescence in army hospitals in France and England; however, in the years afterwards, it was clear that he would never completely recover.

He suffered headaches, chest infections, throat problems and insomnia. Any kind of intense physical exertion gave him tightness in the chest. He had a recurring feeling that something like a piece of corn was stuck in his throat, even though nothing was there. At other times he would feel a 'gripping sensation' around his throat, or feel like someone was pressing against his windpipe. He missed a lot of work due to sick leave, including periods of leave without pay, but there were many more occasions when he would 'soldier on' (as he put it), despite his health conditions.[2]

In 1949, after experiencing chest pains, he underwent an ECG, which revealed a coronary occlusion. Soon afterwards he was bedridden with pneumonia. By December 1953, with worsening health, he had applied for the repatriation benefits available for veterans who suffered ongoing war-related medical problems. A doctor who examined Cecil described him as 'cheerful and intelligent, but somewhat introspective'.[3]

His benefits application was rejected because his health problems were deemed to be age-related rather than war-related. Furthermore, upon looking through his war record, the Department of Veterans' Affairs discovered that on the day he was discharged from the army in December 1917, he was declared to be in good health and 'not suffering from any war-related injuries'. That document, interestingly, did not have Cecil's signature on it but did have the signature of the discharging officer, which obviously was seen as the next best thing.[4]

Cecil appealed the decision. The commission-appointed doctor who reviewed him on appeal investigated his health in detail, noting: 'He looks much older than his stated age, yet is still fairly active.' The review concluded that his non-cardiac health problems were in large part due to allergic rhinitis, but the deciding factor for the review board in rejecting his appeal was that the *Repatriation Act* in force at the time made no allowance for either chest conditions or psychiatric conditions. In the end, whether they were caused by war or not was irrelevant. His medical problems simply were not covered by the Act.[5]

It may well be that Cecil's deteriorating health contributed to Violet's decision to close Sigs and 'retire'. It is just as well that she did, because their time together was running short. On 30 November 1958, Cecil suffered a heart attack and died at home. He was 59 years old.

After he died, Violet bought a ticket to England. She stayed in the United Kingdom for a considerable time, probably in Wales as a guest of Lord and Lady Wakehurst—the former governor of New South Wales and his wife, Peggy— with whom Violet had formed a close friendship during their years in Sydney. It was the first holiday she had had since travelling by ship to the United States to see the Radio World's Fair in 1924.[6]

Six months later, she came home.

32

EX–WRANS

• —••— •— — •—• •— —• •••

There is something about them, difficult to define, but recognizable to anyone who has had the honour to be one of them, however long ago.

Margaret Curtis-Otter, *W.R.A.N.S.*[1]

The inaugural meeting of the Ex-WRANS Association was held at the Dorchester Lounge in Sydney in 1963. The Women's Royal Australian Naval Service had been disbanded in 1947 but re-formed in 1950, and the intention of the Ex-WRANS organisers was to provide an association for wartime WRANS, as well as women in post-war service. The current director of the WRANS, Chief Officer Joan Streeter, was guest of honour.[2]

Many of Mrs Mac's girls were there, including two of the first fourteen at Harman—Jess Prain and Denise Owen—and four of the next eight who had gone to Melbourne: Joan Senior, Dorothy Johnstone, Joan Cowie and Jo Miller. Event organiser Carnie Harrington told those assembled that Mrs Mac had been invited to attend, but was unwell.

When they put together a committee, one of the first items of business was to appoint Violet—who had sent a cheque for an undisclosed sum as a donation to the newly formed association[3]—as 'Patron of the WRANS'. This provided a way for her to participate in the veterans' association without having veteran status.

The following year, Violet was well enough to attend the annual reunion as the guest of honour. In her speech, she made it clear that she thought of *all* ex-WRANS as 'my girls', not just those who had gone through Sigs.

Violet kept in contact with many of her former students, particularly those in the Ex-WRANS Association, and continued to teach privately from time to time. She was known on several occasions to catch a train (she never learned to drive) to visit one of her girls if she learned that they were having a crisis of some kind.[4]

She had always had a lot of books in her house, but the sheer number of them skyrocketed when a friend gave her— or bequeathed to her—virtually a library's worth of books. They were crammed on shelves and stacked wherever they could fit. As there was a regular flow of visitors through her house, particularly ex-Sigs and ex-WRANS women, she instituted a rule that every visitor had to choose and take a book with them when they left. One of her former students, Jean Nysen (nee McKenzie) recalled that she and Sue Timbury (nee Rogers, another Sigs girl) would visit Violet regularly together. As each visit neared its end, Violet would tell them, 'Choose your book! I want you to take another book.'[5] Some of the books that Jean acquired from the Greenwich Point house included *Ismailia*, *The Moods of Ginger Mick*, and *Einstein: His life and times*.

In 1971, the navy hosted a special ANZAC ceremony in Canberra, to mark the occasion of the 30th anniversary of the first fourteen WRANS arriving at Harman. Violet—who had recently turned 80—was invited to attend as the guest of honour.

They offered to bring her to Canberra in a car, but she declined that mode of transport because she had learned that many ex-WRANS were going to travel to the event from Sydney by coach, and she wanted to travel with them. She explained: 'I want to spend the journey talking to my girls.'[6]

A group of ex-WRANS visited her at home a couple of days beforehand, bringing with them a journalist from *The Australian Women's Weekly*, Gloria Newton, who hoped to meet the mythical Mrs Mac for a story that she was writing. The women wanted Newton to understand what Violet had achieved, so they sat around Violet, encouraging her to talk about it: 'Go on, Mrs Mac. Tell how it happened. Tell how you went down to Melbourne and confronted them, and made them take notice.'

But Violet was reluctant. 'You girls go on so, you really do,' she said. 'We were all in it, really. It was an idea we all had.' She then admitted that her role might have been somewhat important. 'I may have pushed it through a little, but then I am not self-conscious, so I didn't let those stern-faced men intimidate me.'

They got her talking eventually. She told Newton that, prior to dealing with the navy board, she had tried to personally contact the local Sydney naval command, 'but those august gentlemen just sat back in their seats and roared with laughter. "Women in the navy!" they said. "Never."'

When she tired of reminiscing about the war, she stood

up, bustled into her pantry and returned with several jars of homemade jam, which she distributed to her guests as gifts. 'My favourite hobby is making jam,' she told them. 'Fig jam.'[7]

Days later, at the podium in Canberra, she addressed the many uniformed women in the audience, as well as the ex-WRANS who had come from around the country: 'I can assure you that there is no such thing as a generation gap. I am at one with all of you, and whether you happened to go to the signalling school or not, you are all WRANS and very, very dear to my heart.'[8]

•—•

The year 1971 was when a young Australian living in London—a feminist of a different stripe—burst onto the world's stage. In her groundbreaking polemic, *The Female Eunuch*, Germaine Greer heaped contempt on the women's movement of the mid-twentieth century, announcing that her book was part of 'the second feminist wave'. Somewhere in between the first wave of suffragettes and the second wave, feminism had lost its way; however, it was now back on track. Greer put it brashly: 'The new emphasis is different. Then genteel middle-class ladies clamoured for reform, now ungenteel middle-class women are calling for revolution.'[9]

The suffragette movement in Britain in the early twentieth century had not been exported to Australia, because women had already achieved the vote in the new Commonwealth in 1902, having first won it in South Australia in 1894. The activism of feminist movements in between, in Greer's view, had been ineffectual: 'They are not much nearer to providing a revolutionary strategy than they ever were; demonstrating, compiling reading lists and sitting on committees are not themselves liberated behaviour, especially when they are still embedded in a context of housework and feminine wiles.'[10]

Greer took a swipe at women's military services, too: 'The women's branches of the armed forces are not soldiers in their own right, but clerical assistants and other kinds of handmaidens to the males.'[11]

Australia's second-wave feminists made a splash and quickly scored some big wins. The biggest success came from the work of the Women's Liberation Movement, which won a legal and political battle for equal pay in 1972. In public discourse, they were called the 'women's libbers', a term that was sometimes used disparagingly.

The monumental victories of the second-wave feminists left the older generation of ex-WRANS unmoved. It was not just that their mid-century women's organisations were being downplayed or forgotten—with only the first wave (the suffragettes) and the new second wave getting airtime—it was, more than anything, that their style was being derided.

Greer herself used coarse and sexually explicit language that they considered offensive. She was relentlessly critical of men, making provocative statements such as 'Women have very little idea of how much men hate them.'[12]

For women like the ex-WRANS, who had spent their formative years counting the dead among the young men they loved, the notion of disparaging men left them cold. They felt no ownership of the successes of this new women's movement.

Other mid-century women's activists held similar views. Mary Wright had been one of the Australian organisers of the first International Women's Day rally in 1936, and in the 1930s she had been a member of the Housewives' Association when Violet had talked to them about electrical appliances. She was critical of the new activists: 'By elevating women, we elevate society. Women's Liberation missed the point. They put man against woman, it was an enmity thing. They wanted to compete against men. We don't want to fight men. We like them. We need them. We just want to be equal citizens.'[13]

But Mary Wright herself missed the point. The second-wave feminists wanted equality, but they believed that the methods favoured by Wright's generation—politeness, deference and gentle persuasion—had failed.

Those methods had not failed for Violet McKenzie. In her speech at the 1975 annual dinner of the Ex-WRANS Association, she reminded the ex-WRANS of their legacy and laid out the importance of what they had achieved: 'WRANS are to be congratulated on the pioneering work they did in the naval service with such a high standard of conduct and efficiency. You have undoubtedly done more to raise the status of women than all the women's libbers could accomplish.'[14]

That same year, journalist and activist Anne Summers published her seminal work on Australian feminism, *Damned Whores and God's Police*. Her book featured an extensive timeline of achievements by and for Australian women, including things such as the gaining of suffrage, sex-discrimination laws and Dawn Fraser winning gold in three successive Olympics.

Women joining the armed forces did not make the cut.

33

THE PILOT FLAG FLYING

— ••••• • •—•• •• •—•• ——— — ••—•••—•• •— ——•
••—••—•• —•—— •• —•——•

*She is regarded as the mother of the WRANS, and will
be greatly missed by them all.*

Marjorie Taylor, Ex-WRANS Association, 1982[1]

Violet had a stroke in 1976 that affected the left side of her
body. She spent several days in hospital, followed by a
recuperation period of several weeks in the nearby Glenwood
Nursing Home, before being discharged.

While recovering, she worried about the welfare of her cat,
Dear Tom-Tom. Jo Miller (the woman who, in 1941, had been
given heavy sailor's boots to help her pass the navy's medical
entry test) reassured her that all 'the girls' were making sure that
Dear Tom-Tom was being looked after. Violet was overjoyed
when she was well enough to be finally reunited with him.

Violet had been in good shape until then. Only a few weeks before the stroke, several ex-WRANS had held an 86th birthday party for her, baking the birthday cake from a recipe in her *All Electric Cookery Book*. Earlier that year, she had attended an ex-WRANS event in Perth. But the stroke had stolen her ability to walk more than a few steps, never far from her wheelchair.

Unfortunately, Cecil's sister—who had moved in some years earlier, and who still lived in the house—was not much help. The two women had fallen out years earlier for reasons that neither would reveal, and the mood between them was frosty. Help instead came from a neighbour named Gwen Hathaway, who had already been assisting Violet with day-to-day chores; now, following the stroke, she stepped up her caring role.

Gwen Hathaway hosted a birthday party for Violet in 1978, perhaps not foreseeing how large it would get. The many attendees included not only the core group of ex-WRANS in close contact with Violet, but also many of her former male students, including NSW Police Commissioner Mervyn Wood. The icing on the birthday cake said 'Happy Birthday' in Morse code. Her 'boys' and 'girls' presented Violet with a scroll bearing all their signatures, plus a plaque in appreciation of her services.[2]

Many of them, having pursued careers as pilots, sailors, ship's captains and radio technicians, owed much to their instruction under Mrs Mac, particularly in Morse code. It was still the international system for distress calls at sea; it was still a required proficiency for radio licences; and it played a critical role in aviation, shipping and telecommunication. But its importance was dwindling. New technologies were obviating the need for the old system of dots and dashes—or, as the people at Mrs Mac's birthday party called them, the *dits* and *dahs*. The air force still used Morse code, but the army had phased it out in 1952, and in the navy it was taught to only a select few.

Over the following two decades, Morse code would be dropped by successive institutions and domains where it had once been prime, including the Australian government, the International Maritime Organization, the air force and the navy. It was still in use, but everyone could see that it was on the way out.

During the celebration of Violet's birthday at Gwen Hathaway's house, several old sailors who remembered each other from Sigs but had lost touch in the intervening years were reunited. They were alarmed by their former mentor's deteriorating health and arranged with each other to stay in contact, so as to organise a more formal event to recognise Mrs Mac's many achievements.

Their plan culminated in a ceremony on 23 May 1980 at The Mission to Seafarers church at Flying Angel House in Sydney, where a plaque was laid in her honour. Violet attended the ceremony and unveiled the plaque.[3]

•—•

By that time, Violet had resigned herself to the reality that independent living was no longer possible, and that she would have to go back to Glenwood Nursing Home, this time permanently.

She made contact with an antiques dealer, Peter Goed, to dispose of as much of her estate as he could. Goed recalls that, when he called at her front door, he met 'a tiny white-haired woman in a wheelchair'. She wasn't completely immobile, venturing out of the wheelchair on errands around the room before returning to it.

Violet gave him a tour of the house so that he could make an estimate of the contents' worth. Gesturing around her, she said, 'This is what I've got. I want to get rid of it. Give me a price.'

He quoted her $2600, which he described as 'a generous sum', but which he was confident he would easily recoup. His eyes had sparkled at what appeared to be highly valuable items, such as an antique grand piano from the 1930s, and an antique car from 1957, which her husband had bought shortly before his death, and which had a mere 7 miles (11 kilometres) on the odometer.

But on a subsequent visit, Goed discovered that the piano was missing its soundboard. When he asked Violet if she had the soundboard, she said that it was faulty, and that she had sent it to the German manufacturer in order to get repairs or a replacement, but the replacement had never come. With a sinking feeling, Goed asked Violet, 'When did you send the soundboard to Germany?'

'In 1938,' she replied. No wonder it had never returned from Germany! Violet added that, by the time the war had finished, the German piano company no longer existed.

As for the car, she explained to Goed that there must have been a misunderstanding, because she had promised it to someone else, and it was never part of their deal. So much for the killing he was going to make on those antiques!

In the garage, Goed made an intriguing discovery: a large amount of radio equipment that all seemed to be in good condition. This was the equipment from Violet's radio station, 2GA. As a boy, Goed had been fascinated by radio, and had often hung around in The Wireless Shop in Sydney (although Violet no longer owned it by then, and its name had changed). He asked her why she still had this equipment.

She said, 'Come inside, and I'll make a cup of tea and tell you all about it.'

He took a seat in the kitchen while the tiny white-haired lady poured him a cup of tea, and then she told him her life's story.[4]

•—•

Gwen Hathaway and some of Violet's 'girls' helped Violet move into Glenwood Nursing Home. There, through the wall, she could hear the unmistakable *dit-dah* sounds of someone sending Morse code. She wondered if she was going senile, but soon discovered that the man in the room next to her was equipped with an amateur radio set and a Morse key.

Naturally, the man assumed that, even if someone heard his transmissions, since they were in Morse code it was unlikely anyone would understand them, and his messages were confidential. Violet kindly informed him that she could hear his Morse transmissions, that she happened to be pretty good at Morse code herself, and that she could understand every single word he sent.[5]

•—•

By 1982, she knew that her time was running out. She talked about her mortality with Jo Miller, who still visited her every week. She told Jo not to be sad or grieve for her after she was gone. She said, 'I have a pilot flag flying and will reach safe anchorage. Please give them my love and blessings.'[6]

Gwen Hathaway visited on 21 May. After fussing around with the blankets and generally cleaning and tidying up, she was satisfied with her work and said, 'Well, it's finished. That's the lot.'

Violet said, 'Yes, it is finished. And I have proved to them all that women can be as good as, or better than, the men.'

That was the last thing anyone remembers her saying. She died in her sleep two days later. She was 91 years old.[7]

Her funeral was held at Greenwich's St Giles Anglican Church, and was conducted by Reverend J.R. Henderson. In his eulogy, Reverend Henderson revealed that Violet—who knew that he would be conducting the funeral—had made some requests about it:

> In talking to Mrs Mac about today—for she did talk about the service we are holding today—she indicated the things she wanted done. One thing she said was that there was to be no recounting of the things she has done, no praise of her is to be said, and I know for many of us that is a real disappointment. I know you would like many things said, but we must respect Mrs Mac's wishes . . .
>
> Mrs Mac also said that this was not to be a sad affair, but we are deeply sad that a person so close to us will not be there for us to talk to. However, we can be joyful for we know that Mrs Mac is now free from her earthly body and the pain it has endured.[8]

Twenty-four former WRANS formed a guard of honour as her coffin was taken away from the church.[9] She was cremated at the Northern Suburbs Crematorium.[10]

ACKNOWLEDGEMENTS

I am grateful for the assistance, knowledge and expertise of many people.

As I indicated in the Preface, journalist Catherine Freyne paved the way. She uncovered and publicised the story of Violet McKenzie in a radio documentary on ABC Radio National's *Hindsight* program titled *Signals, Currents, and Wires: The untold story of Florence Violet McKenzie*, and subsequently in a detailed and extensively researched article for the *Dictionary of Sydney*. I freely admit that the starting point for my research involved retracing her steps, making full use of her extensive references, some of which pointed to obscure sources.

Catherine generously provided me with documents that she had acquired, put me in contact with people to interview, and shared relevant information and insights that had not been incorporated into either her documentary or her article.

In particular, Catherine put me in contact with Peter Goed, who features in the final chapter; Michael Nelmes, the author of Violet McKenzie's entry in the *Australian Dictionary of Biography*; and Paul Wallace, Violet's great-nephew. All three were keen to help. Enthused by my project, Peter engaged in some research of his own and provided me with several useful titbits, including information about Cecil's yacht, the *Pilgrim*. Some of the other leads that he shared were intriguing but proved elusive.

When I contacted Edgar Gold (via a circuitous route), he generously provided me with memorable and moving recollections, which formed the basis of the chapter titled *The Sailor's Lessons*.

John Perryman of the Royal Australian Navy's Sea Power Centre Australia shared his expertise, including (off the top of his head!) a brief history of Morse code in the Royal Australian Navy. Others there, particularly Greg Swinden, were also helpful. Likewise, Captain Damien Allan and Mr Ian Steel of the Spectacle Island Naval Heritage Collections were accommodating.

Cassandra Mohapp's thesis titled 'The Rhythm of Life', which investigated Violet McKenzie's use of music in teaching Morse, was a valuable resource, as was Cassandra herself.

The Ex-WRANS Association helped me in several important respects. Pauline Gribble put me in touch with wartime WRAN Merle Hare and WRANS historian Joan Henstock, both of whom I met; they provided me with useful information. Coral Searle, Ex-WRANS archivist, provided a wealth of material including several of the images. And, of course, the work of those Ex-WRANS who compiled the dossier on Violet McKenzie in 1987, in their unsuccessful attempt to have her recognised for the Australian Bicentenary, was invaluable.

In addition to Merle, I met other wartime WRANS members including Jean Nysen (nee McKenzie), Patricia Johnson (nee Murdoch), Gwenda Garde (nee Moulton) and Marie Davis (nee Munns), each of whom related their wartime experiences and recollections of Violet McKenzie (whom they all referred to as 'Mrs Mac'). Jean Nysen also provided documents and answered additional questions as they occurred to me in follow-up phone calls. I'm also grateful for the hospitality of Jean's daughter, Caroline, as well as Gwenda's daughter, Robyn.

Thanks to the editor of *The Sydney Morning Herald*'s RSVP column for printing my call-out to anyone who could help. I subsequently heard from several people, including three of the Ex-WRANS already mentioned (Marie Davis, Gwenda Garde and Patricia Johnson); Gail Brady; Jo Harris; Noreen McDonald; Diana, Nerida and Rose Saunders; Bill Steele; Mark Sunter; and Joy McManamey (nee Bowers), who served in Britain in both the Women's Land Army and the Women's Royal Naval Service.

Thanks to Anton Kuruc, Jeff Malone, Jenny Edwards, John Smith, Kevin Davies, and Walter Burroughs for taking the time to read a draft and provide feedback.

Thanks to Richard Walsh for championing *Radio Girl* at Allen & Unwin and for early editorial feedback. Thanks also to Elizabeth Weiss, Samantha Kent and everyone at Allen & Unwin for helping to make *Radio Girl* the best book it can be.

My research was enabled by the existence of several excellent archival institutions and the diligence of those who work in them: the Australian War Memorial Research Centre; the Mitchell Library; the National Archives of Australia; the National Library of Australia (and particularly its excellent *Trove* resource); the Royal Australian Navy Heritage Collection at Spectacle Island (mentioned earlier); New South Wales State Archives and Records; the Sea Power Centre Australia (also mentioned earlier); and the State Library of Victoria.

I appreciate the encouragement from members of the Wireless Institute of Australia (WIA), including (but not limited to) Raffy Shammay, Jennifer Wardrop, and John S. Buckley. I hope they forgive my account of a turbulent time for the WIA, where I describe its leadership—while under Ernest Fisk's control—as 'aligned with big business and hostile to the "little bloke"'. That was a transient state. Today's WIA very much supports the 'little' men and women of radio, just as it did a hundred years ago. After attending its 2019 annual conference, I am pleased to report that the WIA is a vibrant, richly talented organisation that tirelessly advocates for the amateur radio community.

Finally, thanks to Jenny Edwards for her support and belief in this project.

NOTES

PREFACE

1 The article that appeared in *The Sun* actually had the printed title, 'Mdlle Edisom' (*The Sun*, 28 March 1920, p. 17), but I could not bring myself to inflict such a subeditorial mishmash on you, particularly so early in the book.

CHAPTER 1: AUSTINMER

1 Louise Lansley & Islay Wybenga, 'Interview with Florence Violet McKenzie'.

2 Norman King, *The Story of Austinmer*, p. 38.

3 Norman King, *The Story of Austinmer*, p. 38; Norman King, *History of Austinmer and Robert Marsh Westmacott in Australia*, p. 3.

4 Marriage certificate, George Wallace and Marie Annie Greville, 28 May 1894.

5 Birth certificate, Walter Reginald Giles, 28 July 1899; Birth certificate, Florence Violet Granville, 28 September 1890.

6 I based this conclusion on genealogical research through online research tool findmypast.com.au; the closest match I could find to her was a baptism record for her in 1874, which lists her birth as being that year, and which gives the same name for her father and same first name for her mother as in later documents. That is my best guess, but I freely admit that I don't know for certain.

7 'The radio girl—Sydney's lone electrician—wireless companionship', *The Sun*, 13 September 1923, p. 13.

8 Norman King, *The Story of Austinmer*, pp. 21, 26, 27.

9 Norman King, *The Story of Austinmer*, pp. 26, 27.

10 Norman King, *The Story of Austinmer*, p. 22.

11 'To 20,000 men and women she's "Dear Mother—Mrs Mac"', *Australian Home Journal*, July 1963, pp. 45–6.

12 Louise Lansley & Islay Wybenga, 'Interview with Florence Violet McKenzie'.

13 Louise Lansley & Islay Wybenga, 'Interview with Florence Violet McKenzie'.

14 'Sydney Girls High School', *The Sydney Morning Herald*, 28 July 1933, p. 13.

15 Lee Jobling, 'The first women graduates'.

16 Louise Lansley & Islay Wybenga, 'Interview with Florence Violet McKenzie'.

17 Louise Lansley & Islay Wybenga, 'Interview with Florence Violet McKenzie'; Richard Begbie, 'The marvellous Mrs Mac—alias F.V. Wallace', p. 7.

18 'Austinmer', *South Coast Times and Wollongong Argus*, 2 December 1910, p. 7.

CHAPTER 2: A TALE OF TWO ENGINEERS

1 Louise Lansley & Islay Wybenga, 'Interview with Florence Violet McKenzie'.

2 'An enterprising woman says little but does much', *Richmond River Herald and Northern Districts Advertiser*, 28 March 1922, p. 1.

3 'Mdlle Edisom', *The Sun*, 28 March 1920, p. 17.

4 Gloria Newton, 'Ex-WRANs plan get-together for 30th Anniversary'.

5 Louise Lansley & Islay Wybenga, 'Interview with Florence Violet McKenzie'.

6 'Obtaining a typewriter by false pretences, Charles Thomas Jones convicted, a complicated fraud', *The Argus* (Melbourne, Vic.), 19 September 1891, p. 6; 'Bishop and undertaker, the case of the Rev Charles Jones, investigation ordered', *The Argus*, 11 December 1896, p. 5; 'The "Rev" Charles Jones', *The Bendigo Independent* (Vic.), 19 December 1896, p. 2; 'Teacher of aviation and undertaker', *The Daily Telegraph*, 16 September 1911, p. 13.

7 'Reverend Charles Jones starts a flickergraph school: pupils run to the police', *Truth*, 23 November 1913, p. 7; 'Quarter sessions', *The Daily Telegraph*, 18 November 1913, p. 6.

8 NSW State Archives Register of Firms, Series NRS12951, Item 2/8544, 'W. R. Wallace & Co'.

9 'Electric woman breaking new ground', *The Sun*, 5 March 1922, p. 17.

10 'Electric woman breaking new ground', *The Sun*, 5 March 1922, p. 17; Rosemary Broomham, 'Florence Violet McKenzie'.

11 *The University of Sydney Calendar*, 1916, pp. 428–30. I am indebted to Catherine Freyne for locating this reference and including it in her extensively researched article, 'McKenzie, Violet', which can be found in the *Dictionary of Sydney*. Violet's result for chemistry is also reported in a newspaper listing, 'The University', *The Sydney Morning Herald*, 11 September 1915, p. 20. There is no paper trail proving that Violet repeatedly applied for the Engineering program, but this is the conclusion I drew based on her own accounts of her early life, for example her claim that she 'always wanted to do engineering', as well as her academic record.

12 Louise Lansley & Islay Wybenga, 'Interview with Florence Violet McKenzie'.
13 'Electric woman breaking new ground', *The Sun*, 5 March 1922, p. 17.
14 'Austinmer', *South Coast Times and Wollongong Argus*, 26 January 1917, p. 14. Her fellow two students who also completed first-year Electrical Engineering were John Pollock and John Magee. See 'Technical education examination results', *The Sydney Morning Herald*, 25 January 1917, p. 6.
15 'Mdlle Edisom', *The Sun*, 28 March 1920, p. 17.

CHAPTER 3: THE WIRELESS SHOP

1 'A woman's letter', *The Bulletin*, 25 December 1924, p. 26.
2 NSW State Archives, Series NRS13658, Item 22644; NSW State Archives, Series NRS12951, Item 2/8549. An article in *Australasian Wireless Review* says that she started dealing in radio parts in September 1921. 'People who are waiting to talk wireless with you', *Australasian Wireless Review*, January 1923, pp. 37–41.
3 'Licence fees reduced', *Brisbane Courier*, 22 November 1922, p 4.
4 Louise Lansley & Islay Wybenga, 'Interview with Florence Violet McKenzie'.
5 Neville Williams, 'Charles D. Maclurcan: Engineer, businessman, hotelier and top Australian amateur broadcaster—1'; Ernest Fisk, 'The possibilities of wireless in Australia', p. 23.
6 Neville Williams, 'Charles D. Maclurcan: Engineer, businessman, hotelier and top Australian amateur broadcaster—1'.
7 His story also demonstrates that wealth could not be taken for granted. In the late 1930s, the Wentworth Hotel (and therefore his family) was almost bankrupted by the constant loud construction of the Sydney Harbour Bridge. Maclurcan kept the family business from going bust by working up to eighteen hours a day and even sleeping at the hotel for several years (see Neville Williams, 'Charles D. Maclurcan: Engineer, businessman, hotelier and top Australian amateur broadcaster—2').
8 'A lady experimenter', *The Evening News*, 13 May 1922, p. 7.
9 Richard Begbie, 'The marvellous Mrs Mac—alias F.V. Wallace'.

CHAPTER 4: THE METROPOLITAN RADIO CLUB

1 'Electric woman breaking new ground', *The Sun*, 5 March 1922, p. 17.
2 Shaw's gripping account of the *Helen B. Stirling* rescue was published under the title 'Calling! Calling! Calling!' in *Smith's Weekly*, 11 February 1922, p. 18. Other details of the event are provided in 'The *Helen B. Stirling*: Details of the rescue: a thrilling sea story', *Newcastle Morning Herald and Miners' Advocate*, 4 February 1922, p. 12.
3 'Wireless hero', *The Newcastle Sun*, 11 February 1922, p. 5.
4 Violet's membership of the WIA is first mentioned in 'Radio telephony', *The Brisbane Courier*, 19 September 1922, p 6.

5 'Mr Raymond H. Shaw', *Australasian Wireless Review,* January 1923, p. 39.
6 'The magic spark: radio news from everywhere: personal and practical notes', *The Evening News,* 18 February 1922, p. 2.
7 Dot Dash, 'The magic spark', *The Evening News,* 3 June 1922, p. 7. This column provides the program for the club from June to the end of the year; Dot Dash's columns regularly provided news on the Metropolitan Radio Club as well as other wireless clubs around Sydney.
8 'Metropolitan Club', *Wireless Weekly,* 4 August 1922, p. 11.
9 Dot Dash, 'The magic spark', *The Evening News,* 15 July 1922, p. 7.
10 'The radio exhibition', *Wireless Weekly,* 29 September 1922, p. 3.
11 Neville Williams, 'Vintage radio magazines: how they came and went, and transmitters BC (before crystals)', p. 48.
12 'Wireless and electrical exhibition in Sydney Town Hall', *Radio in Australia and New Zealand,* 1923, vol. 1, no. 10, p. 232.
13 'Personal', *The Daily Telegraph,* 4 December 1923, p. 6.
14 'Sydney's big radio exhibition', *Radio in Australia and New Zealand,* 1923, vol.1, no. 2, pp. 476–87.

CHAPTER 5: WIRELESS WEEKLY

1 'Wireless Weekly under new editorship', *Goulburn Evening Penny Post,* 11 March 1924, p. 2.
2 'The magic spark: woman delegate', *The Evening News,* 11 November 1922, p. 7.
3 Richard Begbie, 'The marvellous Mrs Mac—alias F.V. Wallace', p. 8; Neville Williams, 'Vintage radio magazines: how they came and went, and transmitters BC (before crystals)', p. 47.
4 F.V. McKenzie, 'The first "Wireless Weekly"'.
5 'Supplying a need: Wireless Weekly takes its bow,' *Wireless Weekly,* 4 August 1922, p. 2.
6 'Dah-da-dah-da-dah!', *Wireless Weekly,* 15 September 1922, p. 4.
7 'Paradise', *Wireless Weekly,* 28 September 1923, p. 17.
8 Richard Begbie, 'The marvellous Mrs Mac—alias F.V. Wallace', p. 9.
9 Neville Williams, 'Vintage radio magazines: how they came and went, and transmitters BC (before crystals)', p. 48.
10 'A talk with Wireless Weekly', *Wireless Weekly,* 11 August 1922, p. 2; 'A talk with "Wireless Weekly"', *Wireless Weekly,* 13 October 1922, p. 2.
11 Cover art, *Wireless Weekly,* 9 November 1923.
12 'Where are those regulations?', *Wireless Weekly,* 3 November 1922, p. 3.
13 'The iniquitous sealed set', *Wireless Weekly,* 1 February 1924, p. 1.
14 Ron Langhans, *The First Twelve Months of Radio Broadcasting in Australia, 1923–1924,* p. 7; Neville Williams, 'Ernest Fisk, the man'.
15 The closing of the contracting business is reported in 'An enterprising woman: says little but does much', *The Richmond River Herald and Northern Districts Advertiser,* 28 March 1922, p. 1.

CHAPTER 6: LOVE AND LOSS

1 'University women in the business life of Sydney', *The Daily Telegraph*, 28 August 1927, p. 28.

2 'The Radio Girl', *The Sun*, 13 September 1923, p. 13.

3 'In the public eye', *The Sun*, 26 February 1922, p. 3.

4 'A woman's letter', *The Bulletin*, 21 August 1924, p. 29. The *Bulletin* article mistakenly claims that the Wireless Shop was in the Imperial Arcade, which was another of Sydney's Victorian shopping arcades of the day.

5 Dot Dash, 'Rest from Radio', *The Evening News*, 23 February 1924, p. 7.

6 'A Dot with a Dash', *People*, 28 January 1953, p. 23.

7 NAA: B2455, McKenzie C R; NAA: C138, M85993, 'McKenzie, Cecil Roland'.

8 'Shipping', *The Daily Telegraph*, 11 September 1924, p. 11.

9 'University women in the business life of Sydney', *The Daily Telegraph*, 28 August 1927, p. 28. In that interview, she refers to the exhibition as the 'New York Radio and Electrical Exhibition'. The demonstration of television is mentioned in 'First radio world's fair', *The Register* (Adelaide, SA), 30 August 1924, p. 7.

10 'Woman electrician', *The Sun*, 10 September 1924, p. 10.

11 Catherine Freyne, 'McKenzie, Violet'; 'Miss Wallace speaks from 2KGO', *Australasian Wireless Review*, December 1924, p. 37.

12 'Miss Wallace speaks from 2KGO', *Australasian Wireless Review*, December 1924, p. 37.

13 Dot Dash, 'Wireless News: KGO at Moruya', *The Evening News*, 15 December 1924, p. 12.

14 'Topics for women', *The Sun*, 1 January 1925, p. 5.

15 Michael Nelmes, 'McKenzie, Florence Violet (1890–1982)'. They lodged the registration of marriage in Gulgong, probably because they were unable to do so before leaving Sydney, since New Year's Day is a public holiday. See: Transcript of marriage between Cecil McKenzie and Florence Wallace, 1925, findmypast.com.au.

16 Marie Dale, 'The Radio Girl: "Tunes in" to many interests'.

17 Catherine Freyne, 'McKenzie, Violet'. According to Freyne, 'The house remains, but has been extensively renovated since the McKenzies lived there.'

18 'The ladies' realm', *The Chronicle* (Adelaide, SA), 19 December 1925, p. 69.

19 'Business changes, etc.', *Dun's Gazette for New South Wales*, 22 March 1926, p. 197; 'University women in the business life of Sydney', *The Daily Telegraph*, 28 August 1927, p. 28.

20 Rex Shaw, 'Ring Me Round with Radio' (song lyrics).

21 'The Radio Girl: new Australian revue', *The Sydney Morning Herald*, 12 April 1926, p. 6.

22 'Births', *The Sydney Morning Herald*, 19 July 1926, p. 10.

NOTES

CHAPTER 7: THE PHILLIP STREET RADIO SCHOOL

1 'Federal Labor campaign in NSW', *The Australian Worker*, 15 August 1934, p. 18.
2 'Well known experimenters', *The Daily Telegraph*, 11 March 1927, p. 4.
3 Garry Wotherspoon, 'Economy'; National Museum of Australia, 'Great Depression'.
4 'Dogs, cats, rabbits, ferrets, goldfish, etc.', *The Sydney Morning Herald*, 28 September 1933, p. 18.
5 F.V. McKenzie, 'Some interesting inhabitants of Sydney's seashores'.
6 'Her mascot "Plug-In" watches woman electrician', *The Sun (Final Extra)*, 14 June 1929, p. 14.
7 See, for example, the daily radio program listing in 'Broadcasting—February 4', *The Sydney Morning Herald*, 4 February 1932, p. 4. Other program listings at about the same time reveal that the title of Violet's fish show was not fixed, but seemed to change from week to week. An example of her appearing in the 2FC program appears in 'Broadcasting for today', *The Daily Telegraph*, 3 September 1934, p. 9. 'How to use your vacuum cleaner' can be seen listed in 'Broadcasting programmes for the week', *The Weekly Times* (Melbourne, Vic.), 25 August 1934, p. 2. Her 'Careers for women' show is mentioned in 'Mrs F.V. McKenzie', *The Australian Women's Weekly*, 3 March 1934, p. 32.
8 Louise Lansley & Islay Wybenga, 'Interview with Florence Violet McKenzie'.
9 'Woman engineer on the job; experimenting with television', *The Australian Women's Weekly*, 24 June 1933, p. 6.
10 'Careers for girls: radio offers wide field', *The Sun*, 1 February 1931, p. 1.
11 Advertisement, *The Sydney Morning Herald*, 28 February 1930, p. 18.
12 'Careers for girls: radio offers wide field,' *The Sun*, 1 February 1931, p. 1.
13 'Careers for girls: radio offers wide field,' *The Sun*, 1 February 1931, p. 1.
14 Advertisement, *The Sydney Morning Herald*, 1 April 1931, p. 26.
15 Neville Williams, 'Readers have their say: What about the "girls" in radio factories and offices?'.
16 'Wireless women: pioneers in the new profession for girls', *The Sun*, 12 June 1932, p. 24.
17 Paul Wallace, interview with David Dufty.
18 Catherine Freyne, 'McKenzie, Violet'; Paul Wallace, interview with David Dufty.

CHAPTER 8: THE ELECTRICAL ASSOCIATION FOR WOMEN

1 'Careers for girls: radio offers wide field', *The Sun*, 1 February 1931, p. 1.
2 'Vacuum cleaner had a loose screw', *The Evening News* (Rockhampton, Qld), 8 September 1931, p. 3.
3 'Safety first lectures (Better living)', *The Sun*, 12 July 1931, p. 2.
4 'Safety first lectures (Better living)', *The Sun*, 12 July 1931, p. 2.

269

5 'Washing machines', *The News* (Adelaide, SA), 17 July 1925, p. 10.
6 Wilfrid L. Randell, *Electricity and Woman*, pp. 19–20. On p. 25, Randell explains that the original name was 'Women's Electrical Association' (WEA), but this led to confusion with another prominent organisation in England at the time, the Workers' Educational Association, so the name was changed in order to create a unique abbreviation.
7 'Common sense and a screwdriver', *The Sun*, 3 May 1931, p. 34.
8 The event was reported in the news the next day, see: 'Distinguished Women, Feminist Club event', *The Sydney Morning Herald*, 31 March 1933, p. 5; confirmation that Violet was one of those honoured can be found in an article about a similar event held twenty years later: 'Lunch will honour Sydney women', *The Sunday Herald*, 22 February 1953, p. 23.
9 'A good servant: women and electricity', *The Courier Mail*, 26 October 1933, p. 20.
10 'A good servant: women and electricity,' *The Courier-Mail*, 26 October 1933, p. 20.
11 'Of interest to women', *The Sydney Mail*, 28 February 1934, p. 20; 'Social and personal', *The Sydney Morning Herald*, 27 October 1934, p. 9; 'New electrical teaching for women', *The Daily Telegraph*, 21 February 1934, p. 10.
12 'New electrical teaching for women', *The Daily Telegraph*, 21 February 1934, p. 10.
13 'Police called in: Electrical Exhibition: Pashometer causes crush', *The Sydney Morning Herald*, 10 March 1934, p. 15.
14 'Electrical association for women', *The Daily Telegraph*, 23 March 1934, p. 10.
15 'Electric equipment; better understanding needed', *The Examiner* (Launceston, Tas.), 1 March 1934, p. 10.
16 'A woman's letter', *The Bulletin*, 28 March 1934, p. 36; Meredith Foley, 'Littlejohn, Emma Linda Palmer (1883–1949)'; Bronwyn Hanna, 'Nosworthy, Ellice Maud (1897–1972)'; Carol Cantrell, 'David, Caroline Martha (Cara) (1856–1951)'.
17 'Electricity—proposed association', *The Sydney Morning Herald*, 13 October 1933, p. 4.
18 'A woman's letter', *The Bulletin*, 28 March 1934, p. 36.
19 Certificate of registration, 'The electrical Association for Women (Australia)', 22 March 1934, copy held in the archives of the Ex-WRANS Association, Spectacle Island.
20 'New electrical teaching for women', *The Daily Telegraph*, 21 February 1934, p. 10.
21 'Electrical association', *The Sydney Morning Herald*, 27 April 1934, p. 4.
22 'Members of the Electrical Association for Women', *The Sydney Morning Herald*, 3 May 1934, p. 6.
23 'Electricity costs: ten breakfasts for 1d', *The Sun*, 12 July 1934, p. 28.
24 'The life of Sydney', *The Daily Telegraph*, 2 August 1934, p. 10.

25 Catherine Freyne, 'McKenzie, Violet'; Barbara Small, 'A woman engineer wrote our first electric cook book'.
26 'More hours of leisure' *The Daily Telegraph*, 12 October 1934, p. 13.
27 'More hours of leisure', *The Daily Telegraph*, 12 October 1934, p. 13; Nikki Henningham, 'The United Associations of Women (1929–)'.
28 'A rich fruit cake', *The Sydney Morning Herald*, 29 November 1934, p. 15.
29 'Xmas luncheon: Electrical Association', *The Sun*, 12 December 1934, p. 25.
30 'Xmas luncheon: Electrical Association', *The Sun*, 12 December 1934, p. 25.
31 'Electrical association for women', *The Sydney Morning Herald*, 13 December 1934, p. 4.

CHAPTER 9: THE BODY ON THE LAWN

1   Mary Tallis, 'Health', *The Armidale Express and New England General Advertiser,* 23 December 1935, p. 7.
2   'Boy electrocuted', *The Sydney Morning Herald*, 28 November 1934, p. 13; 'Social and personal', *The Sydney Morning Herald*, 27 October 1934, p. 9
3   'Electrocuted', *Glen Innes Examiner*, 27 November 1934, p. 1.
4   'Flying to funeral—father's awful death', *The Weekly Times*, 8 December 1934, p. 15.
5   'Air dash to son's funeral', *The Sun*, 28 November 1934, p. 13; 'Dash to attend son's funeral—long trip by plane', *The News* (Adelaide, SA), 28 November 1934, p. 7.
6   'Flying to funeral—father's awful death', *The Weekly Times*, 8 December 1934, p. 15.
7   'Plane crash—father killed flying to son's funeral—down in wild country—double funeral', *Cootamundra Herald*, 30 November 1934, p. 1.
8   'Fatal air trip on way to son's funeral—crash in fog', *The Examiner* (Launceston, Tas.), 30 November 1934, p. 7.
9   'Plane crash—father killed flying to son's funeral—down in wild country—double funeral', *Cootamundra Herald,* 30 November 1934, p. 1.
10 'Flying to funeral—father's awful death', *The Weekly Times*, 8 December 1934, p. 15; 'Was shock—mourners at double funeral—father and son', *The Sun,* 29 November 1934, p. 36. The funeral was conducted by Reverend E. Hart, filling in for the parish minister, Reverend Ross, who was unavailable at the time. St Giles was the church that Violet attended in Greenwich. There are no records indicating whether she attended the funeral; I suspect that she did not.
11 'Switches should be inspected', *Labor Daily*, 11 December 1934, p. 7.
12 'Boy electrocuted—verdict of accidental death', *The National Advocate* (Bathurst, NSW), 11 December 1934, p. 2; 'Switches should be inspected', *Labor Daily*, 11 December 1934, p. 7.
13 'Girl electrocuted,' *The Sydney Morning Herald*, 10 December 1934, p. 9; 'Electrocuted,' *The Gloucester Advocate*, 14 December 1934, p. 3; 'Boy electrocuted', *The Scone Advocate*, 29 January 1935, p. 2; 'Electric shock: eighteen people die,' *Maitland Daily Mercury*, 23 January 1935, p. 2.

14 'Coroner caustic: dangerous electrical installations: need for inspections', *Newcastle Morning Herald and Miners' Advocate*, 13 December 1935, p. 18.
15 Lady Swaythling was born as Gladys Helen Rachel Goldsmid in Belfast on 4 December 1879. She married Louis Samuel Montagu, who held the British title of 2nd Baron Swaythling. After the death of Louis in 1927, she became known as 'The Dowager Lady Swaythling' and became active as a patron of charities and social causes.
16 'Electric shock—advice on resuscitation', *Cairns Post*, 25 January 1935, p. 14.

CHAPTER 10: COOKING WITH ELECTRICITY
1 Frances McKay, 'Foreword'.
2 'Crumbs', *Cootamundra Herald*, 6 June 1952, p. 2.
3 'The life of Sydney', *The Daily Telegraph*, 16 May 1935, p. 15.
4 Louise Lansley & Islay Wybenga, 'Interview with Florence Violet McKenzie'.
5 Barbara Small, 'A woman engineer wrote our first electric cook book'.
6 Barbara Small, 'A woman engineer wrote our first electric cook book'.
7 F.V. McKenzie, *Electrical Association for Women's Cookery Book*, p. 68.
8 F.V. McKenzie, *Electrical Association for Women's Cookery Book*, p. 65.
9 F.V. McKenzie, *Electrical Association for Women's Cookery Book*, p. 229.
10 F.V. McKenzie, *Electrical Association for Women's Cookery Book*, p. 10.
11 Rosemary Broomham, 'Florence Violet McKenzie'.
12 'Model kitchen,' *Labor Daily*, 19 November 1936, p. 11.
13 'By air from Melbourne', *The Sydney Morning Herald*, 5 November 1936, p. 20; 'A woman's letter', *The Bulletin*, 20 January 1937, p. 34; 'Model kitchen', *Labor Daily*, 19 November 1936, p. 11.
14 'From day to day in Sydney', *The Sydney Morning Herald*, 19 November 1936, p. 20.
15 Letter from Electricity Advisory Committee to Mrs F.V. McKenzie, 27 August 1936, held in the archives of the Ex-WRANS Association, Spectacle Island.
16 Louise Lansley & Islay Wybenga, 'Interview with Florence Violet McKenzie'.
17 F.V. McKenzie, *The Electric Imps*, p. 1.
18 Louise Lansley & Islay Wybenga, 'Interview with Florence Violet McKenzie'.

CHAPTER 11: THE AUSTRALIAN WOMEN'S FLYING CLUB
1 'Women in the air', *The Daily Telegraph*, 24 August 1938, p. 4.
2 An initial public meeting had taken place some weeks earlier, on Thursday evening, 7 July 1938, at the Feminist Club, at which Violet was placed on the interim committee; they met the following 12 July, and continued to meet at the EAW until the AGM in August. See 'From day to day in

Sydney', *The Sydney Morning Herald*, 8 July 1938, p. 5; '200 business girls join new women's flying corps', *Labor Daily*, 11 July 1938, p. 2; Michael Nelmes, 'McKenzie, Florence Violet (1890–1982)'; 'Women's flying club organised', *The Sun*, 10 July 1938, p. 9.

3   'Women's flying club: founder on objects', *The Sydney Morning Herald*, 24 August 1938, p. 7.

4   'Women as war birds if wanted', *The Sun*, 19 June 1938, p. 3.

5   'Thorby bars women aces', *Labor Daily*, 20 June 1938, p. 1.

6   William Hazlitt Jr, 'Why must women butt in?'

7   'Woman aviator—first solo flight—pilots a "Moth"', *The Sydney Morning Herald*, 8 February 1927, p. 11; 'First woman air pilot in Australia', *World's News* (Sydney, NSW), 12 March 1927, p. 9; 'Late Mrs. M.M. Bryant—tribute by Aero Club—wreath from the air', *The Sydney Morning Herald*, 7 November 1927, p. 12.

8   'B licence gained: Mrs Terry's long flight', *Goulburn Evening Penny Post*, 14 October 1930, p. 3; 'This week in town', *The Sydney Morning Herald*, 9 October 1947, p. 10.

9   'Miss Amy Johnson welcomed in Sydney', *Australasian*, 14 June 1930, p. 59.

10 'Women as war birds if wanted', *The Sun*, 19 June 1938, p. 3.

11 Margaret Kentley, 'Women's war services' (in MSS0796, 'Kentley, Margaret').

12 Margaret Kentley, 'Women's war services' (in MSS0796, 'Kentley, Margaret').

13 'Women's Flying Club's first general meeting', *The Sydney Morning Herald*, 24 August 1938, p. 16.

14 'Australian Women's Flying Corps activities', *The Sydney Morning Herald*, 15 February 1939, p. 18.

15 'Teaches girls radio and Morse code', *The Australian Women's Weekly*, 4 March 1939, p. 22.

16 Department of Information on behalf of the Council for Women in War Work, *Australian Women at War, 1939–?*, p. 15.

17 The Women's Emergency Signalling Corps never existed as a legal or regulatory entity. Violet created it as 'an activity of the Electrical Association for Women'. From a legal standpoint, it was really just the EAW dressed in different clothes.

CHAPTER 12: THE WOMEN'S EMERGENCY SIGNALLING CORPS

1   Margaret Curtis-Otter, *W.R.A.N.S.: The Women's Royal Australian Naval Service*, p. 3.

2   'Thousands cheer Mr Chamberlain,' *The Argus*, 3 October 1938, p. 13.

3   Professor S.H. Roberts, 'Merely a truce—Germany is Europe's master', *Sydney Mail*, 5 October 1938, pp. 8–9.

4   Greg Flynn, 'Thank you Mrs Mac'.

5 'Mrs Mac is truly special', *Reveille*, April 1979, p. 13.
6 Michael Nelmes, 'McKenzie, Florence Violet (1890–1982)'.
7 'Women's Emergency Signalling Corps', *The Sydney Morning Herald*, 4 May 1939, p. 24.
8 'Teaching the Morse code just in case', *The Sun*, 14 April 1939, p. 9.
9 Marie Davis (nee Munns), interview with David Dufty.
10 'A woman's letter', *The Bulletin*, 7 February 1940, p. 32.
11 'Women's war work', *The Sydney Morning Herald*, 29 August 1940, p. 16 (the model arm is shown in a photograph next to the article, with an explanatory caption under the image); 'Women in uniform', *The Sun* (Section 3), 23 June 1940, p. 1. The 'model arm' was shown to the media a couple of times in 1940, but was not an ongoing part of her teaching system, and seems to have only been used by Violet a small number of times. It was an experimental teaching idea that wasn't as effective as she had hoped, so she moved on.
12 'Women's Emergency Signalling Corps', *The Sydney Morning Herald*, 4 May 1939, p. 24.
13 AWM S00547, '(WR/5) Stevens, Marion', p. 3.
14 'What mother did in the great war', *The Newcastle Sun*, 19 September 1939, p. 3.
15 'What mother did in the great war', *The Newcastle Sun*, 19 September 1939, p. 3.
16 'What mother did in the great war', *The Newcastle Sun*, 19 September 1939, p. 3.
17 Jean Nysen (nee McKenzie), interview with David Dufty.
18 Jean Nysen (nee McKenzie), interview with David Dufty.
19 A copy of the lyrics were provided to me by Joan Henstock.
20 Richard Begbie, 'The metamorphosis of Miss Wallace'.
21 Alison Armstrong, *Oral History*.
22 Richard Begbie, 'The metamorphosis of Miss Wallace'.
23 Moira Millgate, 'According to Galileo'.
24 Richard Begbie, 'The metamorphosis of Miss Wallace'.
25 Catherine Freyne, *Signals, Currents, and Wires: The untold story of Florence Violet McKenzie*.
26 Moira Millgate, 'According to Galileo'.

CHAPTER 13: A SENSE OF RHYTHM

1 Gloria Newton, 'Ex-WRANS plan get-together for 30th Anniversary'.
2 'Women's signal corps invites volunteers', *Wireless Weekly*, 30 December 1939, p. 5.
3 'Army may adopt girls' Morse method', *The Daily Telegraph*, 22 December 1939, p. 6.
4 'Army may adopt girls' Morse method', *The Daily Telegraph*, 22 December 1939, p. 6.

5　'Women also serve', *The Australian Women's Weekly*, 13 January 1940, p. 30.
6　'Wants girls in army as signallers', *The Daily Telegraph*, 21 December 1939, p. 1.
7　'Army may adopt girls' Morse method', *The Daily Telegraph*, 22 December 1939, p. 6.
8　'Not practicable', *The Maitland Daily Mercury*, 22 December 1939, p. 1.
9　'Dot and dash—girls at signals', *The Sun*, 29 February 1940, p. 25.
10　'Girls signalling corps stages first parade', *The Daily Telegraph*, 31 January 1940, p. 5; 'Girl signallers smart on March', *The Daily Telegraph*, 31 January 1940, p. 1.
11　'Nationwide action required—ensuring soldiers' jobs', *The Herald* (Melbourne, Vic.), 21 December 1939, p. 7; 'Women taking jobs?', *The Sunday Times* (Perth, WA), 19 November 1939, p. 3.
12　'Signalling corps', *The Sydney Morning Herald*, 9 April 1940, p. 4.
13　'Girls signalling corps stages first parade', *The Daily Telegraph*, 31 January 1940, p. 5.
14　'Women's emergency signals corps', *The Sydney Morning Herald*, 14 February 1940, p. 6.
15　'Dot and dash, girls at signals', *The Sun*, 29 February 1940, p. 25.
16　'Dot and dash, girls at signals', *The Sun*, 29 February 1940, p. 25.
17　'A woman's letter', *The Bulletin*, 7 February 1940, p. 32.
18　'Sergeant-major drilled signallers, and praised their work: faces meant nothing to him', clipping from unknown newspaper given to the author by Joan Henstock.
19　'Sergeant-major drilled signallers, and praised their work: faces meant nothing to him,' clipping from unknown newspaper given to the author by Joan Henstock.
20　'Signalling test', *The Sydney Morning Herald*, 5 March 1940, p. 4.

CHAPTER 14: WOMEN IN UNIFORM

1　'Girl signallers will help', *The Australian Women's Weekly*, 13 July 1940, p. 2.
2　'Women in uniform—our air girls and signallers', *The Sydney Morning Herald, Women's Supplement*, 26 March 1940, pp. 6–7.
3　'Crude beds at women's camp', *The Daily News*, 26 March 1940, p. 6.
4　'Camp for girls—military but feminine', *The Sun*, 21 March 1940, p. 3.
5　'Dot and dash, girls at signals', *The Sun*, 29 February 1940, p. 25.
6　'Camp for girls—military but feminine', *The Sun*, 21 March 1940, p. 3.
7　'Women in uniform—our air girls and signallers', *The Sydney Morning Herald, Women's Supplement*, 26 March 1940, pp. 6–7; 'Women signallers prepare for national emergency in four days training camp', *The Sunday Sun and Guardian*, 24 March 1940, p. 6.
8　'Choose a wife who does signal service', *The Daily Telegraph*, 26 March 1940, p. 6.

9 'Punishment will make girl signallers cry', *The Daily Telegraph*, 23 March 1940, p. 5.

10 'Punishment will make girl signallers cry', *The Daily Telegraph*, 23 March 1940, p. 5.

11 'Women in uniform—our air girls and signallers', *The Sydney Morning Herald, Women's Supplement*, 26 March 1940, pp. 6–7.

12 The oft-quoted figure of 27,000 deaths does not include the 8000 Australians who died as prisoners of war, which is a terrible oversight.

13 'How you can help win the war', *The Australian Women's Weekly*, 1 June 1940, p. 32.

14 'How you can help win the war', *The Australian Women's Weekly*, 1 June 1940, p. 32.

15 'Learn rifle shooting', *The Sun,* 23 June 1940, p. 1; 'Women in uniform', *The Sun* (Section 3), 23 June 1940, p. 1.

16 'Big array in women's war workers' army: still room for more', *The Telegraph* (Brisbane, Qld), 6 June 1940, p. 8.

17 'How you can help win the war', *The Australian Women's Weekly*, 1 June 1940, p. 32.

18 A WESC examination paper in the Papers of Esme Kurrell (AWM PR00822) tested a range of engineering and science concepts around circuits and electrical theory. Kurrell's papers also contain a practice sheet for letter–number encrypted message groups.

19 'How you can help win the war', *The Australian Women's Weekly*, 1 June 1940, p. 32.

CHAPTER 15: THE WOOLSHED

1 Patrice Dow, *Oral History.*

2 Alison Armstrong (in *Oral History*) says WESC occupied three floors. Other sources say two.

3 'Mrs McKenzie—the woman at the top', *Smith's Weekly*, 5 June 1943, p. 11.

4 Florence McKenzie, 'The Women's Emergency Signalling Corps'.

5 Florence McKenzie, 'The Women's Emergency Signalling Corps'.

6 Florence McKenzie, 'The Women's Emergency Signalling Corps'.

7 'Mascot for girl signallers', *The Daily Telegraph*, 2 June 1940, p. 37; 'Mascot rivals', *The Daily Telegraph*, 15 August 1940, p. 2.

8 Matthew Glozier, *75 Years Aloft: Royal Australian Air Force Air Training Corps: Australian air force cadets*, p. 7; Anzac portal special features, 'A lark on the wing'.

9 Catherine Freyne, *Signals, Currents, and Wires.*

10 AWM S00593, 'WR/21 Starr (previously Blair), Heather Stella (Leading Telegraphist)'.

11 See for example, 'Women's war organisations, orders of the day' in *The Sun, Women's Section*, 14 July 1940, p. 6, which invites women members

to attend 10 Clarence Street, while instructing male RAAF recruits and members of signal units to attend 9 Clarence Street.

12 'Women in uniform', *The Sun* (Section 3), 23 June 1940, p. 1.

13 'Sydney women's efforts in wartime service yesterday', *The Sydney Morning Herald*, 29 August 1940, p. 13.

14 'Rehearsing for revue', *The Sydney Morning Herald*, 29 July 1940, p. 3; 'War work', *The Sun*, 26 July 1940, p. 8.

15 'War dressings for Greeks', *The Sydney Morning Herald*, 20 February 1941, p. 15.

16 'Girls train boy signallers: "lobsterburger" is good word for code', *The Sun*, 3 July 1940, p. 9.

17 'Girls train boy signallers: "lobsterburger" is good word for code', *The Sun*, 3 July 1940, p. 9.

18 Reverend J.R. Henderson, 'Eulogy'.

19 'Women in uniform', *The Sun* (Section 3), 23 June 1940, p. 1; 'Girl signallers test R.A.A.F. recruits', *Pix*, 31 August 1940, pp. 32–3.

20 'Signalling—emergency corps—valuable service', *The Inverell Times*, 22 April 1942, p. 3.

21 The exact date that 9 Clarence Street was vacated isn't known; based on news references and advertisements for WESC, it seems to have been about September 1940, but could have been a month or so after that. Despite ceasing activities under its own name, the Electrical Association for Women continued to exist on paper as a registered association, because Violet had used it as a mechanism to establish the Women's Emergency Signalling Corps.

22 'Signal girls in camp, ready to aid the navy', *The Sunday Sun and Guardian, Women's Section*, 19 January 1941, p. 1.

23 'Signal girls in camp, ready to aid the navy', *The Sunday Sun and Guardian, Women's Section*, 19 January 1941, p. 1.

24 'WESC Programme', in AWM PR00822.

25 'Women signallers ready to aid the navy', *The Sunday Sun*, 19 January 1941 (unknown page). This is a newspaper cutting provided to me bv Joan Henstock. The content is different to the article on the National Library of Australia's Trove service, 'Signal girls in camp, ready to aid the navy', *The Sunday Sun and Guardian, Women's Section*, 19 January 1941, p. 1. The letter referred to here is not in the online version.

26 Patrice Dow, *Oral History*.

CHAPTER 16: WOMEN FOR THE AIR FORCE

1 Geoffrey Hutton, 'Women are now entering the army proper', *The Argus, Weekend Magazine* (Melbourne, Vic.), 16 May 1942, p. 1.

2 'Gatherings in southern capitals', *The Evening News* (Rockhampton, Qld), 4 September 1940, p. 7; 'Women parade in uniform', *The Sun*, 3 September 1940, p. 9; 'Fighting units in Sydney's biggest war rally today', *The Daily*

Telegraph, 3 September 1940, p. 4. *The Courier-Mail* covered the Brisbane
rally in the article 'War rally attended by 20,000', *The Courier-Mail* (Brisbane,
Qld), 4 September 1940, p. 3, and 'Anniversary war rally', *The Courier-Mail*,
4 September 1940, p. 1. The march in Adelaide was reported in 'Fine cere-
monial parade', *The Murray Pioneer and Australian River Record* (Renmark,
SA), 5 September 1940, p. 13.

3   'Women parade in uniform', *The Sun*, 3 September 1940, p. 9.

4   'Eight more attacks on London area', *The Argus* (Melbourne, Vic.),
2 September 1940, p. 1.

5   'Cold blooded massacre of boy scouts', *The Sun*, 16 May 1940, p. 3; 'Jews
interned in Italy', *The Newcastle Sun*, 22 June 1940, p. 6; 'Dachau horrors',
The Sydney Morning Herald, 11 May 1940, p. 10; 'The refugee question',
Cootamundra Herald, 8 August 1940, p. 3.

6   NAA: A595, 735/1, 'Summaries of the decision of the war cabinet', 29 June
1940, p. 51.

7   'R.A.A.F. wants wireless operators', *The Sydney Morning Herald*,
20 November 1940, p. 12.

8   NAA: A2673, VOLUME 3, '295: Minutes of war cabinet, 11 July 1940',
p. 49.

9   NAA: 'Canberra air disaster, 1940—Fact sheet 142'.

10 NAA: A595, 735/1, 'Summaries of the decision of the war cabinet', 29 June
1940, p. 16.

11 AWM ORMF0016, 'History of the WAAAF Part I: Formation', p. 92.

12 AWM ORMF0016, 'History of the WAAAF Part I: Formation', p. 93.

13 NAA: A2679, A2679/1, 'Advisory War Council Minute 63', 8 January
1941.

14 Joyce Thomson, *The WAAAF in Wartime Australia*, p. 66.

15 Joyce Thomson, *The WAAAF in Wartime Australia*, p. 78.

16 AWM 93, 50/2/23/781, 'Notes on formation and organisation of WATC
and WAAAF', pp. 5, 8.

CHAPTER 17: THE ARMS OF THE NAVY

1   Lieutenant Commander Andrew Stackpole, 'Navy women celebrate
70 years of proud history', *Navy News*, 2011, p. 20.

2   'Radio men needed by navy', *The Sydney Morning Herald*, 24 December
1940, p. 6. See also for example a briefer report in 'Telegraphists needed for
navy', *The Sun*, 23 December 1940, p. 3.

3   Iris Dexter, 'Their third year aboard'.

4   Joan Henstock, *Women of the Royal Australian Navy, Part One*, p. 29.

5   Joan Henstock, *Women of the Royal Australian Navy, Part One*, p. 30.

6   Louise Lansley & Islay Wybenga, 'Interview with Florence Violet
McKenzie'.

7   NAA: A2585, 1939/1941/REFERENCE COPY, 'Naval Board Minutes',
30 January 1941.

8   Shirley Fenton Huie, *Ships Belles*, p. 21.
9   'W.R.A.N.S. "Mother"', *Navy News*, 24 April 1962, p. 1.
10 Greg Flynn, 'Thank you Mrs Mac'.
11 'Women ready to serve', *The Sydney Morning Herald*, 26 February 1941, p. 12.
12 Commonwealth of Australia, House of Representatives, *Hansard*, 1941, vol. 13, 25 March 1941, pp. 149–50.
13 Commonwealth of Australia, House of Representatives, *Hansard*, 1941, vol. 13, 25 March 1941, pp. 149–50.
14 'Trainees for WAAAF, small Sydney quota: only five pass', *The Sun*, 25 March 1941, p. 10.
15 'Trainees for WAAAF, small Sydney quota: only five pass', *The Sun*, 25 March 1941, p. 10.
16 'Trainees for WAAAF, small Sydney quota: only five pass', *The Sun*, 25 March 1941, p. 10.
17 'Girl signallers to join navy, says director', *The Sun*, *Women's Section*, 30 March 1941, p. 1. The article erroneously referred to WESC as the 'Women's Emergency Signallers Corps'. I have taken the liberty of correcting the mistake in the text.
18 Commonwealth of Australia, House of Representatives, *Hansard*, 1941, vol. 14, 1 April 1941, p. 382.
19 Commonwealth of Australia, House of Representatives, *Hansard*, 1941, vol. 14, 1 April 1941, p. 382.

CHAPTER 18: HARMAN

1   Margaret Curtis-Otter, *W.R.A.N.S.*, p. 29.
2   NAA: A663, O130/1/781, 'Memorandum to the chairman of the manpower committee, 21 April 1941'; Margaret Curtis-Otter, *W.R.A.N.S.*, p. 4.
3   'W.R.A.N.S. "Mother"', *Navy News*, 24 April 1962, p. 1.
4   AWM S00547, '(WR/5) Stevens, Marion', p. 4.
5   AWM S00547, '(WR/5) Stevens, Marion', p. 11.
6   'W.R.A.N.S. comes of age', *Navy News*, 24 April 1962, p. 1.
7   Shirley Fenton Huie, *Ships Belles*, p. 45.
8   Shirley Fenton Huie, *Ships Belles*, p. 45.
9   'W.R.A.N.S. "Mother"', *Navy News*, 24 April 1962, p. 1.
10 Marion Stevens (AWM S00547, '[WR/5] Stevens, Marion') and Alison Armstrong (in Alison Armstrong, *Oral History*) both refer to a Petty Officer Pennyquick in their respective oral histories (Stevens' was done by the Australian War Memorial, Armstrong's by the NSW 'Australians at war' project). Armstrong said that they were looked after by voluntary defence corps (VDC) men, who were too old for service. The only service record by that name that appears in a search of the National Archives of Australia is an army record for Grieve Pennyquick of the Citizens Military Services, who we can confidently conclude is the same person as the petty officer at Harman.

11 AWM S00547, '(WR/5) Stevens, Marion', p. 14.

12 Alison Armstrong, *Oral History*; AWM S00547, '(WR/5) Stevens, Marion', p. 14.

13 AWM S00547, '(WR/5) Stevens, Marion', pp. 12–13.

14 AWM S00547, '(WR/5) Stevens, Marion', p. 17. The story about Pennyquick's Morse lesson comes from these recollections by Marion Stevens.

15 Bureau of Naval Personnel (United States), 'Radioman 3 & 2, Navpapers 102278-D', p. 97.

16 AWM S00547, '(WR/5) Stevens, Marion', p. 17.

17 'W.R.A.N.S. comes of age', *Navy News*, 24 April 1962, p. 1.

18 AWM S00547, '(WR/5) Stevens, Marion', p. 19.

19 AWM S00547, '(WR/5) Stevens, Marion', p. 20.

20 'A WRANS pioneer recalls struggle to convince men', *The Sydney Morning Herald*, 22 September 1986, p. 7.

21 Joint Standing Committee on Foreign Affairs, Defence and Trade, *The Loss of HMAS Sydney*, p. 180.

22 Joint Standing Committee on Foreign Affairs, Defence and Trade, *The Loss of HMAS Sydney*, pp. 51–3.

23 Jess Doyle (nee Prain), 'Talk given by Jess Doyle to Waverley Rotary club', May 1984, held in the Ex-WRANS archive, Spectacle Island.

CHAPTER 19: AN SOS FROM MARY BELL

1 Douglas Gillison, *Second World War Official Histories—Australia in the War of 1939–1945, Series 3—Air*, p. 99.

2 Douglas Gillison, *Second World War Official Histories, Series 3*, p. 100.

3 AWM 93, 50/2/23/781, 'Notes on formation and organisation of WATC and WAAAF', p. 6.

4 This incident is described by Mary Bell in AWM 93, 50/2/23/781, 'Notes on formation and organisation of WATC and WAAAF'. The data supplied to the Advisory War Council was most likely that reported in NAA A2679, A2679/1, 'Supplement No. 4 to Agendum 1/1940, Formation of Women's Auxiliary to Royal Australian Air Force, 14 May 1941'.

5 Numerous sources state that Violet was awarded the rank of flight officer. One example of many is the article 'Mrs Mac is truly special', *Reveille*, April 1979, p. 13.

6 AWM S00416, 'Air Vice Marshal Henry Neilson Wrigley'.

7 AWM S00416, 'Air Vice Marshal Henry Neilson Wrigley', p. 27.

8 AWM 93, 50/2/23/781, 'Notes on formation and organisation of WATC and WAAAF', p. 11.

9 Douglas Gillison, *Second World War Official Histories, Series 3*, p. 100; Joyce Thomson, *The WAAAF in Wartime Australia*, p. 92; AWM 93, 50/2/23/781, 'Notes on formation and organisation of WATC and WAAAF', p. 12.

CHAPTER 20: THE NEXT EIGHT

1 Margaret Curtis-Otter, *W.R.A.N.S.*, p. 5.
2 Shirley Fenton Huie, *Ships Belles*, p. 170; Louise Lansley & Islay Wybenga, 'Interview with Florence Violet McKenzie'.
3 Louise Lansley & Islay Wybenga, 'Interview with Florence Violet McKenzie'.
4 'Travellers' Aid Society's new quarters', *The Argus* (Melbourne, Vic.), 14 March 1940, p. 10.
5 AWM S00593, 'WR/21 Starr (previously Blair), Heather Stella (Leading Telegraphist)', p. 7.
6 Joan Henstock, *Women of the Royal Australian Navy, Part One*, p. 38.
7 AWM S00593, 'WR/21 Starr (previously Blair), Heather Stella (Leading Telegraphist)',p. 7.
8 AWM S00593, 'WR/21 Starr (previously Blair), Heather Stella (Leading Telegraphist)'; Joan Henstock, *Women of the Royal Australian Navy, Part One*, p. 39.
9 Jo Miller, 'Personal memories of Mrs Mac, 1939–1982'.

CHAPTER 21: MUSICAL MORSE

1 Cassandra Mohapp, 'The Rhythm of Life', p. 72.
2 Louise Lansley & Islay Wybenga, 'Interview with Florence Violet McKenzie'.
3 Louise Lansley & Islay Wybenga, 'Interview with Florence Violet McKenzie'.
4 Cassandra Mohapp, 'The Rhythm of Life', p. 61.
5 'Signal girls in camp; ready to aid the navy', *The Sunday Sun and Guardian, Women's Section*, 19 January 1941, p. 1.
6 'The lady at the top', *Smith's Weekly*, 5 June 1943, p. 11.
7 Jean Nysen (nee McKenzie), interview with David Dufty.
8 AWM S00547, '(WR/5) Stevens, Marion', p. 5.
9 Alison Armstrong, *Oral History*.
10 Catherine Freyne, *Signals, Currents, and Wires*.
11 Catherine Freyne, *Signals, Currents, and Wires*.
12 'Girls in Morse orchestra: new system speeds up telegraphists' training,' *Daily Telegraph*, 14 August 1941, p. 8.
13 'The lady at the top', *Smith's Weekly*, 5 June 1943, p. 11.
14 Gwenda Garde, interview with David Dufty.
15 Gwenda Garde, interview with David Dufty.
16 Gwenda Garde, interview with David Dufty.
17 Alison Armstrong, *Oral History*.

CHAPTER 22: THE GENERAL AND MRS MCKENZIE

1 'Lady Wakehurst at signal rooms', *The Sun*, 22 June 1941, p. 21.
2 'Women's job not in army', *The Mercury* (Hobart, Tas.), 21 November 1941, p. 4; 'Women and war: military training a waste of time', *The Canberra Times*, 21 November 1941, p. 4.
3 NAA: A663, O130/4/134, 'Letter from Chairman to Violet McKenzie'.

4 'Women's emergency signalling corps', *The Sydney Morning Herald*, 4 May 1939, p. 24.

5 'Blamey rouses ire of women in Sydney', *The Sunday Sun and Guardian*, 23 November 1941, p. 11. The article misquoted her as referring to her organisation as the 'Women's Emergency Signallers' Corps'. As it's inconceivable that Violet made such an error herself, I have taken the liberty of correcting the mistake in the quotation here.

6 'Women's job not in army', *The Mercury* (Hobart, Tas.), 21 November 1941, p. 4.

7 NAA: A5954, 768/8, 'Book (Original) Chapter 3—General BLAMEY'S Visit to Australia'.

8 'More recruits, more machines', *Barrier Daily Truth* (Broken Hill, NSW), 12 November 1941, p. 1; 'General Blamey attacks A.R.P.', *The Sydney Morning Herald*, 19 November 1941, p. 6; 'Blamey hits out at lavish A.R.P.', *The Dubbo Liberal and Macquarie Advocate*, 25 November 1941, p. 1.

9 'Blamey reproaches civilians: astounded by "carnival life"', *The Daily Telegraph*, 11 November 1941, p. 2.

10 'The Blamey Papers, No. 8', *The Argus* (Melbourne, Vic.), 7 December 1953, p. 7.

11 'Diggers criticise General Blamey', *The Newcastle Sun*, 17 November 1941, p. 1.

12 'Women's use of uniform—services protected', *The Sydney Morning Herald*, 21 November 1941, p. 6.

13 'Sydney women not perturbed', *The Sydney Morning Herald*, 22 November 1941, p. 12.

14 'Sydney women not perturbed', *The Sydney Morning Herald*, 22 November 1941, p. 12.

15 'Sydney women not perturbed', *The Sydney Morning Herald*, 22 November 1941, p. 12.

16 'Women's uniforms mustn't copy those of forces', *The Sun*, 28 November 1941, p. 2. While it largely occupied the same political space as the modern 'coalition' in Australian political life, the Menzies–Fadden coalition comprised the United Australia Party and the Country Party.

17 'Women's uniforms mustn't copy those of forces', *The Sun*, 28 November 1941, p. 2.

18 For example, a nineteen-year-old man was prosecuted in June 1941 for illegally wearing a uniform ('Wants to see war—youth illegally wore uniform', *The National Advocate* [Bathurst, NSW], 6 June 1941, p. 2).

CHAPTER 23: HARBOUR INTRUDERS

1 John Perryman, 'Japanese Midget Submarine Attack on Sydney Harbour'.

2 NAA: 'United States forces in Queensland, 1941–45—Fact sheet 234'.

3 Aubrey A. Yawitz, *Interview*.

4 Norman Ellison, 'Magnificent Mrs Mac'.

5 'U.S. praise for girl signallers', *The Sun*, 20 April 1942, p. 6.
6 Gloria Newton, 'Ex-WRANS plan get-together for 30th Anniversary'.
7 AWM 188, 42, 'Norman. NAP'; AWM P01612, 'Memoirs of the Naval Auxiliary Patrol'.
8 'Social and personal', *The Sydney Morning Herald*, 11 November 1937, p. 21.
9 NAA: SP338/1, 555/10, 'Applications for Enrolment—Naval Auxiliary Patrol', p. 156.
10 NAA: MP1049/5, 2026/21/79, '[Midget submarine attack on Sydney harbour]', pp. 38, 45.

CHAPTER 24: CORVETTES
1 Jean Nysen (nee McKenzie), interview with David Dufty.
2 'Sydney building corvette for Indian navy', *The Kyogle Examiner*, 14 October 1941, p. 3; 'Australia builds for Indian navy', *The Newcastle Sun*, 17 February 1942, p. 3; Florence McKenzie, 'The Women's Emergency Signalling Corps'.
3 Jean Nysen (nee McKenzie), interview with David Dufty.
4 AWM 012815, 'Photo shows luncheon after launching HMIS *Bengal*. The ceremony was performed by Mrs Curtin, wife of the prime minister'. 'Peg' was Peg Hollier.
5 Jan Visser, 'The Ondina-battle'; R.D. Middleton, 'Time must have dimmed the memories of "Ondina" men'; Jan F.A. Ressing, 'The battle of the "Ondina"—time did not dim memories'; 'Japanese raider sent to bottom of Indian Ocean', *The Northern Star* (Lismore, NSW), 27 November 1942, p. 1; 'The little ships at war', *The News* (Adelaide, SA), 28 June 1946, p. 2.
6 'Senator's daughter as instructor', *The Sun*, 12 March 1942, p. 8.
7 NAA: A6770, Ashley V M; NAA: A6770, McKenzie J J.

CHAPTER 25: THE LADY AT THE TOP
1 'The lady at the top', *Smith's Weekly*, 5 June 1943, p. 11.
2 Gwenda Southcombe, 'Home, home on the range: degaussing'; Shirley Fenton Huie, *Ships Belles*, p. 212; NAA: A6770, Kingsford-Smith S M; NAA: A6770, Cornwallis G M.
3 'The lady at the top', *Smith's Weekly*, 5 June 1943, p. 11.
4 'Signallers still needed', *The Daily Telegraph*, 19 October 1943, p. 8. The article erroneously referred to WESC as the 'Women's Emergency Signallers Corps'. I have corrected the mistake in the text.
5 'A woman's notebook—signallers SOS', *The Sun*, 10 February 1944, p. 6.
6 'U.S. sailors taught signalling', *The Sydney Morning Herald*, 14 September 1944, p. 6; 'U.S. sailors at signals school', undated newspaper clipping estimated to be from 1944, held by NSW Ex-WRANS archives, North Richmond, New South Wales.
7 'SOS answered personally', *The Sun*, 6 March 1945, p. 8.
8 'Signalling from woman', *The Sun*, 1 June 1945, p. 8.

CHAPTER 26: PEACETIME

1 'Mr. Chifley makes announcement', *The Canberra Times*, 16 August 1945, p. 4.
2 Marie Davis (nee Munns), interview with David Dufty.
3 Marie Davis (nee Munns), interview with David Dufty.
4 Marie Davis (nee Munns), interview with David Dufty.
5 'Some souvenirs from Tobruk,' *The Sun*, 9 March 1941, p. 5.
6 Marjorie Wingate, 'Notes for the war workers', *The Sunday Sun and Guardian, Women's Section*, 25 May 1941, p. 5.
7 'Promises flag for signallers', *The Sun*, 21 January 1942, p. 6.
8 'News of members', *The Woman Engineer* (London), March 1942, p. 159.
9 'A woman's notebook—Celebes souvenir', *The Sun*, 24 October 1944, p. 8; 'U.S. map for women signallers', *The Sun*, 29 April 1942, p. 6.
10 'Novel lamp for signallers' "museum corner",' *The Sun*, 16 July 1943, p. 5.
11 'Novel lamp for signallers' "museum corner",' *The Sun*, 16 July 1943, p. 5.
12 Margaret Curtis-Otter, *W.R.A.N.S.*, p. 5; Michael Nelmes, 'McKenzie, Florence Violet (1890–1982)'; Ann Heywood, 'McKenzie, Florence Violet (1890–1982)'.
13 'Women signallers' post-war plan—to open provident fund for members', *The Sun*, 15 December 1941, p. 6.
14 'Planning for future', *The Sun*, 16 February 1943, p. 6.
15 'U.S. sailors taught signalling', *The Sydney Morning Herald*, 14 September 1944, p. 6.
16 Florence McKenzie, 'The Women's Emergency Signalling Corps'.
17 'Sigs chief in peace job', *The Sun*, 10 February 1946, p. 10.
18 Barbara Small, 'A woman engineer wrote our first electric cook book'; Richard Begbie, 'The metamorphosis of Miss Wallace'.
19 'A Dot with a Dash', *People*, 28 January 1953, p. 23.
20 Résumé of F.V. McKenzie's achievements prepared by the Ex-WRANS Association, document held in the Ex-WRANS archive, Spectacle Island.
21 Letter from A.R. Gray to Jess Prain, 31 July 1987, document held in the Ex-WRANS archive, Spectacle Island.
22 Norman Ellison, 'Magnificent Mrs Mac'.
23 Norman Ellison, 'Magnificent Mrs Mac'.
24 'Aircrew licences issued to Florence Violet McKenzie', Commonwealth of Australia Department of Civil Aviation, 1948, copy held in the Ex-WRANS archive, Spectacle Island.
25 The journalist was Catherine Freyne, who was researching Violet McKenzie for an ABC radio documentary about her called *Signals, Currents, and Wires*.
26 'Radio girl seeks job in air', *The Sun*, 27 June 1948, p. 30.
27 Nan Phillips, 'Bayldon, Francis Joseph (1872–1948)'.
28 Mark Sunter, interview with David Dufty.
29 Nan Phillips, 'Bayldon, Francis Joseph (1872–1948)'.
30 'Mrs Mac's services', *The Sun*, 17 August 1948, p. 9.
31 'Mrs Mac's thanks', *The Sun*, 20 August 1948, p. 9.

CHAPTER 27: EINSTEIN'S CORRESPONDENT

1 'What life means to Einstein', *The Saturday Evening Post* (Illinois, USA), 26 October 1929, p. 113.

2 The Einstein archives are accessible through the website <alberteinstein. info.> (Einstein's letters to Violet are lost—the only record of their correspondence are her letters to him, held in the Albert Einstein Archives at the Hebrew University in Jerusalem.)

3 Catherine Freyne, *Signals, Currents, and Wires.*

4 'Old Aboriginal instrument for Einstein', *The Sydney Morning Herald*, 4 November 1949, p. 2.

5 'Prof Einstein puzzled by the didgeridoo', *The Sun*, 10 February 1950, p. 12.

6 'Prof Einstein puzzled by the didgeridoo', *The Sun*, 10 February 1950, p. 12.

7 'Prof Einstein puzzled by the didgeridoo', *The Sun*, 10 February 1950, p. 12.

8 'Stay at our house, says Prof Einstein', *The Daily Telegraph*, 15 March 1953, p. 13.

9 'Stay at our house, says Prof Einstein', *The Daily Telegraph*, 15 March 1953, p. 13.

CHAPTER 28: HONOURS

1 'Career woman trains signallers', *The Sun*, 17 August 1952, p. 46.

2 'Woman thrilled by honors', *The Sun*, 8 June 1950, p. 7. An undated variation of this article, titled 'Women thrilled with birthday list honours', is held in the Ex-WRANS archive, Spectacle Island.

3 Commonwealth of Australia, *Gazette* (no. 35), 22 June 1950, p. 1493; 'Knighthoods to 11 Australians—King's Birthday Honours list', *The Age* (Melbourne, Vic.), 8 June 1950, p. 1.

4 Letter from governor-general to Florence Violet McKenzie, dated 13 May 1950, document held in the Ex-WRANS archive, Spectacle Island.

5 'Congratulations', *The Daily Telegraph*, 15 June 1950, p. 26.

6 'Woman engineer receives OBE', *Radio and Hobbies*, July 1950, p. 9.

7 'All-electric cookery book', *The Advertiser* (Adelaide, SA), 15 June 1950, p. 11.

8 Jo Miller, 'Personal memories of Mrs Mac, 1939–1982'.

9 NAA: A463, 1959/3374, 'Mrs F McKenzie—Honours'.

10 NAA: A6769, Cowie J.

11 Florence Violet McKenzie, Fellow Certificate, Australian Institute of Navigation, document held in the Ex-WRANS archive, Spectacle Island.

12 'Career woman trains signallers', *The Sun*, 17 August 1952, p. 46.

CHAPTER 29: OUT OF THE WOOLSHED

1 Patricia McKinnon, 'A woman taught these men their signals'.

2 'A Dot with a Dash', *People*, 28 January 1953, p. 23.

3 'A Dot with a Dash', *People*, 28 January 1953, p. 23.

4 Michael Nelmes, 'McKenzie, Florence Violet (1890–1982)'.

5 'Column 8', *The Sydney Morning Herald*, 2 October 1952, p. 1.

6   NAA: A705, 151/4/124, 'Minute, Secretary Air', 16 October 1952.
7   NAA: A705, 151/4/124, 'Minute, Secretary Air', 16 October 1952.
8   NAA: A705, 151/4/124, 'Minute, Secretary Air', 16 October 1952.
9   NAA: A705, 151/4/124, 'Minute, Secretary Air', 16 October 1952.
10 NAA: A705, 151/4/124, 'Minute, Secretary Air', 16 October 1952.
11 NAA: A705, 151/4/124, 'Minute Sheet', 24 October 1952.
12 NAA: A705, 151/4/124, 'Minute Sheet', 24 October 1952.
13 D. McNeill, 'Other memories of Mrs Mac'. Violet herself says that she continued the school for nine years after the end of the war.
14 Patricia McKinnon, 'A woman taught these men their signals'.
15 D. McNeill, 'Other memories of Mrs Mac'.
16 'Mrs Mac is truly special', Reveille, April 1979, p. 13. To put that in a modern context, 15 shillings amounts to about $25 in today's currency.
17 'Airline pilots hard to get', The Canberra Times, 21 July 1964, p. 15.
18 'Exciting future of aviation', The Canberra Times, 24 November 1966, p. 36; 'Pilots welcome degree scheme', The Canberra Times, 2 August 1966, p. 14.
19 Letter from A.R. Gray to Jess Prain, 31 July 1987, document held in the Ex-WRANS archive, Spectacle Island.

CHAPTER 30: THE SAILOR'S LESSONS
1   Letter from John Dodwell to Jean Nysen, 1987, document held in Ex-WRANS archive, Spectacle Island.
2   This chapter is primarily based on an interview with Edgar Gold.
3   Letter from John Dodwell to Jean Nysen, 1987, document held in Ex-WRANS archive, Spectacle Island.
4   A sample of views both for and against the Sydney Opera House design can be found in Ronald McKie, 'Winning plan is basis for decades of violent argument'.
5   Edgar Gold, personal communication.

CHAPTER 31: THE WAR'S LONG REACH
1   Jean Nysen (nee McKenzie), interview with David Dufty.
2   NAA: C138, H85993, 'McKenzie, Cecil Roland', pp. 12, 31; NAA: C138, M85993, 'McKenzie, Cecil Roland', p. 23.
3   NAA: C138, H85993, 'McKenzie, Cecil Roland', p. 30.
4   NAA: C138, M85993, 'McKenzie, Cecil Roland', p. 41.
5   NAA: C138, M85993, 'McKenzie, Cecil Roland', pp. 10, 14.
6   'To 20,000 men and women she's "Dear Mother—Mrs Mac"', Australian Home Journal, July 1963, pp. 45–6.

CHAPTER 32: EX-WRANS
1   Margaret Curtis-Otter, W.R.A.N.S., p. 79.
2   'WRANS first reunion dinner', Navy News, 15 November 1963, p. 11.

3 'WRANS first reunion dinner', *Navy News*, 15 November 1963, p. 11.
4 Terry Clark, 'A living legend', p. 35.
5 Jean Nysen (nee McKenzie), interview with David Dufty.
6 Gloria Newton, 'Ex-WRANs plan get-together for 30th Anniversary'.
7 Gloria Newton, 'Ex-WRANs plan get-together for 30th Anniversary'.
8 D. McNeill, 'Other memories of Mrs Mac'.
9 Germaine Greer, *The Female Eunuch*, p. 14.
10 Germaine Greer, *The Female Eunuch*, p. 16.
11 Germaine Greer, *The Female Eunuch*, p. 146.
12 Germaine Greer, *The Female Eunuch*, p. 279.
13 'Women who care about what is going on', *The Australian Women's Weekly*, 5 April 1978, pp. 4–5.
14 Shirley Fenton Huie, *Ships Belles*, p. 27.

CHAPTER 33: THE PILOT FLAG FLYING

1 'Mrs Mac, mother of the WRANS, dies at 92', *North Shore Times* (Sydney, NSW), 9 June 1982.
2 Frank Simon, *A Mariner Remembers*, pp. 71–2.
3 Catherine Freyne, 'McKenzie, Violet'; 'Plaque honours WRANs mother', *The Sydney Morning Herald*, 31 March 1980, p. 3.
4 Peter Goed, interview with David Dufty.
5 Greg Flynn, 'Thank you Mrs Mac'.
6 Jo Miller, 'Personal memories of Mrs Mac, 1939–1982'.
7 Michael Nelmes, 'McKenzie, Florence Violet (1890–1982)'; Catherine Freyne, 'McKenzie, Violet'.
8 Reverend J.R. Henderson, 'Eulogy', pp. 4–5.
9 Catherine Freyne, 'McKenzie, Violet'.
10 'Mrs Mac, signals instructor', *The Sydney Morning Herald*, 27 May 1982, p. 12.

BIBLIOGRAPHY

BOOKS

Curtis-Otter, Margaret, *W.R.A.N.S.: The Women's Royal Australian Naval Service*, Sydney: The Naval Historical Society of Australia, 1975

Gillison, Douglas Napier, *Second World War Official Histories—Australia in the War of 1939–1945, Series 3—Air*, Canberra: Australian War Memorial, 1962

Glozier, Matthew, *75 Years Aloft: Royal Australian Air Force Air Training Corps: Australian air force cadets*, Sydney: Matthew Robert Glozier for Australian Air Force Cadets, 2016

Greer, Germaine, *The Female Eunuch*, London: Paladin Press, 1971

Henstock, Joan, *Women of the Royal Australian Navy, Part One*, Canberra: Joan Henstock, 2017

Huie, Shirley Fenton, *Ships Belles: The story of the Women's Royal Australian Naval Service in war and peace, 1941–1985*, Sydney: Watermark Press, 2000

King, Norman S., *History of Austinmer and Robert Marsh Westmacott in Australia*, Wollongong, NSW: Illawarra Historical Society, 1964

King, Norman S., *The Story of Austinmer*, Wollongong, NSW: Illawarra Historical Society, 1967

Langhans, Ron, *The First Twelve Months of Radio Broadcasting in Australia, 1923–1924*, Sydney: Historical Radio Society of Australia, 2013

McKenzie, F.V., *Electrical Association for Women's Cookery Book*, Sydney: F.V. McKenzie, 1936

McKenzie, F.V., *The Electric Imps*, Sydney: F.V. McKenzie, 1937

Mitchell, Albert, *The Sydney Evening News Handbook*, Sydney: S. Bennett, 1924

Mohapp, C., 'The Rhythm of Life: The perfect rhythm of Morse code', Master's thesis, Sydney: Sydney Conservatorium of Music, The University of Sydney, 2014

Randell, Wilfred L., *Electricity and Woman: 21 years of progress*, London: Electrical Association for Women (London), 1945

Simon, Frank Derek, *A Mariner Remembers,* Sydney: Frank Simon, 2002

Thomson, Joyce A., *The WAAAF in Wartime Australia,* Melbourne: Melbourne University Press, 1991

BOOK CHAPTERS AND REFERENCE ENTRIES

Broomham, Rosemary, 'Florence Violet McKenzie', in Heather Radi (ed.), *200 Australian Women: A Redress anthology,* Sydney: Women's Redress Press, 1988

Cantrell, Carol, 'David, Caroline Martha (Cara) (1856–1951)', *Australian Dictionary of Biography,* National Centre of Biography, Australian National University, <http://adb.anu.edu.au/biography/david-caroline-martha-cara-9906/text17539>, published first in hardcopy 1993, accessed online 13 November 2018

Fisk, Ernest T., 'The possibilities of wireless in Australia', catalogue of Wireless and Electrical Exhibition, Town Hall, Sydney, 3–8 December 1923, Sydney: Wireless Institute of Australia (NSW Division), pp. 17–25

Foley, Meredith, 'Littlejohn, Emma Linda Palmer (1883–1949)', *Australian Dictionary of Biography,* National Centre of Biography, Australian National University, <http://adb.anu.edu.au/biography/littlejohn-emma-linda-palmer-7208/text12473>, published first in hardcopy 1986, accessed online 7 February 2019

Freyne,Catherine,'McKenzie,Violet',*TheDictionaryofSydney,*<https://dictionaryofsydney.org/entry/mckenzie_violet>, 2010, accessed 17 January 2018

Hanna, Bronwyn, 'Nosworthy, Ellice Maud (1897–1972)', *Australian Dictionary of Biography,* National Centre of Biography, Australian National University, <http://adb.anu.edu.au/biography/nosworthy-ellice-maud-11263/text20091>, published first in hardcopy 2000, accessed online 13 November 2018

Henningham, Nikki, 'The United Associations of Women (1929–)', *The Australian Women's Register,* <www.womenaustralia.info/biogs/AWE1023b.htm>, 2004, accessed 7 February 2019

Heywood, Ann, 'McKenzie, Florence Violet (1892—1982)', *The Australian Women's Register,* <www.womenaustralia.info/biogs/AWE0386b.htm>, 2002, accessed 13 January 2018

McKay, Frances, 'Foreword', in F.V. McKenzie, *Elecrical Association for Women's Cookery Book,* Sydney: F.V. McKenzie, 1936

National Museum of Australia, *Great Depression,* <www.nma.gov.au/defining-moments/resources/great-depression>, accessed 6 November 2018

Nelmes, Michael, 'McKenzie, Florence Violet (1890–1982)', *Australian Dictionary of Biography,* National Centre of Biography, Australian National University, <http://adb.anu.edu.au/biography/mckenzie-florence-violet-15485>, published first in hardcopy 2012, accessed online 16 December 2019

Phillips, Nan, 'Bayldon, Francis Joseph (1872–1948)', *Australian Dictionary of*

Biography, National Centre of Biography, Australian National University, <http://adb.anu.edu.au/biography/bayldon-francis-joseph-5159/text8659>, published first in hardcopy 1979, accessed online 3 August 2018

The University of Sydney Calendar, archived electronic copies of past calendars can be found at <http://calendararchive.usyd.edu.au/browse.php>, 1916, accessed 17 January 2018

Wotherspoon, Garry, 'Economy', *The Dictionary of Sydney*, <https://dictionaryofsydney.org/entry/economy>, 2008, accessed 6 November 2018

JOURNALS AND PERIODICALS

Begbie, Richard, 'The marvellous Mrs Mac—alias F.V. Wallace', *Radio Waves*, October 2008, pp. 7–10

Begbie, Richard, 'The metamorphosis of Miss Wallace', *Radio Waves*, January 2009, pp. 33–5

Clark, Terry, 'A living legend', *Amateur Radio*, December 1979, pp. 34–6

Dale, Marie, 'The Radio Girl: "Tunes in" to many interests', *The Australian Woman's Mirror*, 21 July 1925, p. 20

Dexter, Iris, 'Their third year aboard', *Woman*, 3 May 1943 [The original document is held by the NSW Ex-WRANS Association, North Richmond, New South Wales. The page number is missing due to deterioration of the paper.]

Ellison, Norman, 'Magnificent Mrs Mac', *Sky Script*, April 1948, pp. 14–16

Flynn, Greg, 'Thank you Mrs Mac', *The Australian Women's Weekly*, 12 July 1978, p. 41

Hazlitt Jr, William, 'Why must women butt in?', *Table Talk*, 23 June 1938, p. 5

Henderson, Reverend J.R., 'Eulogy', *Ex-WRANS Ditty Box*, June 1982, pp. 4–5

Jobling, Lee, 'The first women graduates', *Record: The University of Sydney Archives*, 2002, pp. 5–6

McKenzie, Florence Violet, 'The Women's Emergency Signalling Corps', *Ex-WRANS Ditty Box*, April 1976

McKenzie, F.V., 'Some interesting inhabitants of Sydney's seashores', *Aquariana*, January 1933, vol. 1, no. 7, pp. 160–2

McKenzie, F.V., 'The first "Wireless Weekly"', *Wireless Weekly*, 5 August 1932, p. 5

McKie, Ronald, 'Winning plan is basis for decades of violent argument', *The Australian Women's Weekly*, 20 February 1957, p. 18

McKinnon, Patricia, 'A woman taught these men their signals', *Woman's Day & Home*, 29 June 1953, p. 7

McNeill, D., 'Other memories of Mrs Mac', *Ex-WRANS Ditty Box*, June 1982, p. 9

Middleton, R.D., 'Time must have dimmed the memories of "Ondina" men', *Dutch Australian Weekly*, 30 December 1966, p. 6

Miller, Jo, 'Personal memories of Mrs Mac, 1939–1982', *Ex-WRANS Ditty Box*, June 1982, pp. 7–8

Millgate, Moira, 'According to Galileo', *Amateur Radio Action*, 1984, vol. 7, no. 7, p. 70

Newton, Gloria, 'Ex-WRANS plan get-together for 30th Anniversary', *The Australian Women's Weekly*, 10 March 1971, p. 15

Ressing, Jan F.A., 'The battle of the "Ondina"—time did not dim memories', *Dutch Australian Weekly*, 27 January 1967, p. 10

Shaw, Raymond, 'Calling! Calling! Calling!', *Smith's Weekly*, 11 February 1922, p. 18

Small, Barbara, 'A woman engineer wrote our first electric cook book', *The National Times*, 26–31 August 1974, p. 45

Southcombe (nee Cornwallis), Gwenda, 'Home, home on the range: degaussing', *Naval Historical Society of Australia*, <www.navyhistory.org.au/author/soutg/>, 1988, accessed 3 March 2019

Stackpole, Lieutenant Commander Andrew, 'Navy women celebrate 70 years of proud history', *Navy News*, 13 October 2011, pp. 20–1

Williams, Neville, 'Charles D. Maclurcan: Engineer, businessman, hotelier and top Australian amateur broadcaster—1', *Electronics Australia*, February 1994, pp. 36–40

Williams, Neville, 'Charles D. Maclurcan: Engineer, businessman, hotelier and top Australian amateur broadcaster—2', *Electronics Australia*, March 1994, pp. 46–50

Williams, Neville, 'Ernest Fisk, the man', *Electronics Australia*, July 1989, pp. 38–41

Williams, Neville, 'Readers have their say: What about the "girls" in radio factories and offices?', *Electronics Australia*, May 1996, pp. 40–2

Williams, Neville, 'Vintage radio magazines: how they came and went, and transmitters BC (before crystals)', *Electronics Australia*, April 1992, pp. 46–51

PERSONAL INTERVIEWS

Edgar Gold, telephone interview, 10 August 2018

Gwenda Garde (nee Moulton), 16 August 2018, Orange, New South Wales

Jean Nysen (nee McKenzie), 3 June 2018, Cremorne, New South Wales

Marie Davis (nee Munns), 8 August 2018, Holt, Australian Capital Territory

Mark Sunter, August 2018, telephone interview

Merle Hare, March–August 2018, Canberra, Australian Capital Territory

Patricia Johnson (nee Murdoch), September 2018, Central Coast, New South Wales

Paul Wallace, May 2018, telephone interview

Peter Goed, 22 May 2018, Redcliffe, Queensland

NATIONAL ARCHIVES OF AUSTRALIA

A2585, 1939/1941/REFERENCE COPY, 'Naval Board Minutes, 1939–1941—Index to Naval Board Minutes 1939—1941'

A2673, VOLUME 3, 'War Cabinet minutes—Minute numbers 343 to 520'

A2679, A2679/1, 'Formation of Women's Auxiliary to Royal Australian Air Force'

A463, 1959/3374, 'Mrs F McKenzie—Honours'

A595, 735/1, 'Summaries of the decision of the war cabinet 1939–1940'

a5954, 768/8, 'Book (Original) Chapter 3—General BLAMEY'S Visit to Australia for Consultations with the Government—November 1941'

A663, O130/1/781, 'WRANS MPC no. 18'

A663, O130/4/134, 'Women's Voluntary National Register, State organisations—expressions of appreciation from Chairman, Man Power Committee'

A6769, COWIE J, 'COWIE JOAN: Service Number—WR/17'

A6770, Ashley V M, 'Ashley Valerie Mary: Service Number—WR/512'

A6770, CORNWALLIS G M, 'CORNWALLIS GWENDOLYNE MARY: Service Number—WR/1635'

A6770, Kingsford-Smith S M; NAA, 'KINGSFORD-SMITH SHIRLEY MAY: Service Number—WR/1636'

A6770, McKenzie J J, 'McKenzie Jean Jervis: Service Number—WR/87'

A705, 151/4/124, 'Mr F V McKenzie (ex civilian instructor) Suggestion RAAF provide suitable accommodations (through Mr Treloar MP)'

B2455, McKenzie C R, 'McKenzie Cecil Roland: SERN 7747: POB Melbourne VIC: POE Sydney NSW: NOK M McKenzie Gertrude Eliza'

C138, H85993, 'McKenzie, Cecil Roland—service number 7747'

C138, M85993, 'McKenzie, Cecil Roland—service number 7747'

'Canberra air disaster, 1940—Fact sheet 142', <www.naa.gov.au/collection/fact-sheets/fs142.aspx>, accessed 21 December 2018

MP1049/5, 2026/21/79, '[Midget submarine attack on Sydney Harbour]'

SP338/1, 555/10, 'Applications for Enrolment—Naval Auxiliary Patrol'

'United States forces in Queensland, 1941–45—Fact sheet 234'

AUSTRALIAN WAR MEMORIAL

012815, 'Photo shows luncheon after launching HMIS *Bengal*. The ceremony was performed by Mrs Curtin, wife of the prime minister', <www.awm.gov.au/collection/C32380>, accessed 16 December 2019

93, 50/2/23/781, 'War of 1939-45. Correspondence with Mrs Mary Bell regarding the formation of the WATC and WAAAF and other information for the official history'

188, 42, 'Norman. NAP [Naval Auxiliary Patrol]—origin, development and activities'

ORMF0016, 'Women's Auxiliary Australian Air Force (WAAAF)'

PR00822, 'Murrell, Esme Kura', Papers of Murrell, Esme Kura (Women's Emergency Signalling Corps)

P01612, 'Gill, Kenneth D', Memoirs written by Kenneth D. Gill entitled 'Memoirs of the Sydney Naval Auxiliary Patrol'

S00416, 'Air Vice Marshal Henry Neilson Wrigley CBE DFC AFC (Ret'd) discusses his career in the Royal Australian Air Force (RAAF), 1921–1946, in an interview with Frank Marshall'. A transcript of the interview can be found at <www.3squadron.org.au/indexpages/AWMWrigley.htm>, accessed 31 December 2018

S00547, '(WR/5) Stevens, Marion (Second Officer), Transcript of oral history recording, interviewed by Ruth Thompson, 21 March 1989', <www.awm.gov.au/collection/C87923>, accessed 10 December 2019

S00593, 'WR/21 Starr (previously Blair), Heather Stella (Leading Telegraphist), Transcript of oral history recording, interviewed by Ruth Thompson, 13 June 1989', <www.awm.gov.au/collection/C87974>, accessed 10 December 2019

NSW STATE ARCHIVES

Register of Firms, Series NRS12951, Item: 2/8544, 'W. R. Wallace & Co.'

Register of Firms, Series NRS12951, Item: 2/8549, 'Briot & McIntosh'

Bankruptcy Index, Series NRS13658, Item 22644, 'Bankruptcy, MCINTOSH Raymond Edgar'

NATIONAL LIBRARY OF AUSTRALIA

[Biographical cuttings on Florence McKenzie, former patroness of the Ex-WRANS Association, containing one or more cuttings from newspapers or journals]

Shaw, Rex, Waltz selection from *The Radio Girl*

MITCHELL LIBRARY, STATE LIBRARY OF NSW

MSS0796, 'Kentley, Margaret'

COMMONWEALTH OF AUSTRALIA PUBLICATIONS

Commonwealth of Australia, *Gazette* (no. 35), 22 June 1950

Commonwealth of Australia, House of Representatives, *Hansard*, 1941

Joint Standing Committee on Foreign Affairs, Defence and Trade, *The Loss of HMAS Sydney*, 1999

VITAL RECORDS

Marriage certificate for George Wallace and Marie Annie Greville, 28 May 1894, NSW Registry of Births, Deaths and Marriages

Birth certificate, Walter Reginald Giles, 28 July 1899, Registry of Births Deaths and Marriages Victoria, record 22442

Birth certificate, Florence Violet Granville, 28 September 1890, Registry of Births, Deaths and Marriages Victoria, record 30595

EX-WRANS ARCHIVE, SPECTACLE ISLAND

Letter from A.R. Gray to Jess Prain, 31 July 1987

Letter from Electricity Advisory Committee to Mrs F.V. McKenzie, 27 August 1936

Florence Violet McKenzie, Fellow Certificate, Australian Institute of Navigation, 13 November 1957

'Women thrilled with birthday list honours', undated newspaper article

Résumé of F.V. McKenzie's achievements prepared by the Ex-WRANS Association

Letter from the Australian governor-general to Florence Violet McKenzie, 13 May 1950

Certificate of registration, 'The Electrical Association for Women (Australia)', 22 March 1934

Letter from John Dodwell to Jean Nysen, 1987

EX-WRANS ASSOCIATION ARCHIVE

Lansley, Louise & Wybenga, Islay, 'Interview with Florence Violet McKenzie at Glenwood Nursing Home, Greenwich, 8 September 1979. Interview conducted on behalf of the Sydney High Old Girls' Union'

AUDIO-VISUAL

Armstrong, Alison, *Oral History*, Australians at War film archive, 19 September 2003, accessed 8 February 2019

Dow, Patrice, *Oral History*, Australians at War film archive, 16 April 2004, accessed 27 February 2019

Freyne, Catherine, *Signals, Currents, and Wires: The untold story of Florence Violet McKenzie, Hindsight* radio program, ABC Radio National, 16 March 2008

Yawitz, Aubrey A., *Interview*, Aubrey A. Yawitz Collection (AFC/2001/001/82152), Veterans History Project, American Folklife Center, Library of Congress

WEB PAGES

Anzac Portal special features, 'A Lark on the wing', The Anzac Portal, <https://anzacportal.dva.gov.au/history/special-features/veterans-stories/great-search-stories/lark-wing>, n.d. accessed 23 November 2018

Bureau of Naval Personnel (United States), 'Radioman 3 & 2, Navpapers 102278-D', <www.navy-radio.com/manuals/rm32-10228D-1964.pdf>, n.d. accessed 9 January 2019

Perryman, John 'Japanese Midget Submarine Attack on Sydney Harbour', Navy Feature Histories, <www.navy.gov.au/history/feature-histories/japanese-midget-submarine-attack-sydney-harbour>, accessed 7 March 2019

Visser, Jan, 'The Ondina-battle', <http://netherlandsnavy.nl/battle_ondina.html>, n.d. accessed 17 January 2019

INDEX